AFTER THE REALIST REVOLUTION

This book extends the existing academic study of American common law to new and previously unexplored areas. Marin Roger Scordato examines the conventional understanding of appellate court lawmaking and the profound change in the common understanding of that activity that occurred during the mid-twentieth century. Scordato argues that this change in the conventional account of common law can be best understood as an authentic paradigm shift akin to those described by Thomas Kuhn in *The Structure of Scientific Revolutions*. The book also sheds light on the ways in which the current instrumentalist approach to appellate court lawmaking is influenced and, in some respects, compromised by the structures and procedures that were created during the prior formalist era. Thorough and insightful, this book is an ideal resource for legal scholars and general readers interested in the nature and evolution of American common law.

Marin Roger Scordato is Professor of Law at the Columbus School of Law, The Catholic University of America. He has been a full-time professor of law in the United States for nearly forty years. During that time, he has published scholarship in the areas of jurisprudence, legal education, legal scholarship, tort law, free speech, and agency law.

After the Realist Revolution

JUDICIAL LAWMAKING IN AN AGE OF INSTRUMENTALIST COMMON LAW JURISPRUDENCE

MARIN ROGER SCORDATO

CAMBRIDGE
UNIVERSITY PRESS

CAMBRIDGE
UNIVERSITY PRESS

Shaftesbury Road, Cambridge CB2 8EA, United Kingdom

One Liberty Plaza, 20th Floor, New York, NY 10006, USA

477 Williamstown Road, Port Melbourne, VIC 3207, Australia

314–321, 3rd Floor, Plot 3, Splendor Forum, Jasola District Centre, New Delhi – 110025, India

103 Penang Road, #05-06/07, Visioncrest Commercial, Singapore 238467

Cambridge University Press is part of Cambridge University Press & Assessment, a department of the University of Cambridge.

We share the University's mission to contribute to society through the pursuit of education, learning and research at the highest international levels of excellence.

www.cambridge.org
Information on this title: www.cambridge.org/9781009589260

DOI: 10.1017/9781009589307

When citing this work, please include a reference to the DOI 10.1017/9781009589307

First published 2025

Cover image: Walter A. Slowinski Courtroom at Columbus School of Law at The Catholic University of America in Washington, DC.

A catalogue record for this publication is available from the British Library

Library of Congress Cataloging-in-Publication Data
NAMES: Scordato, Marin Roger, author.
TITLE: After the realist revolution : judicial lawmaking in an age of instrumentalist common law jurisprudence / Marin Roger Scordato, Catholic University of America, Washington DC.
DESCRIPTION: Cambridge, United KIngdom ; New York, NY : Cambridge University Press, 2025. | Includes bibliographical references and index.
IDENTIFIERS: LCCN 2025000117 (print) | LCCN 2025000118 (ebook) | ISBN 9781009589260 (hardback) | ISBN 9781009589253 (paperback) | ISBN 9781009589307 (epub)
SUBJECTS: LCSH: Appellate courts. | Appellate procedure. | Courts of last resort. | Judge-made law. | Judicial process. | Political questions and judicial power.
CLASSIFICATION: LCC K2123 .S36 2025 (print) | LCC K2123 (ebook) | DDC 347/.03–dc23/eng/20250113
LC record available at https://lccn.loc.gov/2025000117
LC ebook record available at https://lccn.loc.gov/2025000118

ISBN 978-1-009-58926-0 Hardback

For Paula

and for Richard, Victoria, Christopher, Patrick, Dorothy, and Frank

the foundations of a satisfying and exceptionally fortunate life

Contents

Preface and Acknowledgments

This book offers insights and perspectives developed over a period of more than forty years as a full-time faculty member at five different university graduate schools of law in Washington, DC, Boston, Los Angeles, Baltimore, and Tallahassee, Florida. I am grateful to these law schools, my faculty colleagues, and the students I had the privilege to teach throughout this period. The ideas herein are entirely mine and do not represent the views or opinions of any of these schools, their associated universities, or their faculties. All errors and omissions are mine.

I am very grateful to Matt Galloway and the Cambridge University Press for their support and the opportunity for these ideas to become available in book form.

I am deeply grateful to Paula Monopoli – an exceptional legal theorist and scholar – with whom I have discussed the nature of law and to whom I have been profoundly fortunate to be married for longer than I have been either a licensed attorney or a law professor.

Consistent with its nature, this book primarily includes specific citations only for direct quotations and named references to published legal cases. Some chapters of this book are based on work that has previously been published in academic law reviews and journals. Those interested in the extensive footnote support and more detailed elaboration that is typical in academic legal journals may wish to consult the following:

Post-Realist Blues: Formalism, Instrumentalism and the Hybrid Nature of Common Law Jurisprudence, 7 NEVADA LAW JOURNAL 263–300 (2007) (Chapters 4 and 5).

Understanding the Absence of a Duty to Reasonably Rescue in American Tort Law, 82 TULANE LAW REVIEW 1447–503 (2008) (Chapter 8).

Three Kinds of Fault: Understanding the Purpose and Function of Causation in Tort Law, 77 UNIVERSITY OF MIAMI LAW REVIEW 149–212 (2022) (Chapter 9).

Distinction without a Difference: A Reappraisal of the Doctrine of Prior Restraint, 68 NORTH CAROLINA LAW REVIEW 1–35 (1989) (Chapter 10).
Reflections on the Nature of Legal Scholarship in the Post-Realist Era, 48 SANTA CLARA LAW REVIEW 353–440 (2008) (Chapter 11).

1

Introduction

In America's legal system, courts of law, and most especially appellate courts, possess the authority to make binding law. When courts do this directly, without applying law enacted by a legislative body or an administrative agency, the result is typically called common law. Appellate courts have both the authority and the responsibility to function as common law lawmakers.

Courts also have the authority and the responsibility to interpret and apply to the resolution of specific disputes law enacted by other authorized lawmakers like legislatures and administrative agencies. In every case in which the law being interpreted and applied by a court is not unambiguously clear in meaning and interpretation, the court is also engaged, in a very real sense, in making law when it chooses, as it must, one possible meaning over others as the official meaning of a statute or regulation. A court's determination of the official meaning of an ambiguous statute or regulation has the same status and future effect as a court's creation and announcement of new common law.

There exists a long-standing customary practice that courts should consult, and to some extent defer to, the understanding of the original lawmaker when interpreting ambiguous statutes and regulations. As a result, the maintenance and development of common law is a somewhat more direct and more pure instance of lawmaking by courts than is their interpretation of existing law enacted by others. Both, however, are circumstances in which courts are functioning as creators of binding and authoritative law in this country.

So long as a legislature is producing law that does not violate a superior law, like a constitutional provision, the nature of legislative lawmaking is largely procedural. Legislators are chosen through a specified process of general, popular election and these elected persons cast votes under predetermined procedural rules that, when the required procedural mandates have been satisfied, result in the creation of binding statutory law.

Individual legislators may consider and be influenced by a wide variety of factors and arguments. Short of being improperly influenced by something like a bribe, there is no general consensus or understanding as to the appropriate nature of a legislator's consideration and weighing of various possible factors in finally deciding how to cast a vote. The resulting legislative product – the law – is not rationalized and honored based on the analytical approach adopted by individual legislators, but is instead rationalized and honored based on the legislative body being populated in a way that conforms to lawful electoral procedure and those elected legislators casting their votes, and the votes being counted, in a way that complies with the prevailing procedure. Consistent with this, individual legislators are not required, nor expected, to publish formal statements setting forth their rationale for having either supported or not a particular bill. Appropriate procedure produces binding statutory law irrespective of the lawmaking approach or philosophy adopted by individual legislators.

The same is not the case with lawmaking courts. The appellate judges making common law, and interpreting and applying statutory law, are not selected by a process of direct popular election and regular reelection. Their authority does not come from a direct democratic delegation, and then renewed delegation, of formal lawmaking authority. Sometimes, as with federal judges, they serve a lifetime term with no renewal of their formal authority by either popular vote or executive or legislative reconfirmation after their initial appointment.

Given this, the authority vested in appellate judges to make binding law is not adequately rationalized based on procedure and there is an appropriate concern about, and a serious and sustained focus on, the method by which these unelected lawmakers go about the business of creating authoritative law. What they decide should be binding law is respected and honored at least as much because they come to that decision in a particular way and according to a generally agreed upon approach and method as because of who they are; in fact, the result is honored and accepted far more because they adhere to a conventionally accepted method – a particular jurisprudence – than because of how they were individually selected.

So, it is a critical and important inquiry in a democratic republic to ask what kind of lawmaking approach – or jurisprudence – is thought to be sufficient to vest appellate courts with legitimate formal authority to create on their own formal law that binds all of us in this country. The fundamental political legitimacy of unelected lawmakers, and the law that they make, depends upon there being a coherent and widely agreed upon understanding of the appropriate nature of the way in which these particular lawmakers go about the task of ultimately preferring one possible version of a law or legal doctrine over others.

It is not possible to fully understand the nature of American law and the American legal system in the late twentieth and the early twenty-first centuries without appreciating that the activity of lawmaking by the judicial branch is continuing to work through a profound shift in the conventional understanding of the nature of that activity, and correspondingly the appropriate method that appellate courts should adopt when making law; a change that occurred roughly during the middle of the twentieth century. Much of what is currently so opaque and confusing about the operation of courts as lawmakers is a consequence of formal legal structures and procedures that were created under the prior paradigm, where they made logical sense and were largely coherent, that continue to operate largely unchanged under a radically new paradigm in which they make far less conceptual sense.

Moreover, it should be recognized here at the outset that confusion as to the nature and operation of appellate courts as lawmakers should not necessarily be understood as a universally undesired or unwelcome outcome. When courts make new binding law, they are entities possessed of formal societal and political authority publicly exercising that power. It would run counter to our general experience to expect in such situations the person or entity engaged in such an exercise of power to be inclined to be fully transparent and candid about all of the various considerations that played into its decision. At least some mystery and ambiguity surrounding the exercise of power can often be beneficial to those who exercise it. As a result, an accurate understanding of the nature of appellate court lawmaking is unlikely to be available through a straightforward and surface reading of the written explanations offered by the courts themselves – their published appellate opinions.

Still, whether or not fully transparent in the published public explanations that they provide, it continues to matter a great deal how the courts themselves, and the legal community generally, understand the most basic nature of what courts are doing when they make binding law. What counts as a material and relevant consideration, and thus a material and relevant argument, depends upon this understanding. The means by which these arguments and considerations are appropriately scrutinized, analyzed, and weighed against one another also depends upon this understanding. So, too, does the criteria for judging the quality of the courts' decisions, and deciding how much deference to give to the prior decisions of courts.

It is this underlying conceptual understanding of just what appellate courts are doing, and should be doing, when they make law that has undergone such a fundamental transformation over the past century. It is the fact that our American legal system currently operates in the wake of this relatively recent paradigm shift that makes it so difficult to understand many of its contemporary features, and outcomes.

It takes a long time in a legal system such as ours for the basic structures and procedures that were adopted under one paradigm to be reconsidered and changed to conform to a fundamentally new and different understanding. In addition, there is in any radical paradigm shift – especially one that involves the exercise of very substantial formal social power – inevitable winners and losers, and those with influence who are not advantaged by the paradigm shift can be expected to resist – if not to seek to actively impede – the transformation of important internal structures and procedures so that they better conform to, and support, the new paradigm.

All of this results in a circumstance in which a coherent and reasonably clear account of the nature of appellate lawmaking in America is not at all easy to come by. Moreover, such an account, if accurate, is unlikely to be conceptually neat and tidy, describing a system that consistently conforms to a set of widely agreed upon first principles. Nevertheless, this is the challenge that is taken up by the analysis that follows.

2

The Traditional Understanding of Lawmaking by Appellate Courts

From where does authoritative law come in America? In other words, what are the basic sources of binding American law? While the answer to this question is not quite as straightforward as what follows, what follows is sufficient for these purposes. So for these purposes, one can think of there as being four basic kinds, or sources, of American law: (1) constitutional law – law that is set forth in the United States Constitution and the constitutions of the various states; (2) statutory law – law that is enacted by the federal legislative branch and the legislative branches of the various states; (3) administrative (or regulatory) law – law that is created by both federal and state administrative agencies; and (4) common law – law that is created, recognized, and adopted by the federal courts and the courts of the various states.

Courts in our country are empowered to make law on their own when they resolve live disputes among citizens. This is called common law. For a long time, the overwhelming percentage of law that existed in America was common law and not statutory law or administrative law. It was not until the New Deal in the 1930s that this began to meaningfully change; until now, in the early twenty-first century, the ratio has essentially flipped.

It is also the case that courts have the power to interpret the meaning and proper application of constitutional, statutory, and administrative law. When courts do so, they can be said to also be "making law," though in that context they do so under greater constraints than when they engage in traditional common law lawmaking in the absence of legally operative language created by another source.

Early American criminal law, contract law, property law, and tort law were all predominantly traditional common law – created largely by appellate courts through the issuing of publicly announced decisions in actual cases without the existence or influence of constitutional provisions, statutes, or regulations. On what basis did these courts, and the legal community at large, believe that this common law should be determined? By what conceptual process and against what benchmarks should a court go about deciding for its jurisdiction whether the prevailing rule of contract law; for example, is henceforth alternative A, B, or C?

The prevailing view in America until at least the twentieth century was that it was the obligation of the appellate courts to try to identify the best possible rule of law for its jurisdiction consistent with and guided by prior decisions of the courts in that jurisdiction (called precedent). Courts should search the existing precedent in their jurisdiction and determine which of the possible competing versions of a given rule best conformed logically to the pattern of law in that area that already existed and to the general principles of fairness and equity announced by previous appellate court opinions. This approach was supported by a strong practice of discipline that required subordinate courts to faithfully adhere to the prior public decisions of superior courts within a given court system. This is called the doctrine, or the practice, of stare decisis.

Under this understanding of the work of appellate courts, the process of choosing a new rule of common law in a jurisdiction was almost entirely a conceptual exercise with little or no reference to anything other than the facts of the instant case and the existing prior precedent in the jurisdiction. It was predominantly an abstract challenge of legal logic whereby the appellate court sought to determine what specific resolution of a legal issue was most consistent with – or was logically mandated by – the existing pattern of law in that area and by general principles in that area of law embraced and announced previously by courts.

Advocates seeking to persuade appellate courts to adopt the specific rule of law that they preferred would fill their written briefs and their oral arguments with references to the existing precedent. They would try to demonstrate that their preferred position was the product of the correct deductive application of decisions and maxims previously adopted by appellate courts in that jurisdiction.

Consider, for example, a possibly simple issue in contract law. Imagine that a prospective seller sends a telegram to a prospective buyer proposing that the buyer enter into a contract to purchase 1,000 quantity of a certain item at a price of $100 each. While the prospective purchaser writes out the message correctly, the telegraph operator accidently mis-keys it so that what the prospective buyer receives is a message that offers 1,000 quantity of the item at a price of $10 each. The buyer promptly accepts the offer. Has a legally binding contract been formed between the seller and the buyer?

Assume that this specific issue of contract law has not been raised and thus not previously decided in the relevant jurisdiction (and is therefore said to be an issue of first impression in the jurisdiction). During an early period in which an area of law is maturing and still developing and is also predominately common law, appellate courts can be expected to confront such legal issues of first impression rather frequently. How should the appellate court go about deciding whether a contract was formed and is thus legally enforceable?

Because there are not yet any precedents in the jurisdiction that have squarely addressed and resolved this particular issue, the court should seek issues that have previously been confronted and resolved and consider whether those resolutions could be applied analogously to the current one to suggest a consistent result. The court should also look for general principles and maxims of contract law (or law generally) that have been recognized and honored by the courts of this jurisdiction and analyze whether they might be brought to bear to determine an appropriate, logically consistent result in the instant case.

So, just by way of illustration, assume that the jurisdiction in question in this example has a number of previously decided cases that endorse the general notion that a legally binding contract should not be found to exist unless there has been a genuine meeting of the minds between the contracting parties regarding at least the material terms of the contract. Here, the written expression of the offer upon which the prospective buyer based his acceptance was clearly not an accurate expression of the subjective intent of the prospective seller. There was, therefore, no genuine meeting of the minds between the parties, and the resulting offer and acceptance should not constitute a legally binding contract. In logically applying the existing legal principle to this case, the appellate court might determine that no contract was formed and might announce a new rule of contract law (a new precedent) in this jurisdiction that a binding contract is not created where the offer received by the counterparty is not a reasonably accurate expression of the true subjective intent of the offeror.

In this way, the appellate courts of a jurisdiction are, over time, confronted with novel issues and incrementally develop the common law in that area of law by carefully ensuring that the new rules announced are logically consistent with what has come before. By such means, the common law of a given jurisdiction develops and matures in a logically coherent and conceptually consistent manner.

Many of the most basic rules and procedures of appellate litigation can be seen as being a product of this underlying conception of the work of the appellate courts. For example, the fact that the dominant, if not typically exclusive, source of information available to an appellate court as to what the facts of the case are, and what transpired at the trial court below, is the official trial transcript, a highly formal written record produced by the trial court reporter. There is no interview of the trial judge. No interview of any witnesses. No review of video or audio recordings. Just the formal trial transcript.

Also consistent with this underlying conception of the work of appellate courts is the exceptionally limited total inputs to the appellate process: typically, only the trial transcript, the formal written briefs of the attorneys, and, if the court allows, a brief period of live oral argument by the attorneys. That is all of the usual inputs to an appellate process that is purportedly reviewing the full range of legal decisions made by the trial judge during litigation that may well have lasted many years.

Not only are the inputs to the appellate process severely limited, so too are the participants. Only the attorneys for the parties and the panel of appellate judges are necessarily involved. This dramatic restriction on the inputs and the participants in the appellate process is consistent with the idea that the fundamental work of the appellate courts is by nature one of specialized conceptual and logical analysis and not any kind of investigation of the way that the various versions of the new legal rule under consideration might operate in the world as an empirical matter.

Also consistent with this way of understanding the nature of appellate court jurisprudence is the practice of having many appellate court judges appointed by the executive and the legislative branches of government rather than be directly elected by the citizens of the jurisdiction, as are the other prominent makers of law in the system – the members of the legislative branch. No judges in the federal court system ever stand for popular election, or reelection. They are nominated by the President of the United States and confirmed by the United States Senate. Once nominated and confirmed, all federal judges serve for life.

Appellate court judges in a little more than a quarter of the states similarly never stand for initial popular election. These judges are chosen by a variety of facially merit-based methods that include either input, nomination, or selection by either a special-purpose nominating commission, the Governor of the state, or the state legislature. They do not stand for popular election confirmation or for subsequent extensions of their judicial term.

In approximately a third of the states, appellate judges are initially appointed by the same variety of actors and methods as the judges in the states described in the preceding paragraph, and thus become appellate judges for their initial term without popular vote. In these states, however, the judges stand for reappointment at the end of their initial term through popular election. The terms for these judges are typically much longer than for state or federal legislators and can be as much as twelve years in length.

In approximately 40 percent of the states, appellate judges are both initially appointed and then reappointed by popular election. As in the case of judges initially appointed without popular election and then reappointed by such an election, the appointment terms for judges in these popular election states tend to be longer, and often much longer, than the terms of office for state-level legislators, ranging to as much as ten years in length.

To the extent that the professional function of judges, especially appellate judges, is thought to be legally and conceptually technical in nature, then it only makes sense that they be selected based on their perceived technical expertise rather than on their ability to garner and maintain popular political support.

One important conceptual support for this way of understanding the nature of the work of appellate courts is what is often called the natural law view of the law and legal doctrine. This view, which dominated the Anglo–American legal community during the nineteenth century, assumed the existence, at least theoretically, of a more or less ideal set of standards and principles by which human behavior should be governed – a so-called natural law. From this perspective, one critical task of the legal system in a given society is to develop the actual law of the jurisdiction over time so that it more and more closely approximates the ideal, natural law.

This concept of law and the work of a legal system has at least two obvious, and very powerful, influences. The first is the religious tradition, in which there very commonly exist absolute and immutable principles of human behavior, often directives from a deity, which religious communities strive in their various ways to understand, interpret, and apply to specific concrete situations. Much as a particular organized religion may establish a formal structure within which to organize and memorialize its ongoing interpretation of religious doctrine, the natural law paradigm sees the appellate court system as one in which a jurisdiction's understanding of the secular common law is continually reviewed and refined. Both perspectives view this process as one that strives, over time, to align their current interpretations more closely with the ultimately correct meaning and proper interpretation of the ideal standards.

The second profound influence on the development of the natural law view was science and the scientific method. It is no wonder that a high-level intellectual activity like appellate court adjudication and lawmaking would be inclined to see itself as similar in nature to the extraordinarily successful and respected work of the natural sciences and that those seeking a general understanding of the nature of the Anglo–American system of common law might reach for a model to what is among the most profoundly successful and influential human enterprises of the eighteenth and nineteenth centuries: natural science.

Traditionally, it is assumed that the natural world operates according to some set of basic rules and principles – that minerals and chemicals and planets alike possess consistent, stable characteristics and respond to similar stimuli in a similar fashion over time. These basic principles of science are, tellingly, sometimes referred to as the "laws of nature." It is the task of fundamental science to identify and articulate these laws of nature. At any given time, the scientific community will have a working draft, a tentative set of hypotheses, that represents its current best understanding of these actual principles. Through experimentation and the scientific method, by a case-by-case testing of the current hypotheses, science as a whole hopes over time to move its current understanding closer and closer to the actual laws of nature.

Analogously, from a natural law perspective, litigation in a common law system serves as the concrete case-by-case experiments that test the efficacy of current common law doctrine. When application of an existing doctrine to a live dispute produces a satisfying result, the wisdom, and thus the accuracy, of the rule is affirmed and its status as common law is strengthened. When proper logical application of the existing rule results in an unacceptable result, pressure builds to revise the rule or perhaps to create an exception to it. Over the course of hundreds of cases and decades of decisions, the common law of a jurisdiction should significantly improve and evolve ever closer to the ideal, abstract, natural law.

In a common law system based upon such a conception, the primary function of a trial court, after shepherding the litigation through the pleading, discovery, and fact determination stages, is to identify the appropriate general rules of law, ensure that these rules are deductively applied to the specific facts of the case, and announce a result. In a sense, while going about the specific business of resolving genuine disputes among persons, the trial courts also perform the important function of testing the efficacy of existing common law doctrine across a wide spectrum of actual cases. Much like the role of empirical experimentation in the scientific enterprise, the resolution of cases at the trial court level continually tests the correctness of existing common law doctrine by demonstrating the specific consequences of those doctrines in a wide range of actual disputes.

The primary function of an appellate court in such a system is to review the logical soundness of the work of the trial court. Much like a scientific review panel might confirm the basic structure and analysis of a certain experiment before publishing a report of its results, the appellate court's primary task is to "check the math" of the trial court below, to ensure that the appropriate rules of law were selected to resolve the matter and to see that they were accurately applied to the facts to determine the final outcome. Just as the review panel in science is unlikely to perform the actual experiment again, or to audit the accuracy of the empirical data, so, too, do appellate courts refrain from gathering any new facts about the case or engaging in any revision of the facts established during the trial court process.

Occasionally, an appellate court might find that the deductively accurate resolution of a particular case leads to such a manifestly unacceptable result that it will decide instead to make a change to existing common law doctrine. Consistent with the normal progress of the natural sciences, appellate courts operating within this traditional conception should be rather conservative about altering the common law and, in addition, should be more resistant to changing older, well-established doctrine than more recently created law. Moreover, such courts are always particularly mindful of crafting any new doctrine to fit carefully within the existing pattern of precedent. In the same way that one would not expect the scientific community to embrace a fundamental change to previously understood principles on the basis of just a few problematic experimental results, one would not expect the appellate courts of a given jurisdiction to endorse a significant alteration or addition to the existing common law without the pressure of a number of problematic trial level results urging such action.

The evolution of the common law under this traditional conception is, therefore, conservatively incremental and likely to occupy only a small percentage of the time and attention of the appellate courts. The ordinary work of appellate courts under such a view is the routine review and approval, or correction, of the work of the trial courts. Inevitably, such work will entail the refinement and clarification of the existing common law in the jurisdiction. Only rarely, however, would one expect an appellate court opinion to effect dramatic change to existing doctrine or to announce the creation of strikingly new law.

Rather clearly, then, when a supervisory court reviews the usually difficult and subtle work of a subordinate court on the basis of the dry transcript, a few written submissions, and a brief verbal presentation, the superior court is not seriously engaged in a thorough audit of the adequacy of the work of the court below, but is instead more or less "checking the math" of the trial court, reviewing only questions of law to ensure that the trial judge reached for the correct doctrine and applied it to the situation in a logical manner.

Again, entirely appropriate to this conception of the appellate process is the fact that the active participants are all attorneys. Counsel to the parties brief the case and participate in oral argument, and the appellate judges decide. Consistent with the analogy of appellate review to a scientific panel's oversight of an experimental report, only those with expertise in the requisite formal analysis need to participate. In the appellate process, it is only the state certified and licensed experts in legal analysis, the attorneys and the judges, who participate. No one else is thought to be needed for the kind of technical review of the deductive work of the lower court that is contemplated from this perspective.

Placing a label on this traditional understanding of the appellate legal process and appellate court lawmaking can be tricky – and potentially problematic. It can fairly be called a kind of mechanistic jurisprudence in that it relies upon formal logic and legal analysis to identify the preferred legal rule. It can be described as being deterministic in nature in that it presumes the existence of and seeks to discover a particular, specific result that is, at least abstractly, thought to be the ultimately correct and ideal version of legal doctrine. For the purposes of the current analysis, I will call this traditional understanding formalism, even if that term has sometimes also been applied to other, slightly different approaches to jurisprudence.

For many decades, this formalist conception was the primary means by which the Anglo–American legal community understood the function and operation of common law jurisprudence. Trial courts handled all of the work associated with the issue clarification, factual investigation, trial, and disposition of particular cases. The appellate courts reviewed the trial court's handling of questions of law and, in the process, tried incrementally to improve the quality of the common law in the jurisdiction by making occasional, modest changes to it. The fundamentally cautious and conservative nature of the change that appellate courts were expected to make to the common law is illustrated, and also enforced, by the rule of stare decisis that requires subordinate courts to follow as precedent only the holding of prior superior court opinions and not the dicta.

3

The Realist Critique of the Traditional Understanding and the Paradigm Shift from Formalism to Instrumentalism

The dominant formalist conception of common law jurisprudence described in the preceding chapter eventually came under increasingly serious challenge. To more and more participants, as well as observers, the notion of trial courts as mere managers of the case and predictable administrators of existing doctrine failed to describe what was actually happening in the disposition of these cases. Similarly, the actual work of the appellate courts, and the opinions that they issued, did not seem to be captured in a satisfying way by the formalist narrative.

One powerful critique of the formalist account focused on the supposedly tight logical structure of induction and deduction that was said to characterize common law jurisprudence. From a formalist perspective, a common law doctrine begins as the concrete resolution of a dispute, or a series of similar disputes, that is rationalized by an articulated general principle of decision. This generalized principle of decision should, if designed correctly, harmonize and make consistent the varied results in specific cases from which it was induced. This principle of decision, once established, is then relied upon by courts later facing a similar dispute and is deductively applied to reach a disposition in the new cases.

The general legal doctrine that is developed through this process of induction is, then, in a sense, tested to see if it produces an acceptable result each time it is deductively applied to a new situation. Occasionally, on review, an appellate court will be unsatisfied with the operation of the doctrine and will tinker with it by amending it slightly or by recognizing an exception to it. In this way, much like the currently understood principles of science, the body of common law in a jurisdiction, continually tested by the results of empirical experiments, slowly evolves and improves. Just as we hope that our currently understood principles of science move closer and closer to being the actual laws of nature, so, too, we hope in a formalist world that our actual common law moves ever closer to an ideal set of legal principles, sometimes referred to as natural law.

Beginning in the 1920s with writers like Karl Llewellyn and a movement that came to be known as legal realism, the formalist description of the work of the courts was challenged as being unsatisfying and insufficient. The realists claimed that the actual work of both the trial and appellate courts was far more expansive and value laden than was captured by the tight process of logical induction and deduction and the strict discipline of prior precedent, holding, and dicta imposed by the practice of stare decisis.

The legal realists offered a very different account of the structure and process of common law jurisprudence. As much as treatise writers and codifiers might have presented it in that way, the realists did not look at the common law and see a coherent, cohesive, relatively well-organized body of rules analogous to the current state of understanding in a mature natural science like physics or chemistry. Instead, the realists saw the generally accepted common law as more of a cloud of assorted principles, aphorisms, and maxims, some relatively tightly organized around particular topics and issues, and others not much integrated into a larger structure at all. To varying degrees, support existed in the way of established precedent for most all of the many tenets and precepts that constituted the common law. Thus, most all of it possessed some formal status under the doctrine of stare decisis.

The critical feature of the common law that distinguished it from the body of principles that make up a natural science, said the realists, was the fact that some, perhaps many, of the rules and maxims that were contained within the common law were potentially in contradiction with one another, sometimes in direct contradiction. A judge, faced with the task of solving a particular legal issue in a case, could look to the existing cloud of common law in the relevant jurisdiction and likely find two or more honored principles, either of which could be logically applied to resolve the issue, and each of which would, when deductively applied to the problem, yield a different result.

For example, imagine again the earlier example in which a court had to deal for the first time with the problem of an inaccurate offer in contract law, made without the fault of the offering party and interpreted without the fault of the accepting party. Suppose that, in this case, B is a very successful retailer of clothes that are currently quite fashionable and in vogue. In order to gain exposure and access to the large market that B currently enjoys, A, a manufacturer of clothing, sends B an offer to sell certain clothing produced by A for "$1.50 apiece." Due to no intentional mistake or carelessness on the part of A, the message that is received by B states "$1 apiece." B reads the offer, reasonably believes that it is a genuine offer from A, and promptly accepts. Is A bound by B's acceptance of the offer?

When realists consider this circumstance, they point out that a formalist approach to analyzing the issue offers no guarantee, and perhaps not even a likelihood, that a definitive resolution will be reached. Earlier, illustrating a typical formalist approach to the problem, the court invoked the generally accepted contract law maxim that a legally binding contract should only be found to exist where there was a genuine meeting of the minds between the contracting parties. Having invoked this basic principle, the court deductively applied it to the specific issue and determined that since no genuine meeting of the minds in fact took place, there should be no legally binding contract. Once the general governing principle – the precedent – has been invoked, the remainder of the analysis is logically determined and is not within the discretionary judgment of the court.

Legal realists, however, note that the larger precedent invoked by the court is not the only arguably relevant and appropriate general principle of contract law that could be identified and applied in this situation. The court could have instead invoked the equally well-accepted contract law principle that an offeror is the master of his offer. When this general principle is applied to the facts of the case, a contract is found to exist that legally binds the parties. Under this approach, the logically deductive application of a general precedent to the specific issue raised by the case is as solid and sound as in the earlier example. From a formalist perspective, both results are equally sound despite the fact that they lead to diametrically opposite resolutions of the case.

In a strictly formalist system, either decision is technically correct and ought to be upheld on appeal. Both approaches start with widely recognized doctrines of the common law and apply them with deductive accuracy to reach their different results. Neither approach gets "the math" wrong in a way that should invoke an appellate reversal. And yet each approach leads to different resolutions of the exact same issue arising in the same case from a single set of facts.

The thrust of the realist critique on this point was that the formalist conception of common law adjudication was, in practice, largely indeterminate. Not just subtly indeterminate in cases of unusually difficult logical challenges or especially ambivalent facts, but profoundly indeterminate along a wide spectrum of potential issues. One source of this indeterminacy, said the realists, was the co-existence of equally established but potentially contradictory principles and maxims residing within the universe of principles and maxims that constituted the established common law in a given jurisdiction at any given time.

The existence of equally authoritative principles that could result in importantly different outcomes when logically applied to the facts of a specific case meant that the real action in deciding these cases was not taking place in the deductive application of the existing common law to the facts of the case, as was supposed by the formalist model. Instead, it was occurring at the point of choosing which of the possible common law principles should be selected and applied to resolve the dispute. From this perspective, the ultimate resolution of most cases was decided and sealed once the court selected the broader legal principle or rule that was to be applied. In practice, only rarely did a genuine and significant issue exist regarding the logically deductive application of the selected principle or rule to the facts of the specific case.

This characterization of the operation of the common law legal system can be seen as having its counterpart in the larger world outside of law as well. That is to say that a person trying to decide how to proceed in a given situation can reach for one or another of a variety of well-recognized and generally accepted maxims, or principles, of conventional wisdom and can end up deciding to act in either one or another of two polar opposite directions, depending upon the specific maxim that is selected.

Regardless of the larger philosophical status of the conflict between formalism and realism, the legal realist critique of formalism and the realists' alternative account of common law jurisprudence in fact resonated with large numbers of lawyers and legal academics. Before long, the realist conception of the work of the courts became the prevailing perspective. Fewer and fewer observers continued to believe that the primary work of the appellate courts was a more or less technical review of the deductive logic of the lower courts, with an occasional revision of the existing common law. Increasingly, both observers and participants came to view the work of the appellate courts as heavily value laden, involving the selection of specific principles, and thus resultant specific outcomes, from a variety of nearly equal logical possibilities. The values and policies that guided these selections might be more or less explicit, or tacitly underlying, but in either case, they were nevertheless operative in the process.

If the common law were no longer to be seen as analogous to the laws of nature, something that may not at present be in a completely satisfactory form but which we strive to improve upon over time as we test it against the constant flow of cases that are processed by the court systems, what then is a more acceptable concept of it? Why should the courts prefer one possible version of a common law doctrine to another? On what broader principled basis could an advocate try to convince a court to create a new exception to an existing common law rule or to recognize a new common law doctrine? What is the reason for asking an advocate to place their preferred resolution of a case into the structure of a jurisdiction's existing precedent if we did not have faith that the existing precedents represent some settled understanding of the best treatment of a particular issue?

As the formalist paradigm waned under the continuing critical challenge of the realist movement, the emerging perspective that came to replace it viewed the common law not as the current product of a long-term search for the best, the ideal, the natural law, but instead as a social tool, one among many, that could be brought to bear to try to achieve particular social outcomes or solve particular social problems. From such a perspective, the primary purpose of contract law, then, is not so much to discover the abstractly optimal set of rules governing the exchange of promises among members of society, but is instead to maximize beneficial reliance and to minimize friction in executory transactions. Similarly, the goal of tort law is much less to articulate, abstractly, the proper obligations owed by one who harms another than it is to fashion a set of rules that maximizes compensation to victims and deters future harm-producing behavior.

Thus, tort law would be seen much less as a great social statement on the responsibility of citizens for harm caused to others or their property than as a particular social system, operating within a complicated complex of other social systems, such as criminal law, insurance, and government benefit programs, seeking to minimize injury and to provide adequate compensation to the injured. From this perspective, the common law generally is seen primarily as another tool, or another instrument, for attaining desired results in society, not as a grand attempt to accurately capture and articulate the ideally correct principles by which human conduct should be collectively regulated. Thus, this view of the law is often called instrumentalism.

From an instrumentalist perspective, the practical force of precedent in the determination of the outcome of a given case is inevitably far less than it would be under a formalist conception. For the formalist, the existing common law represents the distillate of many decades of articulation, testing, tinkering, and improvement of the doctrine. It is our current best formulation of ideal regulation in the field, and it is not to be disregarded or tampered with lightly. In fact, a court operating within a formalist model would be required to meet a heavy burden before resolving a particular dispute in a manner that was not consistent with the existing pattern of precedent in the jurisdiction.

For an instrumentalist, adherence to the existing precedent in a jurisdiction may be valuable to the extent that it permits parties to anticipate accurately the outcome of disputes, thus reducing the volume of costly litigation brought into the system. It may also be valued because such adherence will result in a more consistent resolution of similar cases brought into the system at different times or decided by different courts within the same system, thus advancing an important kind of fairness. On the other hand, adherence to an existing precedent from an instrumentalist perspective is a hindrance to the extent that it slows the alteration of the common law to achieve desired outcomes more effectively, or it makes more difficult the changing of existing common law to reflect new goals or to respond to new problems.

For the formalist, the existing common law is a carefully constructed social canon in which decades of painstaking thought and practical testing have been invested. To the instrumentalist, it is a tool, one whose primary value is its ability to be used at a given time and place to respond to the currently understood needs of society. If the tool is no longer doing the job that is currently required, then the obligation of the user is to modify the instrument until it performs more effectively.

The function of a judge in such an instrumentalist system, especially at the appellate level, is to ensure that the application of discrete doctrine in specific cases advances the intended social purposes behind that doctrine, to monitor the overall effectiveness of existing common law in achieving the desired social consequences, and to alter the existing law as needed to better serve the underlying social goals. Far from operating as the detached analytical technician envisioned by the formalists, judges in a realist world are thought to be enmeshed in value-laden choices regarding the identification of important social goals and the best means of achieving them.

For the realists, a change in law was typically necessitated not by a desire to move it closer to some abstract ideal, but to better respond to new social challenges or to changes in the regulated environment. The reasons why a legal doctrine should embrace any one of a number of logically possible versions had everything to do with the relative desirability of the practical social consequences likely to be generated by each possible version of the doctrine. Thus, for example, tort law's decision to adopt or not adopt an affirmative duty to reasonably rescue a stranger in peril should not be made on the basis of which version of the rule best articulates abstract notions of social obligation or best conforms, as a logical matter, to the existing pattern of affirmative duties. Instead, the decision should be made based on the relative desirability of the likely practical consequences of either adopting an affirmative duty to aid or refraining from doing so.[1]

The shift from formalism to instrumentalism was very much like the kind of occasional profound paradigm shift in the natural sciences that has been famously described by Thomas Kuhn in *The Structure of Scientific Revolutions* (2012). By the mid-1980s, less than fifty years had passed since the serious start of the realist movement. The initial intellectual excitement occasioned by the shift in the conventional paradigm of how law was understood to operate was still evident. Academic energy naturally flowed to projects designed to apply this new perspective across the broad spectrum of legal doctrine. Scholars eagerly worked at developing the fundamental instrumentalist rationale for each substantive area of law. Contract law, for example, stopped being about identifying meetings of the mind and defining the abstract obligation to make good on a promise and began focusing on maximizing socially beneficial reliance and efficiently allocating the risks of promissory transactions.

The heated debates in the late twentieth century among the critical legal theorists, the devotees of law and economics, and other competing schools of thought were primarily intramural battles. Despite their many differences, most all of these intellectual movements shared a thoroughly modern instrumentalist conception of the law, especially the common law. The arguments were overwhelmingly over the accurate identification of the underlying social purposes and the practical social consequences of legal doctrine.

By the decade of the 1990s, most law schools were overwhelmingly instrumentalist in their understanding and presentation of the law. No longer was it particularly noteworthy to include considerations of policy and social purpose in your presentation of a course, it was more or less expected. Standard casebooks, and even popular commercial outlines, by this time included a very significant amount of practical, empirical policy rationale for existing law and legal doctrine. Rare was the article published by a prestigious law review that did not delve deeply into the social goals and consequences of the legal doctrine under consideration.

1 See Chapter 8 herein.

Even though instrumentalism has become the dominant perspective within law schools and in the academic literature of law, it is still, as a newly emerging paradigm, relatively young. While it may not be quite the revelatory journey that it seemed twenty-five or thirty years ago, many students still come into first-year law school courses harboring expectations about the hard determinacy and the mechanistic nature of legal rules. Much of the popular culture, especially in depictions of the operation of the criminal law, conveys at least an implicit message of objectivity and traditional formalism.

More significantly, political actors at the highest levels of government continue to espouse the most deterministic version of formalism. These kinds of pronouncements typically take center stage during the nomination and confirmation of federal judges, particularly the United States Supreme Court justices. For example, in 2005, when nominating Samuel Alito to be an Associate Justice of the Supreme Court, President George Bush said, "He has a deep understanding of the proper role of judges in our society. He understands that judges are to interpret the laws, not to impose their preferences or priorities on the people."[2] Chief Justice John Roberts – in the opening statement of his confirmation hearing before the Senate Committee on the Judiciary – said, "Judges and justices are servants of the law, not the other way around. Judges are like umpires. Umpires don't make rules; they apply them."[3]

Erwin Chemerinsky, then chaired Professor of Law and Political Science at Duke University and now Dean of the School of Law at the University of California Berkeley, referred to this when he spoke at a 2006 symposium titled "The Role of the Judge in the Twenty-First Century." Professor Chemerinsky decried the continued persistence of formalist rhetoric to describe the nature of judging and the process of judicial review. He concluded his presentation by saying, "we should abandon the misleading rhetoric of discretion-free judging and talk about judging as it actually occurs."[4]

Perhaps one reason for the dominance of instrumentalism in law schools and among legal academics is that for a certain generation of legal academics the shift away from formalism is still clearly remembered, or it was tacitly absorbed in the mix of instrumentalist and traditional formalist professors that they encountered in law school. For these individuals, the energy of the realist critique may still be vivid, and the notion of turning a critical eye on instrumentalism itself seems somehow retrograde, an expression of a possible yearning for, or defense of, a now discredited and old-fashioned formalist past.

2 Press Release, Office of the Press Secretary, President Nominates Judge Samuel A. Alito as Supreme Court Justice (Oct. 31, 2005), http://www.Whitehouse.gov/news/releases/2005/10/2005/1031.html.

3 Confirmation Hearing on the Nomination of John G. Roberts, Jr., to be Chief Justice of the United States: *Committee on the Judiciary, United States Senate, 109th Congress* 55 (2005) (Statement of John G. Roberts, Jr.).

4 Erwin Chemerinsky, *Seeing the Emperor's Clothes: Recognizing the Reality of Constitutional Decision Making*, 86 *Boston University Law Review* 1069, 1081 (2006).

Most current law faculty members were likely schooled by professors who were themselves nearly all enthusiastic instrumentalists and who, outside of a possible jurisprudence elective, may not have wished to spend class time self-consciously identifying and justifying their instrumentalist approach to the material. The dominant, if implicit, message to these students was that the only meaningful way to understand legal doctrine was through an appreciation of how that doctrine advanced certain social values and disfavored others.

Given the depth of the shift of perspective from a formalist to an instrumentalist paradigm on the lawmaking work of appellate courts, there exists a striking lack of published appellate court cases that directly address the question of whether the court should adopt a formalist or an instrumentalist approach to its work. There are, in fact, no such widely cited and discussed cases. There exists no period of American jurisprudence during which appellate courts themselves take up this issue directly and argue in their published opinions for the superiority of a formalist or an instrumentalist paradigm. Why might this be the case?

The answer to this question lies in large part in the dominantly descriptive nature of the paradigm shift, and concomitantly in the degree to which the shift was not normative in nature.

The conception and practice of appellate court lawmaking under a strong formalist paradigm was neat and satisfying from a normative perspective. The analogy to the scientific method prevailed and was flattering and attractive. Appellate court judges were understood to be doing technical, conceptual analysis in an abstract and largely value-neutral way. They were selected based on their perceived technical, legal, and analytical expertise. They were not in the business of openly balancing and weighing often competing societal interests and concerns when determining the proper substance of the common law – no more than natural scientists were doing so in discovering the actual laws of physics or chemistry – and so they were appropriately insulated from the contaminating pressures of direct election and regular reelection by citizens.

The inputs to the common lawmaking process in appellate courts were, consistent with this model, severely limited to an official report of the proceedings in the trial of the matter being considered and formal written and oral arguments offered by similarly licensed and experienced experts in abstract legal analysis and doctrinal synthesis.

When the realist challenge arrived, it was not based primarily on a series of objections to the consequences of the formalist approach, or to its doctrinal product per se. The most successful thrust of the realist critique was not that formalism had produced incoherent and unworkable versions of common law torts, contracts, property, and agency law, for example. The critique was not normative in that sense.

Instead, the powerful and persuasive thrust of the realist critique of formalism was that appellate judges were not, in fact, doing what they said they were doing, and what they thought they were doing, when deciding what the common law should be. They were not choosing to formally adopt one version of a legal rule or doctrine over other possibilities because only one was logically and deductively consistent with existing law and established legal principles. Such an analysis, when carefully scrutinized, rarely produced only one acceptable or preferred logical possibility among others. The formalist approach, in fact, lacked the necessary kind of determinacy and constraint to adequately account for and rationalize common law lawmaking within a formalist paradigm. Whatever the basis was for appellate judges ultimately selecting one possible version of legal doctrine over others to be the authoritative common law doctrine in that jurisdiction, it was simply not accurately described, explained, accounted for, or rationalized by traditional formalism.

This is a fundamentally descriptive critique, not a normative one. In this way, the paradigm shift away from formalism in common law was like the paradigm shifts in physics and other natural sciences described by Thomas Kuhn in *The Structure of Scientific Revolutions*. Once one sees and appreciates the deep inadequacy of a prevailing paradigm in accurately characterizing and accounting for a given phenomenon, it cannot be unseen. Once the consensus of professional opinion in law came to intellectually appreciate that formalism did not really account for the choices made by appellate judges in fashioning and creating the common law, a kind of civic faith in the formalist paradigm was lost; not by normative choice so much as by intellectual necessity.

In Kuhn's account of scientific revolutions, an existing explanatory paradigm is supplanted by an alternative explanatory paradigm that better accounts for the known data in a given field. Cartesian and Aristotelian accounts of basic physics increasingly fail to explain experimental results and come to be replaced by Newtonian physics.

With the formalist understanding of the creation of common law and the nature of appellate courts in common law lawmaking, its fall from general acceptance was less a function of a successful challenge from a competitor paradigm than it was a growing understanding that formalism simply did not describe in an acceptably accurate way what it was that appellate courts were actually doing when they created and maintained common law. It was an increasingly unavoidable perception that the previously understood and publicly embraced basis for officially preferring some possible versions of legal rules and doctrine over others was not, in fact, the case; that it could not, in most cases, be true, even if the practitioners themselves believed that was what they were doing.

Thus, the shift from formalism to instrumentalism was not characterized by extended arguments and debates over which was the normatively superior approach to common law lawmaking. It was not a question of that. Formalism was almost certainly more elegant and normatively superior in many ways, and similarly most consistent with democratic values and manageable appellate practice. But it was not what was actually happening, and its normative superiority absolutely depended upon its descriptive accuracy.

Similarly, the claim for the superiority of instrumentalism over formalism was not based on some asserted greater determinism or consistency with respect to specific results or appellate court decisions. Different courts attempting to identify the version of a legal rule likely to result in the most attractive mix of practical costs and benefits could not be expected to necessarily agree on that judgment. The same court, either with the same decision-makers in place or not, might not decide consistently on the preferred version of a legal rule when the external circumstances in which the rule operated changed dramatically.

The core of the claim for instrumentalism over formalism was not that it offered greater determinism. The core of the claim was that in actual operation formalism was itself not nearly as logically bound and thus as logically determined as it pretended to be. Something else, something unacknowledged and unstated, was motivating the appellate judges to choose one possible general legal rule or principle over others to bring to bear in deciding a given matter. Something else was influencing and directing the preference for one ultimate outcome in the case over others. The sin of formalism was that it was obscuring that choice and that analysis under a thick façade of false assertions about the logically determined and value-neutral nature of the choice itself.

The fatal flaw of formalism was, therefore, not a lack of hard determinism, which it could not avoid nor escape from, but a lack of transparency. Like a magician, formalist appellate judges were engaged, conscious or not, in misdirection. While focusing the spotlight on the process of logical deduction by which the selected larger legal rule or principle was applied to the facts and the issues in the case to result in a specific resolution, the process by which one larger principle or maxim was chosen over other equally appropriate possibilities to begin the overt analytical process was often obscured.

The great advantage of instrumentalism over formalism is that unelected wielders of formal lawmaking power – appellate court judges – are encouraged, if not required, to be explicit about the value-laden choices that they are making, and about why those choices were preferred over other possible alternatives. This approach more often results in published appellate court opinion that provides far more accurate information about the actual assumptions, factors, and analysis that guided the court's ultimate judgments. Such opinions better hold the unelected decision-makers accountable in the exercise of their formal societal power. They also provide a far better guide to courts confronted with the task of having to confront and think through similar issues in the future.

It was not so much a matter of instrumentalism supplanting formalism in terms of offering a more compelling and attractive claim either normatively or descriptively. It was more a matter of formalism losing the foundational confidence of the legal, and larger intellectual, community and thereby failing to maintain its status as the shared conventional understanding of the nature of appellate court common law lawmaking. Instrumentalism more filled the consequent void than it affirmatively toppled the prior regime.

4

What Does Appellate Court Lawmaking Look Like within an Instrumentalist Paradigm?

The Tarasoff *Case as an Exemplar*

On July 1, 1976, the Supreme Court of California issued its final opinion in the case of *Tarasoff v. Regents of the University of California.*[1] A leader in the development of tort law operating at the zenith of its influence, the court was fully aware of the national and international attention the opinion was likely to attract. Indeed, *Tarasoff* is among a handful of the best-known tort law cases in American jurisprudence, particularly outside the legal community. It has been the subject of debate and analysis for nearly fifty years.

Doctrinally, the case made new law by recognizing, for the first time in any American jurisdiction, the existence of a legal duty on the part of a therapist to use reasonable care to protect a third person from serious danger of violence posed by the therapist's patient, thereafter commonly known as the "*Tarasoff* duty." Prior to the *Tarasoff* case, an individual owed no duty to act reasonably to protect a third person from harm inflicted by another adult unless the defendant was in a specially recognized legal relationship with the harm producer at the time the harm was caused to the victim. Thus, prior to *Tarasoff*, unless the patient harmed the victim in the therapist's waiting room, or in the therapist's presence, or while under the therapist's direct care and control, the therapist owed the potential victim no legal obligation to warn her about the possible danger posed to her by the therapist's patient.

While there are many interesting aspects of the case that have been well noted and discussed, at least one aspect of the opinion has received far less attention: the strikingly modem jurisprudential approach that the court adopted to analyze the legal problem presented to it. Just twenty years before, an appellate court faced with the prospect of creating a significant new common law doctrine, especially in a high-profile case, could have been expected to devote the great majority of its published opinion to the identification and analysis of relevant precedent, to thoroughly discuss analogous existing legal doctrine, and to make a determined

[1] 551 P.2d 334 (Cal. 1976).

effort to place the newly recognized duty in the broad, comforting context of existing rules and approaches. Not so in *Tarasoff*.

The facts of the *Tarasoff* case are as simple as they are sad. Dr. Lawrence Moore was a psychologist working for the Cowell Memorial Hospital at the University of California at Berkeley. On August 20, 1969, during the course of his treatment, Prosenjit Poddar, a patient and a graduate student at the university, indicated to Dr. Moore his intention to kill Tatiana Tarasoff upon her return to the United States from Brazil, which he expected at the end of the summer. Moore was apparently convinced of the genuineness of Poddar's stated intent because he, along with two other colleagues, sought to have Poddar committed for observation in a mental hospital. This effort was thwarted when members of the campus police department who were enlisted to detain Poddar found him, questioned him, and then physically released him in exchange for his assurance that he would leave Tatiana alone. Two months later, on October 27, 1969, Prosenjit Poddar killed Tatiana Tarasoff.

Tatiana's parents filed suit against Dr. Moore and his colleagues, the campus police, and the University of California at Berkeley. They claimed that the defendants negligently failed, during the slightly more than two months between Poddar's stated intent and the actual fatal assault, to warn Tatiana of the danger posed to her by Poddar. They also claimed that the defendants were negligent in failing to confine Poddar successfully when they tried to do so on August 20, 1969. The California Superior Court in which the case was initially filed granted the defendants' demurrers to both of the plaintiffs' theories of liability without leave to amend. The California Court of Appeal upheld the Superior Court's ruling. The Supreme Court of California sustained the Superior Court's judgment with respect to the plaintiff's failure to detain theory. However, in the part of the opinion that has made it so famous, the Court reversed and remanded regarding the failure to warn claim.

The holding of the *Tarasoff* case is succinctly stated in the fourth paragraph of the majority opinion. The court writes, "[w]hen a therapist determines, or pursuant to the standards of his profession should determine, that his patient presents a serious danger of violence to another, he incurs an obligation to use reasonable care to protect the intended victim against such danger."[2] This was the first time in California, or in any American jurisdiction, that a court had formally recognized such a duty.

And so, the *Tarasoff* case emerged in the summer of 1976 as a significant new addition to the common law of torts, issued by a nationally influential court with the likely ambition to change long-standing tort law doctrine across the country. By all measures, it is an important case, decided by a court that was well aware of its importance. What was the nature of the analysis that led to the court's conclusion in the case? What arguments mattered? What did the court consider when it contemplated creating a new tort law?

[2] *Id.* at 340.

One might expect a court facing an issue like the one in *Tarasoff* from a formalist perspective to devote a very significant portion of its opinion to a description of the already settled tort law doctrine surrounding the issue, a consideration of the most salient cases, and a careful characterization of the newly announced rule as residing harmoniously within the existing pattern of precedent. While the majority opinion in *Tarasoff* does briefly address the then – current case and statutory law in California, no real argumentative energy is expended in the debate among the majority, the concurrence, and the dissent regarding the characterization of existing case law; nor in a demonstration that the newly announced rule can or cannot be seen as a logical extension of already established doctrine. There is, in short, little deference shown to a traditional formalist approach to the problem.

Instead, the court in *Tarasoff* – majority, concurrence, and dissent alike – most eagerly view the problem as one of discerning the likely practical consequences of either adopting or rejecting the new doctrine and balancing the anticipated costs of these likely consequences against the expected benefits. Should a brand-new duty be recognized? "In analyzing this issue, we bear in mind that legal duties are not discoverable facts of nature, but merely conclusory expressions that, in cases of a particular type, liability should be imposed for damage done," the majority writes. Moreover, "[duty] is not sacrosanct in itself, but only an expression of the sum total of those considerations of policy which lead the law to say that the particular plaintiff is entitled to protection."[3] On this point the majority and the dissent agree, with the dissenting opinion stating flatly that, "[p]olicy generally determines duty."[4]

And so, thoroughly modern and instrumentalist in its approach, the court sets out for itself the task of identifying and weighing the practical benefits and costs of a formal legal duty being imposed upon psychiatrists to warn others of a serious threat of violence posed by one of their patients.

In this analysis, the plaintiffs' side of the case enjoys a more straightforward presentation. The basic thrust of the argument for the plaintiffs is that there will be fewer deaths and serious physical injuries if psychiatrists in the position of defendant Dr. Moore respond to credible threats made by their patients by reasonably warning the intended victims rather than failing to do so. Even if harm cannot be averted in every case, there is little question that permitting the victim at least the possibility of flight, fight, or watchfulness would result in less overall harm to such victims.

In addition to this very traditional tort law argument that the existence of a formal legal duty will result in less harm and more compensation, the plaintiffs can argue that such a duty accurately articulates the preferred moral stance on the issue. Here there is invoked the image of the psychiatrist, having heard a credible threat by a

3 *Id.* at 342.

4 *Id.* at 358.

patient against another, going about the remaining routine of his day: seeing other patients, returning phone calls, completing paperwork, driving home, having dinner, all while his patient stalks and kills the intended victim. Who could morally justify the doctor's failure to engage in merely reasonable efforts to try to warn the unwitting innocent victim under such circumstances?

Even if a case for refraining from warning could be constructed, it is hard to ignore that complete inaction is an easier option for the doctor than engaging in any effort to help. Moreover, the issuance of a warning to the intended victim aligns the psychiatrist, at least in the patient's mind, on the side of a stranger and against the patient, who is, after all, often the source of professional revenue for the doctor's practice. A therapist who develops a reputation for issuing warnings to third parties about potential threats to them posed by the therapist's patients might well, over time, encounter difficulty attracting and retaining a clientele sufficient to maintain their professional practice.

The case against the creation of a therapist duty to warn is far more complicated. It begins with an appreciation of the social cost incurred when a physician issues a formal warning to a third person that a patient under his care has threatened to inflict upon the recipient of the warning a serious bodily injury or to cause his death. Once a formal legal duty to issue such a warning is in place, psychiatrists will be advised to maintain a careful record of all such warnings issued, so one might expect the great majority of such warnings to be either immediately or eventually issued in writing.

The following is the text of an actual post-*Tarasoff* warning letter, with names redacted:

> Dear _____:
>
> As required by the *Tarasoff* decision, we must notify those persons whose lives have been threatened. This is to advise you that _____ has made threats against your life.
>
> We have notified the Police Department and the Mental Health Authorities of this and we strongly advise you to take precautions in the event that _____ is discharged from the hospital. One of the avenues available to you is in obtaining a restraining order from the District Attorney's Office in _____.
>
> Our plan is to discharge _____ upon stabilization, which may take up to 17 days. May we strongly advise you to take precautions in the event that he is released, as we are not able to force a person to leave the city.
>
> For further information and/or assistance, you may contact this office at _____ during work hours; after hours you may call to speak to the "ON CALL" Psychiatrist at _____ (to have him paged), the Police Department, and/or the nearest Mental Health Clinic in your area.
>
> Sincerely,
>
> Chief of Psychiatry

Imagine being the recipient of such a letter. Assume that you are the spouse, parent, child, close friend, supervisor, or co-worker of the patient who presumably poses to you a threat so serious that such a letter is thought by the Chief of Psychiatry to be necessary. Imagine further that you are the patient about whom the letter is sent to some combination of spouse, parent, child, friend, or co-worker. One can hardly doubt that the issuance of such a warning carries with it enormous social cost within the community of the patient's relations, friends, and co-workers – a cost that will likely last for years, and quite possibly a lifetime.

If lives are saved, or serious physical injury averted, then all the pain and social disruption involved can be seen as necessary. But what if the warning was, in fact, not necessary? What if the patient would never have actually tried to act out the threat? In such cases, the enormous social harm caused by each unnecessary warning would have to be viewed as a cost of the rule that must be balanced against its expected benefits.

Unsurprisingly, opponents of a formal *Tarasoff* duty have argued that psychiatrists and other therapists are not good at predicting the likelihood of a particular patient acting out on hostile, physically aggressive feelings that the patient may have toward another. Their training and experience focus on treatment and healing and hardly at all on the making of accurate predictions of specific future patient behavior. Thus, they argue, the imposition upon therapists of a duty to warn of such future behavior will surely result in large numbers of false warnings and the corrosive social consequences that will inevitably follow.

This line of argument is embraced by both Justice Clark in dissent, and by Justice Mosk, who is both concurring and dissenting in the *Tarasoff* case. Justice Clark writes, "[b]oth the legal and psychiatric communities recognize that the process of determining potential violence in a patient is far from exact, being fraught with complexity and uncertainty."[5] Justice Mosk asserts that, "[p]redictions of dangerous behavior, no matter who makes them, are incredibly inaccurate, and there is a growing consensus that psychiatrists are not uniquely qualified to predict dangerous behavior and are, in fact, less accurate in their predictions than other professionals."[6]

The majority in the case does not dispute that the recognition of a duty to warn will likely result in false warnings, nor does it engage with the dissenting Justices on the issue of psychiatrists' relative ability to predict the future violent behavior of their patients. Instead, it implicitly accepts the problematic nature of psychiatrists' predictive abilities and, nevertheless, maintains that, "professional inaccuracy in predicting violence cannot negate the therapist's duty to protect the threatened victim." Implicitly, the majority balances the cost of false warnings against the benefit of genuine warnings and concludes that, "[t]he risk that unnecessary warnings may be given is a reasonable price to pay for the lives of possible victims that may be saved."[7]

5 *Id.* at 346.
6 *Id.* at 354.
7 *Id.* at 346.

A second important theme of objection to a formal duty to warn highlights the many costs to the therapeutic process that might be experienced once such a duty becomes law. Essentially, this line of argument recognizes that a formal legal duty places both psychiatrist and patient in a difficult position. Both are likely to respond to difficulties they face in ways that will be detrimental to the therapeutic process.

Again, the starting point is an appreciation of the profound social cost to the patient that will be generated by the issuance of a *Tarasoff* warning. Psychiatrists have no choice but to be concerned about the possibility of legal action brought by a patient who has suffered such consequences and who feels that the doctor issued the warning on an insufficient basis. Indeed, the court in *Tarasoff* makes it clear that such an action would be viable when it writes: "[T]he therapist's obligations to his patient require that he not disclose a confidence unless such disclosure is necessary to avert danger to others, and even then that he do so discreetly, and in a fashion that would preserve the privacy of his patient to the fullest extent compatible with the prevention of the threatened danger."[8]

A therapist is thus placed between the rock of possible liability to the victim if the therapist does not warn and the patient, in fact, harms the victim, and the hard place of possible liability to the patient if the therapist warns unnecessarily. Faced with these twin exposures, therapists would be well-advised to disclose fully in advance to their patients the possibility that a warning will be issued if, in the course of treatment, the therapist believes that a credible threat exists. In effect, at the very start of the therapeutic relationship, the healer turns to the afflicted and makes it clear that if their conversation turns in the wrong direction, the healer will cause profound damage to at least one of the patient's most intimate relationships.

Whether aware of this possibility in advance or informed of it at the start of therapy, one might expect the existence of such a serious risk to operate as a powerful deterrent for some persons to seek or continue psychiatric treatment. In fact, because they face the greatest risk of triggering the warning and paying the resulting price, it is exactly those persons who are struggling with issues of hostility, aggression, and violent ideation, and who might pose the greatest risk of actually inflicting harm on others, who are presented with the strongest deterrent to seek treatment. For all such persons who respond to this disincentive by failing to seek help or who discontinue treatment, the possibility of preventing them from harming another as a result of effective therapeutic intervention is completely eliminated.

Even for those patients who do seek treatment, a powerful incentive continues to exist to withhold from the therapist any disclosure of hostile thoughts, feelings, wishes, or dreams that might possibly trigger the issuance of a warning. To the extent that such disclosures are a valuable component of the therapist's ability to diagnose and act, the effectiveness of the treatment experienced by the patient will be significantly compromised.

8 *Id.* at 347.

Moreover, one would expect that a patient's ability to place his trust fully in the therapist would decrease along with the patient's understanding that the therapist may be forced to issue a *Tarasoff* warning and thereby cause him great harm. Again, to the extent that a patient having trust in the therapist is important to the mode of therapy employed, the effectiveness of the patient's therapeutic experience will most likely be diminished as a result of the existence of a formal duty to warn. And again, this undesirable effect will operate most powerfully in the case of just those patients who could most use therapeutic intervention to help them avoid doing harm to others.

From the perspective of therapists, the prospect of legal liability attached to the decision to warn or not to warn whenever a patient indicates that he may pose a threat to another makes the treatment of such patients relatively undesirable. If given a choice, one would expect therapists to choose to avoid such patients in favor of others who do not present symptoms of hostility and aggression.

As relatively undesirable patients, people struggling with violent impulses may have difficulty finding therapists willing to treat them. Those who do find treatment are likely to find it among therapists who have little or no choice in the selection of their patients. Moreover, therapists who do find themselves treating such patients may be tempted to engage in measures designed to minimize their risk of *Tarasoff* liability. Such measures might include especially vigorous advance warnings to the patient of the possibility of the therapist having to issue a warning, steering conversation with the patient away from problematic topics, or subtly signaling to the patient in other ways that the therapist would find discussion of hostile impulses toward others unwelcome.

Viewed in this way, the adoption of a formal *Tarasoff* duty to warn can be seen as aligning the self-interest of both the patient and the therapist in the effort to avoid circumstances in which the obligation for the therapist to issue such a warning might arise. Patients may avoid treatment or avoid making any revelations during the course of treatment that are likely to trigger the obligation. Therapists may avoid problematic patients altogether or discourage any such patients that they treat from discussing thoughts or feelings that could be interpreted as constituting a threat. Each of these responses to the existence of a formal duty to warn will make it far less likely that persons wrestling with violent impulses toward others will be moved away from the path of acting out those impulses by effective psychiatric treatment.

Further, because neither therapists nor patients can know in advance with much certainty whether their interactions will lead into this dangerous territory, the chilling effect on the willingness to seek treatment, on the selection of patients, and on the unfettered range of issues explored during therapy can be expected to exert its influence, to varying degrees, across the full spectrum of psychiatric practice. This is especially true with respect to the reduction in trust invested by patients in therapists once they learn that the therapist could, conceivably, be forced by law to reveal their confidences in a way that is almost certain to cause them great pain. Thus, the existence of a *Tarasoff* duty can be argued to impose harm on the efficacy of psychiatric care far beyond the specific patients who are likely to trigger an actual *Tarasoff* warning.

A third broad front of argument that can be mounted against the creation of a formal duty to warn revolves around the possibility of involuntary civil commitment. Now, as in California at the time of the *Tarasoff* case, it is possible for a person to be physically detained against his will without having engaged in any criminal activity, nor even having raised in anyone a reasonable suspicion of having committed a crime. This possibility, a rare hole in the fabric of constitutional doctrine designed to limit the possibility of incarceration to, and even within, the criminal justice system, is created by the existence of what are commonly known as involuntary civil commitment statutes. These statutes typically authorize the unconsented incarceration of a person thought to be mentally ill for the purpose of psychiatric evaluation and possible treatment.

The existence of involuntary civil commitment is relevant to an analysis of a formal therapist duty to warn in at least two ways. One is the much greater attractiveness to therapists of the involuntary commitment option in the presence of a formal therapist duty to warn. Imagine a patient who behaves in a way that raises a reasonable suspicion that the patient may pose a risk to another in a jurisdiction that has adopted a therapist duty to warn. The therapist understands that from this point on he faces the twin-horned dilemma of either issuing a *Tarasoff* letter that may subsequently be determined to have been unnecessary or choosing not to warn and face the risk of the patient actually inflicting harm on another. With these two unappealing prospects looming, the therapist may see the involuntary commitment of the patient as an appealing option. He could avoid issuing a potentially unnecessary warning to the possible victim and, at the same time, ensure that the patient is not physically able to cause harm, at least during the period of involuntary commitment.

Not only will the patient be physically unable to inflict harm during the period of involuntary commitment, but the patient's physical confinement is likely to occur, if at all, quickly after the threat is manifested and thus might provide a critical cooling off period, reducing further the risk of eventual harm. Moreover, even an unsuccessful attempt to commit the patient may be beneficial to the therapist inasmuch as it creates a record of a formal determination that the patient's condition does not satisfy the standards for involuntary civil commitment, and thus may not rise to the legal requirement of issuing a *Tarasoff* warning. In addition, therapists operating in a *Tarasoff* jurisdiction are likely to be more sensitive and attentive to their patients' expressions of hostility toward others, and this, too, may lead to an increase in involuntary civil commitments.

For all of these reasons, therapists operating under a duty to warn regime may find the option of seeking the involuntary civil commitment of problematic patients significantly more attractive than therapists who do not operate under such a duty. To the extent that the involuntary commitment of mentally ill persons represents an undesirable, even if arguably necessary, exception to the usual constitutional protections against incarceration without criminal fault, the creation of an incentive for therapists to seek such commitments in larger numbers and with greater vigor must be viewed as a social cost generated by the creation of a therapist duty to warn.

The second way in which the existence of involuntary civil commitment statutes influences judicial determinations regarding a formal therapist duty to warn is more internal to the deliberations of, and the political constraints inevitably faced by, appellate courts. Given their unusual nature and the history of severe abuse associated with them in other countries, it is not surprising that involuntary civil commitment statutes have been the target of controversy and sustained constitutional challenges for more than fifty years. At the time of the *Tarasoff* case, and at present, the basic standard for the constitutionality of such statutes is that they must, at a minimum, require a determination by a psychiatric professional that the person subject to civil commitment poses a present danger to himself or to others and that this determination be reviewed and adjudicated before a neutral magistrate within three days of the start of confinement.

Any court, including the California Supreme Court in *Tarasoff*, comes to a case that raises the prospect of a formal duty to warn with an awareness of the rich history of constitutional litigation involving involuntary civil commitment statutes. As a result, the justices must understand that no matter how factually persuasive they may find the argument that psychiatrists and therapists are not trained for, not experienced in, and not competent to make accurate predictions of future violent behavior by their patients, it would be jurisprudentially awkward to publicly base a decision not to adopt a formal duty to warn on this rationale when the prevailing constitutional standard for involuntary civil commitment statutes relies upon just such predictive competence by psychiatric professionals. Any published opinion in the duty to warn area that acknowledged the problematic aspects of therapist predictions of future harmful behavior by their patients could be expected to be quickly taken up by opponents of involuntary civil commitment in an effort to reopen that constitutional controversy.

Thus, a very important line of argument against the adoption of a formal therapist duty to warn – starting with therapists' lack of training, experience, and competence in the prediction of dangerous behavior, moving on to the high level of false warnings that are likely to be produced as a result, and then recognition of the enormous personal and social cost generated by these false warnings – is burdened by the consequence that embracing these arguments is likely to have on a largely unrelated area of jurisprudence. Moreover, this burden is wholly unrelated to the factual accuracy of the argument or to the courts' perception of the actual number of damaging false warnings likely to be issued as a result of the adoption of a duty to warn rule.

One further area of concern regarding the adoption of a formal therapist duty to warn is also somewhat internal to the operation of the rule within the common law court system. Appreciation of these concerns begins with recognition that, in many ways, the specifics of the *Tarasoff* case present to the courts a nearly ideal set of facts upon which to ground the creation of a therapist duty to warn. In the *Tarasoff* case, a patient currently under the care of a fully licensed psychiatrist disclosed to the doctor a concrete plan to kill a specifically named individual in the near future, and, in fact, actually caused that person's death within the announced time frame. The court then finds that under these circumstances, the doctor had an obligation to inform the individual of the impending danger, and, consequently, a formal legal duty to warn is born.

However, one can hardly expect most of the cases that will come before the courts requiring adjudication under the *Tarasoff* duty to be as factually simple and as clean as the *Tarasoff* case itself. Hence, the adoption of this new duty will inevitably require the courts to confront variations of facts that will push the new duty, and its more precise definition, along a number of dimensions.

For example, what kind of harm must be threatened by the patient in order to trigger the therapist's formal duty to warn? *Tarasoff* involves a threat of death, but what about a threat of bodily harm that does not pose a risk of permanent physical injury or death? What about a threat of a moderate physical beating, or a single punch, or a slap across the face, or a shove, or a trip? What about a threat to the intended victim's emotional well-being? Or to her property? Or her reputation?

Prosenjit Poddar indicated to Dr. Moore his intention to kill Tatiana Tarasoff. What if another patient indicated to his therapist his intention to kill a specific, but unnamed, individual? Or if the patient never specifically named the intended victim but the therapist deduced or could have reasonably deduced the identity? What if the therapist might have identified the victim with some modest investigative efforts, including non-therapeutic interrogation of the patient? If the patient threatens serious physical injury to "my family," or to "my enemies at work," or to "those lawyers," does the therapist have a legal duty to warn a threatened group of people, and of up to what size?

The threat in *Tarasoff* was communicated to, and thus the duty descended upon, a fully licensed medical doctor of psychiatry. What if the caregiver learning of the threat was a licensed therapist who was not a medical doctor, or a working therapist who did not require a license to practice in the jurisdiction, or a psychiatric nurse? Does, or should, the formal duty apply to a university or school counselor, a professor or a teacher, a licensed physician not providing psychiatric care to the patient, an attorney, a family member, or a best friend? Though none of these many difficult questions need to be answered, or even confronted directly, in order to impose a formal duty to warn in the *Tarasoff* case itself, the court's adoption of a general duty in that case inevitably commits the jurisdiction to a future encounter with these many unresolved aspects of the doctrine. In addition, until these open issues are dealt with by courts, or by the legislature of the state, those who may be affected by the duty must operate under uncertainty and speculation as to the ultimate contours of the rule.

5

Problematic Aspects of Instrumentalist Court Lawmaking within a Formalist Framework

Given the preceding arguments in Chapter 4, both in favor and against the adoption by the law of a formal therapist duty to warn, one can see the rather dramatic difference that the choice of a formalist or an instrumentalist approach to the problem would make. A formalist court would focus primarily upon the degree to which a newly recognized duty to warn could be found to have antecedents in the tort jurisprudence of the jurisdiction, whether it could be determined to be consistent, at least analogously, to broader tort principles and maxims, and how it might reside harmoniously among the existing precedents in the area. An instrumentalist court, on the other hand, would focus primarily on identifying and balancing the likely practical benefits of the new duty against its costs, as did the California Supreme Court in *Tarasoff*.[1]

The realist revolution, over the years, produced a fully developed analysis of the many problems inherent in a formalist regime. As the newly ascendant and currently dominant paradigm, the instrumentalist approach has not yet been subjected to nearly as pervasive a critique. The *Tarasoff* case can serve as a useful and appropriate vehicle for a start at identifying some of the more obviously problematic aspects of the instrumentalist approach.

Perhaps the most pervasive problem with the approach adopted by the *Tarasoff* court to the question of whether there should exist a formal duty to warn imposed upon therapists is that it engages in a primarily instrumentalist endeavor within the confines of a court structure and appellate procedures designed and built for a formalist world. In other words, the court in *Tarasoff* and appellate courts generally operating within the instrumentalist paradigm are committed to engage in analysis about the likely practical consequences of competing versions of legal doctrine without the benefit of any regular structured means by which to identify and scrutinize such consequences.

One threshold difficulty in appellate courts engaging in instrumentalist analysis is that the individuals engaging in that analysis – appellate court judges – are not

[1] Tarasoff v. Regents of the University of California, 551 P.2d 334 (Cal. 1976).

selected based on, and cannot be expected to necessarily possess, any particular talent, experience, or skill in identifying and weighing the practical consequences of one version of legal doctrine compared to another. Almost nothing in law school training, or the assignment of grades in law school, focuses on that kind of exercise of practical judgment. Nor do law schools typically look for indicia of such aptitude in their admissions criteria. An appellate court judge might easily have been an undergraduate philosophy major and earned high grades in law school without possessing any particular interest, or developing any particular competency, in assessing the practical, real-world consequences of various doctrinal alternatives to a legal issue. Adeptness at understanding and manipulating abstract concepts in themselves and in relation to other abstract concepts would be fully sufficient for such success. Thus, virtually nothing exists in the current system by which appellate court judges are selected and confirmed that even increases the likelihood, let alone ensures, that these lawmakers possess the kind of professional skill upon which instrumentalist legal analysis depends.

Moreover, appellate courts engaged in instrumentalist analysis are required to ground their decisions in an analysis of the likely pragmatic consequences of those decisions in regulated communities about which the members of the court may have little or no actual knowledge or experience. Given the broad range of human activities to which the law, by its nature, applies, appellate judges might well be called upon to identify the anticipated costs and benefits of various possible versions of a legal rule in an enormously wide range of different factual circumstances, including within widely varying communities and specialized subcommunities.

For example, in the *Tarasoff* case, it is clear that one critical element in an instrumentalist analysis of the issue is the determination of the extent to which the creation of a formal duty to warn will cause therapists to issue more false warnings than they would otherwise. Even more critically, the court must estimate the number of false warnings that will be issued by therapists in response to the duty compared to the number of valuable warnings that the existence of the duty will provoke. In other words, how will the ratio of false warnings to necessary warnings be altered when the jurisdiction moves from there being no duty to warn to the embrace of a *Tarasoff* duty?

Whether or not the judges confronted with this task enjoy any meaningful facility with utilitarian analysis generally, they may have no direct experience whatsoever with psychiatrists or therapists, with their patients, or with the therapeutic process. Worse still, perhaps, they personally may have had some direct personal experience with therapists and psychiatric therapy and, as a result, are tempted to over-extrapolate from this very specific personal experience to therapists, patients, and therapy in general. Moreover, this utterly uncertain and wholly random possession of specialized knowledge and experience regarding the activity affected by the legal doctrine at issue characterizes as much the attorneys who develop and deliver the arguments to the court as it does the judges who evaluate those arguments and ultimately decide.

The court in the *Tarasoff* case explicitly acknowledges that the problem of false warnings that may be triggered by the existence of a formal duty to warn is a significant possible cost of the legal rule under consideration and a key factor in deciding whether such a duty should be part of California's tort law. The majority in the case weighs the cost of increased false warnings against the benefit of encouraging a potentially increased number of accurate and helpful warnings and ultimately concludes that "[t]he risk that unnecessary warnings may be given is a reasonable price to pay for the lives of possible victims that may be saved."[2]

On what possible basis, other than some kind of generic and generalized exercise of personal intuition, can the California Supreme Court embrace that conclusion? On what basis could any appellate court come to such a conclusion? These courts are populated by decision-makers who may or may not possess even an ordinary capability to identify practical consequences likely to flow from a change in applicable doctrine and who, in a large number of instances, have little or no actual experience or knowledge regarding the regulated community to which the legal rule under consideration will apply.

Even if appellate decision-makers do, in a particular instance, possess experience or knowledge regarding the relevant regulated community (in this case, professional therapists and their patients) sufficient to ground a conclusion like "[t]he risk that unnecessary warnings may be given is a reasonable price to pay for the lives of possible victims that may be saved," note how very quickly such experience and knowledge is attenuated when the court is confronted with no more than a slight variation in the legal issue before them.

What if the next case after *Tarasoff* requires the court to decide whether to recognize a formal duty to warn that applies to those who provide individual therapy to clients and who are not fully licensed psychiatrists (as were the therapists in *Tarasoff*) but are instead situated somewhere along the broad spectrum of licensed and unlicensed psychologists and psychiatric therapists, nurses, aides, and mental health support providers that exist in the United States? What if the case after that requires consideration of a formal legal duty to warn applied to school counselors, or to immediate family members, or to close friends, or to bartenders, or to sellers of weapons? Even a subtle shift in the contours of the legal rule under consideration is likely to call upon quite different kinds of experience and knowledge of widely varied practical circumstances in which the rule will effectively operate. And this must be done within the confines of a relatively narrow issue (the inclusion or not in specific circumstances of an obligation to warn as part of the duty of reasonable care element in the negligence claim) situated rather deep in the interstices of just one area of law (torts).

With just an occasional exception, the overwhelming majority of both state and federal appellate courts in this country are courts of general jurisdiction rather than

2 *Id.* at 346.

appellate courts of limited and specialized jurisdiction. Similarly, the overwhelming majority of common law issues brought before appellate courts of general jurisdiction reside along wide spectrums of different substantive areas of law and have practical consequences along the full spectrum of actors and activities in society. Thus, most common law in this country is created and maintained by appellate courts of general jurisdiction that must confront, analyze, and resolve questions of legal doctrine that will span dozens of different areas of common law and that will operate within and affect a vast scope of human activity taking place in a staggering variety of more and less specialized communities.

The only reasonably accurate and fair conclusion that can be drawn in this regard, then, is that any given appellate judge, and thus any given appellate court, will very likely come to an instrumentalist analysis of a given common law issue possessing virtually no, or very little, practical experience or knowledge regarding the regulated community in which the legal doctrine under consideration will primarily operate. This is a very serious impediment to the pursuit of effective instrumentalist analysis by such courts, and it calls into serious question the likely accuracy of such analysis, and thus the degree of legitimate faith and reliance that should be invested in the resulting substance of the common law.

Not only is it unlikely that those engaging in instrumentalist legal analysis will possess much meaningful experience or prior knowledge about the practical nature of the regulated communities in which the law they create will operate, but the materials upon which their judgments are based are not designed to provide them with much meaningful information about the practical nature of those communities. These participants are nearly always full-time practicing lawyers. Typically, the only people meaningfully involved in appellate litigation are the attorneys representing the parties to the litigation and the appellate judges assigned to the case. Unlike a trial court, and unlike legislative and regulatory bodies, appellate courts do not hear from witnesses and do not accept evidence. The typical inputs to appellate litigation are: (1) formal written legal arguments (known as briefs) submitted by the attorneys representing the parties in the case, and also very occasionally briefs submitted by other interested persons (known as friends of the court, or amici curiae) who may offer to the court formal legal arguments in the form of what is known as an amicus curiae brief; (2) a specialized written transcript describing what took place in the litigation at the trial level (known as the record of the case); and, perhaps (3) a brief period of oral argument by the main attorneys before the appellate judges (very rarely more than two hours total in length).

So, in a case like *Tarasoff*, the active participants in the process of determining whether the jurisdiction should adopt as part of its tort law a formal legal duty to warn borne by therapists – with all of the practical consequences for some individuals that such a determination entails – are no more than a relative handful of individuals, all of whom were trained in the law and are professionally active as either practicing attorneys or jurists. This handful of lawyers will argue, debate, and analyze the likely practical consequences of legal rules in a wide variety of specific (and often sophisticated, complicated, and not entirely transparent) real-world contexts in which none of them will necessarily possess personal experience or significant expertise. Moreover, they will do so based only on a small number of written legal materials prepared predominately by attorneys and without the routine or required participation of actual participants or substantive experts in the area of activity being regulated.

The California Supreme Court in *Tarasoff* did not itself hear any direct testimony, including no testimony regarding empirical data or evidence, in an effort to gather information or advice from those with either experience or expertise in: the nature of persons who seek therapeutic help in response to having violent impulses; the number of such persons who actually express violent intentions to their therapists; the number of persons who eventually act out on violent impulses, expressed or not; the ability of most therapists to accurately predict who such patients will be; the impact on an identified possible victim of receiving a *Tarasoff* warning from the therapist; the burden placed by the possibility of the therapist being legally required to issue a *Tarasoff* warning on the efficacy of the therapeutic process itself; and the many other practical considerations that should appropriately be taken into account when deciding whether the existence of a *Tarasoff* duty will likely be a net benefit or net detriment to the relevant jurisdiction. The appellate court will not seek such information on its own, and there are virtually no procedural mechanisms by which such information will be reliably provided to the court.

In the overwhelming number of appellate court cases in this country, the appellate court receives legal briefs only from the attorneys representing the parties to the case and receives no amicus curiae submissions. The length of the briefs submitted by the attorneys for the parties (and also for the amici curiae, if there are any) are strictly limited in length (often in the neighborhood of no more than thirty pages or its word count equivalent), and they are required to spend a meaningful amount of these limited words and pages on matters that do not address any kind of instrumentalist analysis of the desirability of one possible legal rule or another; matters like a statement of the standard of appellate review, an articulation of the questions presented to the court, a recitation of the facts of the case, and a table of authorities. There is neither opportunity nor expectation that a legal brief submitted to an appellate court can offer to the court anything like sufficient factual background or argument upon which to base a serious empirical analysis of the likely practical consequences of the court choosing to embrace one possible version of a legal doctrine over others. The same is true of the oral arguments in the case, if there are any.

Whether an appellate court adopts a traditional formalist approach or an instrumentalist approach to fashioning the common law for its jurisdiction, the practice of stare decisis still applies with respect to relevant prior decisions existing within that same court system. Therefore, the attorneys in the case must devote some significant portion of their argumentative resources in both their briefs and their oral arguments to trying to persuade the court that the legal rule, and the resolution of the case, that most benefits their client and that the attorney is urging the court to adopt also acceptably satisfies the doctrine of stare decisis with respect to existing prior decisions in the jurisdiction.

For all of these reasons, neither the formal legal briefs, nor the oral arguments, nor the two taken together, are likely to provide an appellate court with anything like a sufficient factual or analytical basis for engaging in the kind of often complicated and subtle analysis that is the foundation of an appropriate instrumentalist approach to creating and maintaining the common law.

Note again that appellate courts overwhelmingly work only with three kinds of inputs: the written briefs of the parties (and perhaps amici curiae), the oral arguments of counsel, and the record of the proceedings in the lower courts. Attorneys in the case may make assertions regarding the likely consequences of one interpretation of a legal doctrine or another, and these assertions may be footnoted in the briefs, but they are not permitted to bring persons with relevant expertise or experience into the appellate proceedings to testify and be cross-examined for the benefit of the appellate court. Similarly, appellate courts do not have available to them a procedure by which to seek independent experts to educate and advise them as to the likely practical consequences of their decisions.

While the kind of expert testimony and factual investigation that is essentially no part of the appellate process is, indeed, a regular part of trial court procedure, the fact-finding process at the trial level is narrowly focused on the specific history of the parties and their disputes and has little or no concern with, and makes no investment in, determining the degree to which the specific facts of the instant case fairly represent the regulated community as a whole. An appellate court reviewing the legal decisions made in the subordinate courts below and having access only to the formal written record of the case might well have no basis for determining whether the particular facts of this case, including the actions of the parties and their specific consequences in this instance, represent a typical example of more general behavioral dynamics in this regulated community or instead represent a rare and uncommon outlier.

Even if the actual facts of a specific case could be considered to be reasonably representative of the larger community affected by the legal doctrine at issue, there are many aspects of trial procedure that make it unlikely that the legal facts developed to determine the eventual outcome of the case at the trial level and that are included in the formal written record of the case will provide the appellate courts with a good and sufficient factual basis for instrumental analysis. In other words, there are many reasons to believe that the factual representation of any specific case that comes before an appellate court in the written record of the case enjoys only a modest correspondence to the actual factual incidents that transpired among the parties. As a result, there is even less reason to believe that the factual version of the case presented to the appellate courts bears strong correspondence to the usual experience of participants in the regulated community.

The dynamics by which the actual facts of a dispute may differ significantly from the presentation of those facts to an appellate court begin with the inevitable sophistication of parties who become regular and recurring, even if reluctant, participants in litigation. Such parties learn fairly quickly, often under the advice and guidance of experienced attorneys, to develop their methods of recording facts and to design their systems for maintaining, organizing, and purging factual records in a manner that provides them with the maximum strategic advantage in possible future litigation. Thus, in such cases, the framework within which the basic facts of a transaction are gathered, maintained, and made available for legal discovery is oriented far less toward historical or empirical accuracy than it is toward the tactical advantage of the party who creates those factual records.

Once litigation commences, the process of factual investigation is undertaken exclusively by the interested parties themselves. In the pursuit of factual discovery the parties are, of course, motivated far more by a desire to uncover or conceal information that is strategically relevant to the litigation rather than by any ambition to develop a full and accurate factual picture of events. Thus, the process of factual investigation in a litigation setting is heavily influenced by, indeed, it operates entirely within, the specific contours created by the relevancy of information as determined by the legal doctrines likely to be applied to the case and by the admissibility of that information as determined by the rules of evidence. Moreover, the accuracy and thoroughness of the factual picture developed by the discovery process are also compromised by the financial limitations faced by the parties. These limitations place pressure on the attorneys to focus their investigative efforts narrowly on only the most strategically valuable information.

Even beyond the distorting effect of possible future litigation on the maintenance of factual data and the vast difference between an objective empirical investigation and the legal discovery process, there are a plethora of legal doctrines that routinely come into play during litigation that cause the official version of facts in a trial to vary significantly from the actual historic events. Included among these devices are factual stipulations entered into by the parties and admissions, both of which are routinely encouraged by trial court judges, and neither of which are required to be empirically accurate in order to become an undisputed part of the factual record of the case. In a similar way, other doctrinal devices such as formal presumptions and burdens of proof, while critical aids to fairness and efficiency, alter the operation of the fact-finding process in litigation so that it potentially operates quite differently than would an objective empirical investigation.

Witness testimony is still another area of concern. To the extent that the primary mode of presentation at trial is the live testimony of witnesses, the dependability of the factual result will suffer from the notoriously problematic accuracy of the testimony of witnesses, many of whom are unaware of the importance of the events in question at the time they observed them, who may have made the observations years before they testify about them at trial, and who by the date of their court appearance are typically hyper-aware of the consequences of what they might say.

Procedures and rules at the trial level of litigation are designed primarily to provide a fair forum for the resolution of specific disputes between actively litigating parties. As such, they are poorly suited to create a record that provides appellate courts with a factual picture that is accurate or representative of the regulated community as a whole. When the process of developing an accurate and complete account of the facts, even in the instant case, let alone representative of the regulated community generally, conflicts with the interest in providing the parties with a competitively fair and balanced basis for resolving the disputes between them, the law of evidence and trial practice consistently favor fairness over factual accuracy and comprehensiveness. As a result of this policy orientation, the facts of a situation brought forward at trial may not include many of the salient features of the actual situation due to the existence of standard rules of evidence that exclude clearly relevant and material information from the finder of fact and from the formal written record of the case.

Sometimes otherwise valuable evidence is excluded because of a concern that, while probative, it is also unacceptably prejudicial to a party. For example, imagine a situation in which A is being prosecuted for the crime of shoplifting. A has previously been convicted of committing the crimes of assault and arson. An objective decision-maker might find the fact that A previously committed more than one crime as indicating that A generally possesses a criminal disposition and, therefore, increasing the likelihood that A committed this particular crime in this instance, at least in contrast to a circumstance in which A had never previously committed any crime. This chain of inference might not necessarily be dispositive, but it would at least be relevant to the judgment that must be made.

Nevertheless, it is highly unlikely that evidence of these prior criminal convictions of A will be permitted in this circumstance to be introduced as evidence in A's shoplifting trial. The reason for this is that the court in the case is likely to determine that while these prior convictions may be relevant, their probative value is outweighed by the likelihood that the finder of fact in the shoplifting case will be unduly prejudiced against A after learning of these prior convictions and might be inclined to convict him of shoplifting in this case because he is a repeat criminal and a bad guy even if there does not exist direct evidence beyond a reasonable doubt that he actually engaged in shoplifting in this instance. Because a ruling excluding the prior convictions would not be a difficult or a close call under the current rules of evidence, it is most likely that the prosecution will not seek to introduce it, the defense will not need to object to it, and the trial court will not need to rule on it, thereby resulting in A's prior convictions not appearing anywhere in the formal written record of the case that will be made available to an appellate court.

In addition to accurate and relevant information sometimes being excluded from a case because the court determines that the probative value of that information is outweighed by its prejudicial effect, other, accurate and relevant information regarding a case may be excluded because the admission of that evidence will arguably compromise other important societal values and norms that may have nothing to do with the case itself or with the larger legal issues raised by the case. These kinds of exclusions usually operate through various evidentiary privileges.

Typically, a privilege will operate to exclude otherwise relevant, material, and admissible information because maintaining the possible confidentiality of this information, even in an active litigation setting, is thought to support free and uninhibited communication of that information from one person to another under certain circumstances in which undeterred and unfettered communication is thought to be important. Thus, formal evidentiary privileges cover communications between spouses, between physicians and patients, and between attorneys and their clients.

In all three of these instances, the law recognizes that other important societal interests may, under certain circumstances, override the truth-seeking function of a trial. While long-standing, well-recognized, and generally uncontroversial, these evidentiary privileges nevertheless have the consequence of causing the formal legal record of facts in a given case to deviate, possibly quite significantly, from the actual factual experience of the parties.

Finally, even after the conclusion of all trial activity and the issuance of a final judgment, it may not be at all clear to an appellate court from the record of the case what precise version of disputed facts was adopted by the finder of fact. For example, in a case that is tried before a jury that returns a general verdict, the appellate court receives the trial record containing evidence presented by the parties, some of it potentially conflicting and contradictory, and also sees the jury's general verdict. From these materials, there is often no way for the appellate court to know what version of disputed facts was relied upon by the jury in reaching its verdict. In fact, the appellate court has no real guarantee that the jury as a group actually agreed on a specific, coherent characterization of the facts of the case.

For all of the reasons mentioned in this chapter, appellate courts cannot confidently assume that the facts presented to them in any given case accurately reflect the actual factual history of the parties. Moreover, the appellate courts have no serious factual basis for believing that the presented facts of any given case represent the typical behavior of similarly situated parties, or in any way present a reasonably accurate picture of the regulated community at large. In the absence of such assurances, the development of important legal doctrine on a case-by-case basis by appellate courts employing an instrumentalist approach seems, at best, to be highly problematic.

6

Other Aspects of Current American Law that Reflect the Paradigm Shift from Formalism to Instrumentalism

The way in which those who participate in a legal system view its basic nature makes a critical difference in the way in which that system actually operates. Overarching conceptions, basic understandings, and philosophical constructs have functional, pragmatic consequences.

In what significant ways would one expect a common law legal system operating under an instrumentalist paradigm to differ from one operating under a formalist paradigm? In other words, what meaningful changes might be expected to take place, at least over time, when the participants in a given legal system shift from viewing it as being primarily formalist in nature to being primarily instrumentalist at its core?

6.1 THE RELATIONSHIP OF COURTS TO THE LARGER EMPIRICAL WORLD

Under a formalist conception of law, courts need to reach out empirically into the world when parties to an action cannot agree on the facts of a case. Competing evidence of what actually transpired is brought into the litigation process by the opposing parties and the neutral decision-makers – the judge, jury, or both – come to a conclusion regarding the legally operative version of events.

Under formalism, appellate courts – involved in the process of reviewing the work of the trial courts below – are largely isolated from direct contact with the real world. Reflecting this feature of formalism, there continues to exist a long-standing rule of appellate practice that limits the power of appellate courts to review and to possibly reverse only the legal issues decided by the trial court. Because it is only at the trial court level that evidence is presented, witnesses observed, and cross-examination conducted, appellate courts are not granted the authority to reverse a factual finding made at the trial court level. In this way, it is the primary function of the appellate courts only to "check the math" of the trial court judge, by reviewing only the disputed legal decisions for doctrinal accuracy.

Under an instrumentalist conception of law, trial courts must still look out to the empirical world and resolve the parties' conflicting versions of what actually transpired between them. However, unlike under formalism, an instrumentalist conception of the work of the appellate courts also inevitably involves empirical engagement with the world outside legal doctrine and legal sources as part of the appellate court's common law lawmaking function. If the conventional understanding is that the common law is the product of an analysis that identifies and balances the likely practical consequences of one version of common law doctrine against others and selects as controlling the version that offers the most attractive combination of costs and benefits, then the appellate courts, in reviewing and developing the common law, must embrace some notions of how, empirically, one version of legal doctrine or another will affect the behavior of relevant actors in society.

For example, an appellate court in the modern age considering whether to adopt or reject a formal tort law duty to reasonably rescue a stranger in peril would be expected to consider a whole range of practical costs and benefits likely to be associated with such a rule.[1] Would the adoption of such a doctrine increase the number of rescues attempted? Would increasing the number of rescues attempted result in less overall harm to those in peril? Does there already exist a high, or at least a sufficient, number of rescue attempts in the absence of an affirmative legal duty?

Once these kinds of questions become relevant to the determination of the proper legal rule, as they do under an instrumentalist conception of common law, then pressure inevitably exists for appellate courts to empirically engage the world beyond the law library. This, in turn, is likely to increase the attention paid to those legal doctrines and customs dealing with the introduction and management of empirical evidence in the court system, especially evidence that purports to describe how the world works in general terms.

Not long after the realist critique of formalism began to gain traction, a pioneering attempt to change the nature of the formal written submissions made by parties to appellate courts took place. This occurred in a United States Supreme Court case titled *Muller v. State of Oregon*.[2] In 1907, social reformers Florence Kelley and Josephine Goldmark retained Goldmark's brother-in-law, Louis Brandeis, later to become a United States Supreme Court Justice, to file a brief supporting an Oregon law regulating the number of hours women were legally allowed to work. The brief, which was more than hundred pages in length, contained only two pages of traditional legal argument, with the remainder comprised of a compendium of scientific literature and social science studies by which Brandeis sought to empirically describe to the Court the actual conditions and experience of women in the workplace. This empirical evidence was not introduced at the trial and was nowhere contained in the formal record of the case. This effort has famously become known as the "Brandeis brief," and it is clearly a logical extension of a larger shifting paradigm from formalism to instrumentalism.

1 See Chapter 8 herein.
2 208 U.S. 412 (1908).

As meaningful as the attempt, so too was the Supreme Court's response to the brief. In deciding the *Muller* case, the Court noted that while the materials presented in the Brandeis brief "may not be, technically speaking, authorities ... they are significant."[3] The Supreme Court again famously recognized the legitimacy and appropriateness of appellate court arguments based on extra-record empirical evidence in the famous case of *Brown v. Board of Education*.[4]

The technique of offering to an appellate court the background empirical evidence relevant to the lawmaking function of the court and not introduced at the trial court below is now a standard part of modern appellate practice. "The 'Brandeis brief,' which brings social statistics into the courtroom, has become a commonplace."[5]

There has also been, since the middle of the twentieth century, a veritable explosion of case law and commentary on the management of scientific evidence in court proceedings. For nearly seventy years, the seminal case in this area was *Frye v. United States*, decided in 1923.[6] According to *Frye*, evidence of this sort should be admitted at trial if the underlying science is "sufficiently established to have gained general acceptance in the particular field in which it belongs."[7]

The admissibility of scientific evidence was not a topic of much concern or controversy for many years following the issuance of the opinion in *Frye*. The decision was cited only thirteen times in the first twenty-five years following its publication and not at all in the first ten years. It was cited only eighty-three times in the next twenty-five years. However, "by the 1980s, it was being cited as much each year as it had been in its first fifty years."[8] This sharp increase in attention to the status and qualification of empirical scientific evidence is fully consistent with the shift from a formalist to an instrumentalist paradigm.

In 1993, the United States Supreme Court set forth a new standard for the admissibility of scientific evidence in federal courts. In the case of *Daubert v. Merrell Dow Pharmaceuticals*, the Court instructed federal judges to admit scientific testimony only when they have determined that the underlying science is valid.[9]

The shift from *Frye* to *Daubert* is subtle, but profound. While both approaches ultimately seek to determine the validity of the science at issue, *Frye* positions the trial judge as an outsider to the process of validation, looking to the relevant scientific community for the substantive determination of general acceptability. In contrast, *Daubert* places the trial judge at the very center of the validation process,

3 *Id.* at 420.
4 347 U.S. 483, 494, n.11 (1954).
5 Rivera v. Division of Industrial Welfare, 265 Cal.App.2d 576, 589, footnote 20 (1968).
6 293 F. 1013 (D.C. Cir. 1923).
7 *Id.* at 1014.
8 David L. Faigman et al., Modern Scientific Evidence: The Law and Science of Expert Testimony, section 1:3, footnote 8 (2006).
9 509 U.S. 579 (1993).

requiring the court to directly determine for itself the validity of the underlying science. Trial judges may not simply refer to the current consensus in the relevant scientific field but are to roll up their sleeves and hold hearings designed to sufficiently inform them to make their own independent judgment on the validity of the science at issue. The Federal Court of Appeals for the Tenth Circuit has clearly stated that "a district court, when faced with a party's objection, must adequately demonstrate by specific findings on the record that it has performed its duty as gatekeeper."[10]

The shift from the 1923 *Frye* standard, seeing the court as being engaged in a legal process entirely different from the pursuit of science and needing only to consult the appropriate scientific community for its judgment, to the 1993 *Daubert* standard conceiving of the court as fully engaged in the process of understanding how the world works and capable of engaging in an independent determination of scientific validity, is completely consistent with the larger replacement of a formalist paradigm with instrumentalism. This shift in the formal standards of admissibility of scientific evidence accurately reflects the broader change in the legal culture's understanding of the relationship of judicial processes to the larger world. No longer isolated within the formalistic practice of technical legal analysis, trial and appellate courts alike are thrust into the larger culture and expected to seriously consider the likely practical consequences of their decisions.

Once the process of creating and maintaining the common law is seen as necessarily involving the identification and balancing of instrumentalist consequences of competing versions of legal doctrine, then it is inevitable that much greater importance will be attached to the empirical understanding of the world in which that doctrine will operate and to the models that we adopt to help predict the changes likely to be caused by one version of a legal rule rather than another. Thus, it is not surprising that there has been enormously high and sustained interest in the validity and admissibility of scientific evidence starting shortly before the decision in *Daubert* right up to the present.

This line of analysis can be extended at least a little further. It is entirely consistent with the paradigm shift from formalism to instrumentalism that much greater attention will be paid to the status of scientific evidence in our legal system and that courts will be seen as being more actively engaged in attempts to understand how the larger world operates. Moreover, and more specifically, the shift to an instrumentalist view of the creation and maintenance of common law doctrine places pressure on appellate courts to embrace, either explicitly or implicitly, some set of understandings, or models, of the operation of the regulated community to which the common law under consideration will apply.

For example, an appellate court engaged in instrumentalist analysis must have some sense of whether and how people are likely to provide affirmative aid to a

[10] Goebel v. Denver Rio Grande Western Railroad Co., 215 F.3d 1083, 1088 (2000).

stranger in the presence of, or in the absence of, a coercive legal rule in order to properly determine whether such a formal duty should be adopted as part of the common law.[11] Similarly, the Supreme Court of California had no choice but to adopt some model of the actual nature and dynamics of therapeutic relationships when it announced a formal therapist duty to warn in the famous case of *Tarasoff v. Regents of the University of California*.[12]

Here lies a pressure for courts to confront empirical knowledge different from the one addressed by *Frye* or *Daubert*. The need for scientific understanding in this context goes not to a resolution of a specific factual dispute between the parties in a given case; instead, it is needed to support the larger analytical task of crafting the applicable common law itself. And for these purposes, appellate courts cannot rely upon trial courts to hold the relevant hearings and to create a useful record.

Thus, inexorably, in a shift from formalism to instrumentalism, pressure will build for appellate courts to independently seek out information about the regulated communities most directly affected by the common law at issue. An appellate court outside of California confronted with the question of whether or not to adopt a *Tarasoff* duty in its jurisdiction will naturally want information on the nature of therapeutic relationships, the likelihood of patient violence, the ability of therapists to accurately predict violent behavior, and a host of other empirical, non-legal issues as a part of reaching the optimal result on the ultimately legal question of duty or no duty.[13]

Independent research by appellate courts on non-legal aspects of a case before them for decision is not a part of the heritage or custom that has come to us from our formalist past. And yet it is a question of appellate practice that is inescapable in an instrumentalist world. Thus far this discussion has only recently begun, and it had arisen, appropriately enough, in the context of appellate review of trial court decisions on the admissibility of scientific evidence. Understood in its broader context, however, it can be expected that this issue will expand over time to generate a vigorous debate over the appropriateness of independent appellate court research in a wide range of circumstances.[14]

6.2 VARIATION AND UNCERTAINTY AS TO THE APPROPRIATE ARGUMENTS TO MAKE TO APPELLATE COURTS

One important consequence of the shift from formalism to instrumentalism is greater variation, and thus greater uncertainty, in the kinds of arguments regarding issues of law that courts consider appropriate and persuasive. Within a formalist conception of common law jurisprudence, it is widely understood that appropriate

[11] See Chapter 8 herein.
[12] 551 P.2d 334 (1976); see Chapter 4 herein.
[13] See Chapter 4 herein.
[14] See, for example, Edward K. Chang, *Independent Judicial Research in the Daubert Age*, 56 Duke Law Journal 1263 (2007); Elizabeth G. Thornburg, *The Curious Appellate Judge: Ethical Limits on Independent Research*, 28 Review of Litigation 131 (2008).

arguments on issues of law consist primarily of attempts to analogize the instant case to prior precedents and generally accepted legal principles. Attorneys on each side seek to persuade the court of the appropriateness of their preferred precedents and demonstrate how the proper deductive application of those precedents and principles to the instant case should result in the resolution they favor. Of course, different courts may differ on the kinds of precedent that they are most persuaded by, or the degree of looseness of analogous reasoning that they will tolerate, but all courts operating within a formalist paradigm pretty much speak, and recognize, the same language of precedent, principle, analogous reasoning, and deduction.

In the shift from a formalist to an instrumentalist perspective, and especially during the current period of transition from one dominant paradigm to another, there is much greater variation in what different courts view as useful and persuasive arguments on issues of law. For the purposes of this point, assume an oversimplification that assigns the term "precedent" to the kind of argument that most naturally flows from a formalist approach and the term "policy" to the kind of argument that is most naturally persuasive from an instrumentalist perspective. One can then say that compared to a largely homogeneous formalist system, the present system of transition from formalism to instrumentalism displays a far greater and less predictable mix of court tolerance for, and receptiveness to, arguments of precedent and policy.

Again, while subtle differences in the proclivities of different courts have always existed, attorneys practicing within a dominantly formalist system knew that most every court before which they argued would expect to hear arguments of precedent, and pretty much only arguments of precedent, on issues of law. Currently, this is not the case. While some courts may still wish to hear only, or predominately, arguments of precedent, many courts would consider a presentation on a significant issue of law to be wholly inadequate without the inclusion of policy arguments, and other courts, while they may patiently tolerate arguments of precedent, are really interested in, and only potentially persuaded by, arguments of policy.

This variation is sometimes broadly seen as corresponding to certain characteristics of a court. So, it might be generally assumed that arguments of precedent would play a larger and more persuasive role in arguments at the trial court level while arguments of policy would take a place of greater prominence at the appellate level, and more so as one moves up the appellate court hierarchy in a given system. In the middle and latter part of the twentieth century, when many judges were still initially schooled in a heavier mix of formalist approaches to law, it might be assumed that older judges and justices, especially at the trial court level, would be less patient and less persuaded by pure policy arguments than would younger judges. It might be assumed that arguments of policy would carry greater persuasive force before a federal court than a state court, especially at the intermediate appellate court level, so that a savvy advocate might, for example, craft a significantly different brief on the exact same issue of law when appearing before the Virginia Intermediate Court of Appeals as contrasted with the United States Court of Appeals for the Fourth Circuit.

Each of the aforementioned assumptions regarding the preferred mix of precedent and policy arguments are broad simplifications, and as such they can hardly serve as reliable guides in any particular case. The point is not that these overgeneralized perceptions are accurate, or even valuable, it is instead precisely that they are not. A litigating attorney in today's environment who faces the need to prepare effective points and authorities on a disputed issue of law before a trial court is aware that a wide disparity exists among trial judges regarding the relative value of precedent arguments and policy arguments. However, unless they are familiar with the specific judge in question, attorneys cannot reliably know in advance what mix they will encounter in any particular instance.

This variation in the blend of formalism and instrumentalism embraced by different jurists in different courts carries some significant system costs. One is the compromise of basic due process values that necessarily occurs when different judges, and different courts, are bringing to bear quite different notions of appropriate argument and analysis when deciding essentially the same issues of law. This is more than the inevitable variation in bottom-line judgment that will occur among different decision-makers. It is a situation in which the most basic notion of what counts as a relevant and material consideration in the analysis varies widely from one decision-maker to another.

Even among courts that are receptive to policy arguments, it is difficult for advocates who lack specific experience with the court to know how much empirical support to present for their instrumentalist claims. If an argument is made that therapists will not be very accurate at predicting the future harmful behavior of their patients and that, as a result, a large number of false warnings will be issued under a *Tarasoff* duty, should the attorney advancing that claim support it with empirical evidence? Should attorneys offer expensive expert testimony to the trial court initially considering the argument? Should they provide exhaustive citations to relevant empirical studies to the appellate courts? Do, or should, attorneys have the same ethical obligation to make the court aware of empirical studies that are negative to their argument in the same way that they do negative precedent? And what is the appellate court to make of such citations, especially in the absence of live expert testimony explaining their significance and tested by cross-examination?

These are among the open issues faced by a common law system engaging in instrumentalist analysis within a formalist procedural structure. As yet, little consensus has developed as to how these dilemmas should be resolved, and as a result, there is an enormous variation in approach. Different courts view very differently not only the preferred mix of precedent and policy arguments on issues of law, but also view very differently the kind and quantity of empirical support that should accompany policy arguments.

Not only does this situation compromise basic due process values, it also places a premium on a litigating attorney's specialized knowledge and experience with a particular court. Because courts differ widely along this critically important dimension, and because they do not differ predictably or systematically, a party wishing to maximize their opportunity for success before a particular court in a specific case would be well advised to retain an attorney who possesses deep experience with that court and who could say with confidence what mix of precedent and policy arguments, and what kind of empirical support for policy arguments, the court prefers.

The importance of such experience narrows very significantly the number of attorneys who will be sought by sophisticated parties to argue before a given court, and will also narrow dramatically the range and diversity of attorneys from whom the court regularly hears. Neither consequence is desirable, or healthy, for the maintenance of a vibrant common law jurisprudence in a given jurisdiction.

Moreover, the acquisition of the necessary experience by an attorney before a particular court takes considerable time to acquire and is, therefore, expensive. Thus, to the degree that access to a fundamental feature of the court's operation requires a party to purchase such experience, it causes the system of common law jurisprudence to be deeply regressive, making effective participation much more difficult for those without considerable wealth. And since the common law system not only resolves discrete disputes but also generates binding law, this dynamic threatens, over time, to skew common law doctrine itself regressively in favor of moneyed interests.

6.3 LESS CONSISTENCY IN THE SUBSTANCE OF COMMON LAW DOCTRINE ACROSS DIFFERENT JURISDICTIONS

Another consequence of the shift from a formalist to an instrumentalist approach to common law jurisprudence involves greater variation in the common law doctrine that is produced by the system. When courts move from regarding the common law as the logical working out of the details, and the fact-specific application, of historic precedent and basic first principles to viewing it as a means by which to influence the behavior of affected persons and thereby achieve certain social goals, one would expect greater variation among states in the substantive doctrines that are produced.

One might expect that different jurisdictions, located in different regions of the country, would subscribe to subtly different social values, and thus seek to achieve somewhat different social goals. Under an instrumentalist regime, these differences would result in the development of correspondingly different common law doctrines. In addition, speculation on the likely practical effects of a given version of common law doctrine and non-empirical cost-benefit analyses of those possible consequences is a rather imprecise business, likely to lead to quite different conclusions by different decision-makers. For both of these reasons, one would expect greater variation in the substance of the common law in terms of more significant splits among jurisdictions under an instrumentalist regime than a formalist one.

Consider, for example, the question of whether a defendant should be allowed to use deadly force in self-defense before retreating, if reasonably possible, in the face of an imminent threat posed to him by the plaintiff. Technically, this is a somewhat subtle question of the scope of the self-defense privilege in both tort and criminal law. There is, however, from an instrumentalist perspective, really nothing technical about it. The resolution of this issue depends largely on the underlying cultural values of the jurisdiction in which it is considered. Thus, it is of little surprise to find that at least three distinct positions on this question have developed across the United States, each enjoying a regional following, and each corresponding roughly to the broad reputation of these regions regarding their attitudes on individual self-reliance and the ownership and use of guns.[15]

Formalism looks predominately to the past and to the abstract as its touchstone for analysis. In contrast, instrumentalism looks to the predicted human behavior in the world projected out into the future. One consequence of this difference is that common law legal doctrine under an instrumentalist approach is likely to be less stable across different jurisdictions than is doctrine maintained under formalism.

6.4 INCREASED MOVEMENT TOWARD UNPUBLISHED OPINIONS

While the work of appellate judges and appellate courts is rarely easy, it is likely the case that such work is relatively easier under a formalist paradigm than under an instrumentalist paradigm. In circumstances in which an appellate court operating within a formalist paradigm has a fairly strong instinctual feel for the appropriate resolution of a legal issue, the written opinion announcing and rationalizing that judgment can often cite a controlling precedent or a controlling legal principle and declare the court's decision in the case as being logically consistent, if not logically required, by that precedent or principle. Under an instrumentalist paradigm, there is inevitable pressure for the court to, or to also, explain how the anticipated practical costs and benefits of the court's preferred rule or resolution of the case compare favorably to other plausible alternative rules and resolutions. Clearly, much more work for the court is involved under the instrumentalist paradigm than under formalism.

Moreover, there is a much greater chance that the court's published analysis and rationale will, over time, be proven to be erroneous in some or all respects within an instrumentalist paradigm as contrasted with a formalist approach. Under formalism, the appellate court cites prior precedent or principle and asserts that its decision in the instant case is at least logically consistent with that principle or precedent. The validity of this claim of logical consistency should be fairly apparent on the surface of the court's published opinion, and it is not difficult for the court to get right, at least technically.

What is not apparent from a surface reading of the court's formalist opinion is if there existed one or more alternative precedents or equally honored legal principles

[15] See Jason W. Bobo, *Following the Trend: Alabama Abandons the Duty to Retreat and Encourages Citizens to Stand Their Ground*, 38 CUMBERLAND LAW REVIEW 339 (2008).

that could have been chosen by the court to bring to bear on the matter and that would have resulted in a different resolution of the matter. A standard appellate court opinion in a formalist world need not, and rarely did, identify other plausible precedents and principles and explain why the court chose the one that it did rather than a possible alternative. (The exposing of these often unannounced and unanalyzed background choices was a significant part of the realist critique of formalism.)

In contrast, under instrumentalism, the appellate court bears at least an expectation that it will support in its published opinion the choice of legal doctrine that it makes in its decision by analyzing to some extent the anticipated practical costs and benefits of its preferred rule. This instrumentalist analysis, by its very nature, involves a prediction of various practical consequences that will result in the future from adopting the preferred position as binding law. Read some years later, the court's opinion can be seen as having been more or less prescient – more or less accurate – simply by comparing the analysis (the court's predictions regarding the practical effect of the chosen rule) offered in the text of the opinion with the now current state of affairs. The degree to which the court's instrumentalist analysis was accurate or not is far more apparent from a surface reading of the opinion than in the case of a standard opinion written under a formalist paradigm.

The much greater reputational risk that is borne by appellate courts under instrumentalism compared with formalism and the greater effort required to produce a typical instrumentalist appellate opinion than a formalist one both mean that powerful incentives exist for appellate courts to, if possible, more vigorously seek to avoid the production of published opinions when the prevailing paradigm shifts from formalism to instrumentalism. Just such a movement by appellate courts in the United States has clearly and strikingly taken place starting in the latter half of the twentieth century.

For example, in California, appellate courts can decide on their own whether their opinions are published or not.[16] If an appellate court chooses to issue an opinion and not publish it, it means that the opinion may not be cited nor relied upon in subsequent cases, even though the court's decision and opinion serve as a fully authorized and binding resolution of the instant case. In effect, in California, in a large number of other states, and in the federal court system, an appellate court may do the work necessary to respond to the case at hand and at the same time opt out of the usual and traditional obligation to publish a statement of that decision that is included in the jurisdiction's body of precedent and that is subject to the rule of stare decisis.

The opportunity for an appellate court to produce an unpublished opinion is a product of the latter part of the twentieth century and it is consistent with the risks and incentives created by a paradigm shift from formalism to instrumentalism. Also consistent with these risks and incentives is the popularity of the unpublished

[16] Cal. R. Ct. 8.1105, 8.1115.

opinion option among appellate courts. "As of September 2007, over 80% of U.S. courts of appeals opinions per year were unpublished."[17]

There are some seriously problematic aspects to the use of unpublished opinions by appellate courts, most especially when they are used more than sparingly, and a continuing and vigorous controversy surrounds the practice.[18]

6.5 INCREASED POLITICIZING OF JUDICIAL APPOINTMENTS

In part because formalism was the dominant paradigm for so long, and because most all of our basic court structures and procedures are based upon it, formalism has enjoyed a powerful hold on the public's image of the operation of common law courts. One prominent feature of a formalist paradigm is that it characterizes appellate judges as primarily being technical experts in formal legal analysis. It is thought that their dominant function within the common law system is to review the legal decisions of lower courts and to audit those decisions against the existing array of legal principles, maxims, and specific precedents in the jurisdiction, correcting lower court errors of deductive logic and occasionally inductively extending prior law to new circumstances.

However, as the shift from formalism to instrumentalism has solidified, and as instrumentalism's reign lengthens, public perception is changing as well. It is the understanding of increasing numbers of persons that decisions of appellate courts are very frequently the product of an instrumentalist cost-benefit analysis, even if the courts do not always label it explicitly as such.

One important consequence of the public's increasing perception of the instrumentalist nature of common law jurisprudence is the dramatically increased politicizing of the appointment of appellate court judges. This phenomenon is most obviously seen regarding the United States Supreme Court, though it has been occurring with lower federal court and state appellate court appointments as well.

It is now commonplace, for example, for mainstream news media to identify the President who appointed a federal judge when reporting on a newsworthy matter coming before that judge, and to similarly identify the makeup of federal appellate court panels hearing such cases. In addition, some prominent states, such as California, have statutes in place that create the possibility of an appellate judge,

[17] Erica S. Weisgerber, *Unpublished Opinions: A Convenient Means to an Unconstitutional End*, 97 Georgetown Law Journal 621, 624 (2009), citing James C. Duff, Admin. Office of the U.S. Courts, Annual Report of the Director: Judicial Business of the United States Courts 39, Table S-3 (2007).

[18] See Johanna S. Schiavoni, *Who's Afraid of Precedent?: The Debate over the Precedential Value of Unpublished Opinions*, 49 UCLA Law Review 1859 (2002); David C. Vladeck & Mitu Gulati, *Judicial Triage: Reflections on the Debate over Unpublished Opinions*, 62 Washington & Lee Law Review 1667 (2005) (Introduction to Symposium: Have We Ceased to Be a Common Law Country?); and Shenoa L. Payne, *The Ethical Conundrums of Unpublished Opinions*, 44 Willamette Law Review 723 (2008).

including a justice on that state's highest court, being removed from office by a recall election among all state voters. Other states have systems in place by which state appellate judges, initially selected by gubernatorial appointment, are then subject to a popular retention election. Additional measures have been proposed in other states, including the adoption of initiatives that would impose term limits on judges and require appellate judges to be elected from specified districts in which they must reside.[19]

Moreover, the nature of these popular elections regarding judges has been observed to be moving in the direction of popular elections for other lawmakers, such as legislators: "Judicial elections in the United States have undergone a dramatic transformation.... Over the past quarter century, and especially in the past decade ... a rise in campaign spending, interest group involvement, and political speech has disturbed the traditional paradigm. In the 'new era,' as commentators have dubbed it, judicial races routinely feature intense competition, broad public participation, and high salience."[20]

Though the increased politicizing of the judicial appointments process, and the accompanying close scrutiny of judicial candidates' ideology and political commitments, is often decried and criticized, it can be seen as a logical consequence of the paradigm shift from formalism to instrumentalism. If appellate court judges are crafting the common law based on their perception of current social needs and the potential for one version of legal doctrine or another to better meet those needs, then it is only logical that those who are interested in the outcome of appellate court cases, and in the substance of the common law, would turn their sustained attention to the views that judicial candidates hold on current social problems and preferred legal responses thereto. It would be a willful act of ignorance for persons interested in the common law and who understood its fundamentally instrumentalist nature to do any less.

6.6 DECLINING AUTOMATIC CREDIBILITY AND AUTHORITY OF JUDGES AND COURTS

One consequence of a dominantly formalist conception of common law lawmaking is a profound separation between elected legislators as lawmakers and appellate judges as maintainers and developers of the common law. While the actions of both result in authoritative, binding law, and while virtually all of the common law at any given moment could theoretically be codified by legislators into statutory law, the two kinds of lawmakers are thought to operate in radically different ways in a formalist world. Unlike legislators, appellate judges adhering to formalism are thought to be tightly constrained in the exercise of their lawmaking judgment by

[19] Molly McDonough, *Voting on the Law*, 5 No. 43 American Bar Association Journal E-Report 1 (2006).

[20] David E. Pozen, *The Irony of Judicial Elections*, 108 COLUMBIA LAW REVIEW 265 (2008).

the vast web of already accepted legal principles, axioms, standards, and precedents that exist in the jurisdiction. Moreover, the law that is made by formalist judges is presented as being tightly justified by its logical consistency with those already existing principles, axioms, standards, and precedents. In its strongest form, formalism conceives of the more specific and incremental lawmaking engaged in by appellate judges as being essentially value neutral, much like an umpire calling balls and strikes in the approving analogy of Justices Roberts and Kavanaugh.[21]

Under such a formalist conception, the law created by appellate judges is appropriately owed respect and obeisance because it is not the mere expression of the policy preferences of the individual judges themselves but because it is instead a necessary logical extension of long-established and long-honored legal principles and precedents; a logical elaboration of the natural law. Formalist appellate judges are said to function primarily as objective and technical experts engaged in the task of clarifying and modestly extending an already vast body of existing and consensus-endorsed common law. Thought to be operating in this way, appellate judges are deemed worthy of more or less automatic societal respect, and are invested with automatic credibility, in a way not similarly enjoyed by appellate judges operating within an instrumentalist paradigm or by elected legislators.

As a product and consequence of the realist critique of formalism, instrumentalism at its core rejects the formalist claim that common law lawmaking by appellate judges is a value-neutral, preference-free endeavor. It may be hoped that appellate judges do not bring to their lawmaking work commitments to a political party, ideology, and specific constituencies in the way that elected legislators are understood to do, but no matter how free of such influences, appellate judges operating within an instrumentalist paradigm are seen as having no choice but to exercise value-laden preferences when choosing between alternative possible common law rules that promise different mixes of practical costs and benefits. Operating in this way, appellate judges are perceived as functioning more like elected legislators than the perception of appellate judges held under a formalist paradigm. Along with the instrumentalist perception that appellate judges operate in some respects like directly elected legislators comes too an inevitable reduction in the automatic and default respect that is invested in the common law lawmaking process and its results, and that is correspondingly afforded to appellate judges.

Some of this phenomenon is a function of the greater mystique that formalism wraps around the creation of common law. From a formalist perspective, the work of appellate courts is highly technical and is dependent upon special training in distinctively legal analysis and deep expertise in the substance of the existing common law,

[21] In May of 2024, at a judicial conference, Justice Kavanaugh was reported as saying "Chief Justice Roberts famously said judges are like umpires" and then calling the phrase "four of the most important words ever uttered." Adam Liptak, *Justice Kavanaugh on the Presidency, the Court and Taylor Swift*, New York Times, May 10, 2024.

and is therefore largely beyond the common understanding and evaluation of the public at large. In contrast, in many areas, such as whether potential victims of psychiatric patients should be legally provided an advance warning by an aware therapist or whether there should exist a formal legal obligation to provide reasonable assistance to a stranger in peril, the likely practical consequences of one resolution or another of the issue is not beyond the comprehension and evaluation of the public at large. With an ability to understand the nature of the analysis and to possess policy preferences of their own comes a far less automatic grant of respect and default deference to the work of appellate courts, and to appellate judges.

An additional wrinkle exists here. One area of commonality between a formalist paradigm and an instrumentalist paradigm is the allocation of professional responsibilities and activities between appellate judges and trial judges. While trial judges must necessarily make the initial decision regarding all disputed legal issues in a given case, trial judges typically have only a very modest percentage of their total workload occupied by the creation of new common law. Most all of the common law lawmaking that takes place in a particular jurisdiction takes place in its appellate courts and not in its trial courts.

In this way, while legal realists were harshly critical of the formalist notion of appellate judges being analogized to referees and umpires in sport – just calling balls and strikes and neutrally enforcing existing rules – the comparison to trial judges is not nearly as objectionable. A great deal of the regular work of trial judges involves the neutral management of litigation on their docket and the largely value-neutral ruling on various party motions and objections.

However, while, in fact, the professional roles of trial judges and appellate judges are very different, there is little reason to believe that this distinction is appreciated by the public at large, who likely think of judges as judges, whether they are state judges, federal judges, municipal judges, or trial or appellate judges. As a result, the kind of reduction in the automatic and default respect and deference accorded to appellate court decisions that is, in part, a function of the shift from formalism to instrumentalism likely also applies to the work of trial judges. This is the case even though there is little or nothing about the paradigm shift from formalism to instrumentalism that suggests any significantly different or contrasting understanding of the nature of the work of trial judges.

For example, during the criminal prosecutions of former President Trump in 2023 and 2024, mainstream media routinely identified the prior political affiliations and appointment history of the trial judges assigned to those cases, much as they would for appellate court judges, including the United States Supreme Court justices. This framework for viewing the work of an appellate judge was applied to these trial judges and has been applied to both state and federal trial judges presiding over other high-profile, newsworthy cases, even though neither formalism nor instrumentalism would suggest that the performance of a trial judge is likely to be meaningfully influenced by such factors.

7

Stipulations, Clarifications, and Elaborations

7.1 IT'S NOT ALL, AND THEN NOTHING

The creation of American common law is a collective enterprise engaged in by many individual appellate judges working in a large number of different courts in dozens of different states and the federal court system, all over a long period of time. To say that this prodigious collective societal enterprise has experienced over more than 100 years a profound paradigm shift from formalism to instrumentalism is not to say that at one point in time every appellate court and every appellate judge in America was a strict formalist and that at some later point in time every appellate court and every appellate judge in America was an equally strict instrumentalist. The activity of large groups of different persons operating largely independently can almost never be accurately characterized in such absolute and stark terms.

A rough analogy is available with the environmental movement. When it first came to prominence in America in the 1950s, the movement – large, diverse, and not tightly organized – focused primarily on isolated ground and air pollutants as hazards to human health and quality of life. Over time, the focus shifted to the consequences of various human activities on the physical condition of the whole of the earth and its atmosphere so that it is now the case in the early part of the twenty-first century that the environmental movement is focused primarily upon, if not dominated by, a concern for global climate change. This is accurately characterized as a very significant and foundational shift in environmentalism that has taken place since the 1980s.

This characterization, and this understanding, of the environmental movement since the middle of the twentieth century is no less accurate, and no less meaningful, if some scientists and authors in earlier times could be found who voiced concern about what is now called climate change and some currently could be found who publicly deny its existence, or cause, or importance. The activity under examination is far too widespread, disparate, diverse, and lacking in central management or organization to reasonably expect that kind of uniformity, even with respect to an overall sea change that is genuine and real. Someone who concluded on the basis of the presence of some occasional work on climate change prior to the 1980s and the occasional presence of climate change denial thereafter that no meaningful shift in the nature of the environmental movement along this dimension took place between the first half of the twentieth century and the present would completely miss this critically important difference in the nature of the environmental movement over that period.

The situation is the same with regard to common law lawmaking in America over the last 100 years. The overall and dominant paradigm shift from formalism to instrumentalism is no less real even if one can seek and find something that could be characterized as instances of instrumentalist analysis in some appellate court opinions that were produced before the realist revolution.[1] Similarly, no effective challenge to the characterization of the present as being a dominant age of instrumentalism arises if some current appellate court opinions contain elements of formalist analysis. (See more on this in Section 7.6.)

7.2 "THE LIFE OF THE LAW HAS NOT BEEN LOGIC; IT HAS BEEN EXPERIENCE"[2]

The fact of a foundational paradigm shift in common law lawmaking from formalism to instrumentalism means that the legal realist critique of formalism was exceptionally successful. It has been widely accepted by the American legal community, most especially by legal academics who focus their professional attention most intensively on the nature of common law and who, as noted in Chapter 11, overdetermine how nearly all new attorneys first encounter and come to understand the nature of law and appellate jurisprudence. However, the fact of this widespread popular success does not mean that the legal realist critique necessarily refuted, in some bedrock philosophical sense, the basic commitments of formalism, especially the commitment to the presence and importance of a natural law that embodies an objectively superior and ideal set of legal principles.

This natural law is thought to consist of an eternal and unchanging canon – an array of precepts and tenants – that operate as the only true basis for the governance of human beings. One way of understanding legal formalism is as a conception of common law lawmaking that views the proper function of appellate courts as being the logically deductive application of the natural law to the myriad specific legal issues that are brought before the courts. The primary function of appellate courts, according to this view, is the long, careful elaboration of the natural law, the working

[1] See Brian Z. Tamanaha, Beyond the Formalist-Realist Divide: The Role of Politics in Judging (2010).

[2] Oliver Wendell Holmes, Jr., The Common Law 1 (1881).

out of the details of the natural law as it is logically applied to more and more previously unresolved legal issues.

From where does this supposed natural law come? What is its source? Some answers have been offered to these questions in more or less the following way: the current natural law is the slowly developed and accumulated wisdom of human beings as they have tried to govern themselves through the creation and enforcement of general laws going back at least as far as ancient Greek civilization.

One feature of a natural law arising from such a source is that there is likely to be reasonable disagreement about just what constitutes such accumulated wisdom, especially when the substance of that wisdom is any more specific and substantive than a collection of broad, generic bromides. Thus, the substance of the natural law can be uncontroversial and enjoy consensus agreement if it is sufficiently abstract and vague (for example, "the law should be designed to maximize the dignity (or the 'personhood' or the 'inherent potential') of all humans"), in which case it is highly unlikely that the application of such a broad principle will result in the identification of a univocal, distinct, and logically required resolution of a specific and concrete legal issue, at least any nontrivial issue. The highly abstract and generic quality of such natural law pronouncements is what allows for multiple possible, plausible, and equally logical applications of such "law" to more specific legal issues. Thus, some other ways and means by which a court must select among the plausible alternatives is required for authoritative resolution of these issues. And yet, it is this abstract and generic quality of the natural law that makes it possible for it to possibly enjoy some consensus status as the accumulated wisdom of mankind.

Alternatively, the asserted substance of the natural law can be sufficiently concrete and specific to reasonably limit the range of outcomes that result from its logically deductive application to an actual legal issue requiring resolution by the courts. But in such a case the asserted natural law is unlikely to enjoy broad and consensus agreement as the unquestioned distillate of the human experience in law and legal regulation. When there is meaningful disagreement regarding the substance of the natural law, there must be some basis by which courts select the preferred competitor, and that basis cannot coherently be the natural law itself (unless the bit of natural law chosen to resolve this competition is highly abstract and generic, in which case the court is thrown back to the inherent indeterminacy described in this chapter).

Either common law rulemaking based on the existence of an asserted natural law and an asserted strictly logical formalist application of that law to the resolution of current legal issues employs a natural law substance that is highly abstract and general and therefore fails to generate a logically definitive resolution of the current issue – thus requiring some other, usually unstated, basis for choosing among the logically consistent applications – or it reaches for a more specific version of the natural law that is unlikely to enjoy broad general support and agreement as being part of some universal and eternal legal canon. Either way, in order to come to a resolution of a current legal issue from a formalist perspective, the deciding court must employ some means of choice – some means of preference – that is not a uniquely logical application of a widely agreed upon and essentially universal legal precept. Thus, the formalist approach on its own does not yield definitive resolutions of current legal issues. It requires some additional basis for determining preferences and choices among possible alternative resolutions. One of the main and most effective claims made by the legal realists was, and is, that traditional formalism systematically obscures whatever that other basis for ultimate choice may be, sometimes perhaps even from the decision-makers themselves.

7.3 THEISTIC SOURCES OF NATURAL LAW

One way of addressing the indeterminacy of formalism and a natural law-based jurisprudence is to identify a basis for the legitimacy of a particular version of the natural law as the embodiment of the one true and eternal guide to the regulation of human behavior that is independent of the consensus agreement of humans on that point. Historically, theistic sources of origin and authority have served this function. If one accepts the possible existence of a natural law and further believes that a given version of natural law carries the imprimatur and endorsement of God, then such a version of natural law need not enjoy broad agreement and support among humans for its authority and it may therefore become specific and detailed enough to limit the range of logically deductive outcomes that it permits.

When one reads the current literature seeking to defend formalism and to maintain intellectual opposition to the classic legal realist critique, one gets the impression that the energy behind such efforts is less about saving formalism per se than it is about preserving a belief in the existence of natural law, and that impulse appears to be a product of a larger religious commitment and faith. Given this source of motivation, one might expect that attempts to defend formalism, and especially the idea of natural law, will continue irrespective of the broader reception that this view is afforded in the larger legal culture. For those who possess the appropriate religious faith, the idea of a one true natural law that is universal and eternal is real. Such a person could hardly believe otherwise than that such a natural law would serve as the best possible basis for the creation and further development of all human law, including common law.

7.4 THE POWER OF THE LEGAL REALIST MOVEMENT WAS ITS UNCOVERING OF FORMALISM AS ADVANCING A FALSE NARRATIVE OF APPELLATE COURT DECISION-MAKING

As noted in this chapter, a paradigm shift in a given activity can take place without the prior paradigm necessarily having been definitively debunked. It is also the case that a paradigm shift can take place without the new paradigm having affirmatively proven itself to be an overall superior alternative to the prior one.

In this respect, shifts in paradigms can work differently in a field of practice like law than they do in the natural sciences. According to Thomas Kuhn's account, a paradigm shift takes place in a natural science when the existing data in an area of study is increasingly better explained and accounted for by a newly emerging paradigm than by the existing one.[3] At some point the accumulated body of observations that are not well accounted for by the existing paradigm and that are well explained by the emerging, competing paradigm reach a tipping point and the larger shift from one conceptual framework to another occurs. Thus, at some point, classical Newtonian physics gives way, through a paradigm shift, to a fundamentally different relativistic Einsteinian physics.

A field of actual ongoing practice, like law, can in this way operate differently from an explanatory science like physics. Faith can more easily be lost in a particular conception, or understanding, that underlies a prevailing practice without there necessarily being a new and competing understanding that sparks and drives the resulting conceptual revolution.

So, with the loss of belief in the previously prevailing formalist understanding that appellate courts were making new common law based on the largely value-neutral logical application of preexisting principles and doctrines of a universal and uncontroversial nature, the revolution was sparked. And it was driven by the legal realist exposure that appellate courts were, in fact, making such law based on the embrace of assumptions and on the preference of some societal values and outcomes over others that were not being acknowledged, revealed, or discussed in their published opinions. Formalism provided a satisfactory conceptual framework for the creation in a democratic republic of authoritative, binding law by unelected individuals based on an exceptionally narrow and limited set of resources. Legal realism revealed to a relatively broad audience that what these appellate court lawmakers were, in fact, doing did not – and likely could not – conform to the idealized practice that formalism espoused.

The realist movement, in effect, caused the legal community at large to lose its faith in the legitimizing myth of strong formalism. It did this without championing an alternative to formalism that better explained what appellate courts were actually doing and also satisfactorily justified unelected common law lawmakers creating binding law without any systematic access to reliable empirical data or evidence. In this way, the paradigm shift from formalism to instrumentalism was importantly different from paradigm shifts in explanatory natural sciences.

It is possible that many appellate judges were not fully conscious of the value-laden choices they were required to make when creating new common law. It is possible that some of them were applying value-laden choices that they considered a matter of common sense, that reflected the particular values and social attitudes of

[3] Thomas S. Kuhn, The Structure of Scientific Revolutions (4th ed., The University of Chicago Press 2012).

their class and their race, or that derived from an organized religion to which they were adherent. The power of the legal realist exposure and critique did not, and does not, depend upon what specific value-laden judgments are made by appellate judges. Instead, its power comes from its demonstration that some value-laden choices are nearly always, in fact, being made and that those choices and preferences were being obscured by the false façade of formalism.

Once the realist exposure of formalism took root and was accepted by the overwhelming majority of the legal community, there existed a void and a vacuum that no new explanatory conception of common law lawmaking automatically occupied. The legal realists successfully established that formalism was an inaccurate and false account of the nature of appellate court lawmaking without necessarily establishing that a different explanatory account was both accurate and also provided the politically and socially legitimizing benefits of formalism.

In the face of this void, the natural default was to equate the appropriate approach of appellate courts to common law lawmaking with a somewhat idealized version of what legislative and regulatory lawmakers are thought to do – identify and balance the known empirical benefits and costs of various possible versions of a legal rule, or no rule at all, and elevate to the status of binding law that alternative which promises the most attractive practical combination of consequences. This is instrumentalism.

It is not the case that the legal realists, or anyone else, sought to demonstrate that during the long formalist period in America appellate court judges were closet instrumentalists who were covertly and consciously making common law on an instrumentalist basis and then concealing that practice by authoring published opinions that justified those decisions on formalist terms. Nor is it the case that the legal realists, or anyone else, argued that instrumentalism was an understanding of appropriate appellate court lawmaking that offered, as compared with formalism, a better and more satisfying fit with the practice of unelected lawmakers creating binding law based on either a very limited, or highly suspect, or nonexistent empirical basis. Instrumentalism was the conceptual approach that the American legal community adopted, by default, when the prior faith in formalism was no longer tenable. At the time of legal realism's ascent, and to this day, no real alternative to instrumentalism as a replacement for formalism exists.

7.5 THE DESCRIPTIVE CLAIMS OF THE LEGAL REALISTS ARE ACCEPTED AS TRUE BY A BROAD CONSENSUS OF THE PROFESSIONAL LEGAL COMMUNITY

The nature of formalism, instrumentalism, and the paradigm shift from the former to the latter described in Chapter 3 helps to explain two interesting aspects of the current situation regarding American common law.

One is the impression one might have from reading both the academic literature and some appellate court opinions that the intellectual struggle between formalism and instrumentalism is somehow unresolved. A small but steady stream of academic writing continues to seek to relitigate the legal realist critique of formalism and, especially, to reclaim a respected and influential role for the idea of a universal, objectively true natural law. More than a few appellate court opinions continue to contain rationalizations and to offer lines of justifying argument that are essentially formalist in nature.

With respect to the academic literature and commentary, it is useful to recognize a distinction between a descriptive aspect of the legal realist critique of formalism and a normative aspect. Descriptively, legal realism sought to demonstrate that the formalist explanation offered by appellate courts for the judgments they made, and for choosing to create the common law that they did, failed to establish that those choices were uniquely determined by logical, preference-free analysis. The realists showed time and again that in a large number of instances appellate courts could have reasonably started from different first principles that would have logically resulted in a different final result or that the first principles chosen by the court were so abstract and generic in substance that the application of deductive logic could result in more than one, unique, conclusion. This descriptive claim of the legal realists proved over time to be compelling to the legal community at large. About this there is virtually no meaningful disagreement.

Separate from this descriptive claim, it is possible that the legal realist critique could also seek to establish – to effectively prove – that the formalist account of common law lawmaking could not ever possibly be accurate and true. This would be a normative claim, and this normative claim would obviously be very much more difficult to establish than the descriptive claim. Commentators who wish to maintain some debate between formalism and realism frequently focus on an asserted lack of a definitive normative refutation of formalism or of the idea of natural law.

First, no normative claim of realism was required to fuel the realist revolution and the paradigm shift from formalism to instrumentalism. That appellate courts overwhelmingly and over a long period failed to provide a satisfying and defensible account of their decisions in a way that demonstrated that those decisions and judgments were logically required, or often even meaningfully logically constrained, was enough for the legal community to lose its faith in the formalist paradigm. Second, at some point, the lack of actual success in the formalist legal project over a significant period goes some way to suggest that it may not be normatively feasible, even if affirmative philosophical proof of that negative proposition has not yet been produced.

Moreover, because formalism is tied to the idea of natural law, and because natural law is closely associated with some systems of religious belief, including some that are deeply involved in the sponsorship and support of academic work, one can expect the sustained appearance of some academic commentary that seeks to defend and to promote the idea of natural law and, to the extent then necessary, the idea of formalism. This continued strain of academic commentary can be expected to exist independent of the degree to which those without religious conviction and motivation find either legal formalism or natural law to be plausible concepts.

The motivation for appellate courts to continue to include elements of formalist analysis and justification in their published decisions is rather obvious and clear. While some appellate judges in an earlier age may have felt discomfort and some cognitive dissonance when producing formalist opinions that they could sense, or that they knew, did not adequately or thoroughly reveal the bases for those decisions, and while some may still do, the political benefit to unelected appellate judges of presenting appellate court decisions within a formalist framework is quite apparent. Formalism operates to obscure the politically and socially awkward practice of unelected persons, persons who are also overwhelmingly among the societal elite, formally exercising political power in a way that requires them to rely upon significant value-laden preferences. Instrumentalism exposes and highlights that uncomfortable reality. It is no surprise, then, that appellate courts would continue to present their decisions in terms that minimize the degree of value-laden judgment and discretion that is required in coming to those decisions for as long after the legal realist revolution as possible.

So, neither the existence of academic commentary nor appellate court opinions that can be read to seek to maintain formalism in the face of the legal realist revolution should be regarded as an indication that some serious, substantive, unresolved debate between formalism and legal realism continues, or that any meaningful current uncertainty about the implausibility of formalism as a widespread understanding of appropriate appellate court practice still exists. There is no present pressure or need to assert that formalism and natural law have been definitively debunked in some bedrock philosophical sense. Serious attempts to reconsider formalism and to establish the viability of the idea of natural law should be welcomed. But none of this should obscure the unassailable fact that as a practical matter at present, the legal realist revolution has been entirely successful in its attempt to all but remove from the mainstream of both practicing and academic legal life the previously widespread notion that appellate courts exercise their political power in a value-neutral, discretion-free, formalist manner.

7.6 WHY SO SLOW? LINGERING DENIAL AND RELUCTANCE REGARDING THE PARADIGM SHIFT FROM FORMALISM TO INSTRUMENTALISM

The second interesting aspect of the current situation regarding American common law that can be better understood in light of the aforementioned analysis is the exceptionally slow pace at which the new instrumentalist paradigm is being digested by the American legal community.

Again, as aforementioned, significant paradigm shifts in either the sciences or law involve the activities of a large number of different individuals, many of them highly trained and experienced professionals, acting largely independently and without tight coordination or close management. A paradigm shift in such circumstances is usually the consequence of a movement over some time in consensus community attitudes and opinions, and not the result of a one-time pronouncement by some governing body. While the adoption of a new paradigm may well be gradual and cautious, once the consensus of the relevant community has, in fact, clearly shifted, one would then expect vigorous efforts to commence in developing the new paradigm. This is what Kuhn describes as occurring in the natural sciences. For example, once it is broadly understood that relativity-based physics is a more promising framework through which to understand and predict the subject of that scientific discipline than traditional Newtonian physics, then resources move reasonably rapidly toward new work developing observational data and refining theories within the Einsteinian framework.

However, this expectation, arising from the observation of paradigm shifts in other fields, has not played out in the same way with respect to the paradigm shift from formalism to instrumentalism in law. It has been at least fifty years since the legal realist critique of formalism has clearly taken hold and instrumentalism in some form became the default consensus understanding of the nature of common law jurisprudence, at least within the legal profession. And yet, strikingly little attention has thus far been directed to the degree to which instrumentalist common law analysis operates uneasily, if not with serious difficulty, within an appellate court structure, and with appellate court procedures, designed during a dominantly formalist era. Virtually no resources or energy have been directed to a serious consideration of changing this structure or these procedures so that they are more compatible with, and more productive in, an instrumentalist age. On the surface this disparity might be puzzling, but there exist a number of factors that together help to make it more understandable.

One hugely significant factor in what could be fairly characterized as a kind of sustained denial in the law about the consequences of the paradigm shift to instrumentalism is the degree to which it is far more difficult to accommodate and to justify formal decision-makers who are largely unelected and who are employing the practical and explicitly value-laden, cost-benefit approach of instrumentalism to wield considerable political power. It would be difficult to overstate the importance of this factor.

How does one justify in a democratic republic a permanent structural element of formal lawmaking that is systematically insulated from democratic pressure and is both encouraged and expected to be unresponsive to broad popular sentiment? While one might imagine the possibility of a sophisticated theory that would justify the need for such an undemocratic source of power within a larger democratic republic, and while one could even imagine being persuaded by such an argument, that discussion is little present in the current period. This is true even with respect to the United States Supreme Court, for which the prior formalist mythology of objective, value-free decision-making is rapidly evaporating, even among the broad general public.

One of the problems, of course, is that any kind of justifying rationale possessing even a modest degree of sophistication or complexity would be a hard sell on a popular political basis. Furthermore, if the larger political culture were to openly acknowledge the undemocratic implications of judicial instrumentalism and fail to persuade the public that such a formal source of unelected power within a democratic republic was justifiable or necessary, then there would likely follow a genuine crisis in which broad faith and respect in the work of appellate courts would badly erode, if not dissipate entirely. In fact, it is arguable that such a shift in attitude toward judicial lawmakers has already begun, especially with respect to the highest profile appellate court in this country, the United States Supreme Court. A sharp and sustained reduction in popular faith in, and respect for, the decisions made by the courts in this country would indeed be a serious and profound national predicament. This alone might be enough to account for the sustained denial of judicial instrumentalism.

Even beyond that factor, court procedures based on a formalist understanding of appellate lawmaking pervade our judicial system. As detailed in Chapter 5, appellate court procedures are a poor match for, and are unsuited to support, appellate lawmaking on an instrumentalist basis. The rules by which trial courts create the formal written record in the case are designed far more to provide competitive fairness to the disputing parties than to provide to the appellate courts a full and accurate picture of what transpired in the case, and of the factually relevant background. Moreover, virtually no current appellate procedures operate to provide appellate judges with a reasonable factual picture of the larger context in which these kinds of disputes typically arise and upon which a generally applicable common law could be effectively fashioned. Extensive, disruptive, and expensive changes would need to be made to long-standing appellate procedures and to traditional customary practices in order to refashion and reconstruct current appellate practice to suitably support instrumentalist common law lawmaking.

Not only is the nature and extent of the required changes daunting, it is also the case that the key players required for any possibly successful initiation and implementation of such changes – appellate court judges – face few incentives to begin or to seriously pursue such a project. For example, why would sitting and established appellate court judges wish to focus attention on, and to openly call into question, the far less than directly democratic basis upon which they obtained their lawmaking power and upon which they continue to possess it? In fact, in contrast, appellate courts face a rather obvious incentive to continue to present to the general public in their published opinions the idea, or at least the implicit suggestion, that the basis of their lawmaking work is as objectively determined and as logically required as they can while still presenting a straight face to the professional legal community. To the degree that published judicial appellate opinions set forth the rationale for their judgments, especially the judgments required in the creation of new common law, in the practical cost-benefit terms of explicit instrumentalism, the more the perception of their professional and societal role and that of directly elected politician-legislators narrows, to their obvious detriment.

And so, any serious structural and procedural transition from common law formalism to instrumentalism involves an expansive, disruptive, and expensive program of fundamental reforms carried out primarily by profoundly reluctant actors. No wonder we are close to a century into the postrealist, postformalist shift of conceptual paradigm to instrumentalism with only modest recognition beyond the academic literature and virtually no structural or procedural transition having begun.

One might note that some similar kinds of disincentives to acknowledge the occurrence of a paradigm shift and to implement a transition probably exist in the sciences as well. Surely, important investments are made based on an existing paradigm, and those having made those investments can be expected to be reluctant to publicly recognize or to support the movement toward the different understandings and different methods offered by a new paradigm.

In this respect, the societal system that generates common law differs from the sciences in at least two ways. One is that the sciences, and the natural sciences in particular, operate within a framework in which large and powerful organizations, including prominently the federal government, manage the flow of investment in scientific work through an elaborate aggregate of grant programs by which research scientists must successfully convince a funding source that the intended direction of the scientific inquiry is promising and worthy of investment. While not entirely centralized, there are only so many meaningful funding sources operating at any one time in a given area of scientific research. If these few major funding sources become convinced that, for example, the Einsteinian paradigm is a more promising approach than the traditional Newtonian one from which to understand and explain phenomena in the field of physics, then the field at large can be moved rather quickly to shift focus and to engage in fresh work developing the new paradigm. No such dynamic exists with respect to the work of appellate courts and the production and maintenance of the common law in this country.

Second, significant rewards await scientists and laboratories that are able to newly explain previously anomalous observational results and phenomena. These rewards, and the intrinsic desire of scientists to correctly understand and explain a given field, operate as motivators for researchers to abandon their existing investments and efforts in a previous paradigm and to transition their work to a more promising new paradigm. Again, no similar dynamic exists with respect to the work of appellate courts.

Neither formalism nor instrumentalism effectively prevents appellate judges from applying their instinctive sense of the world and their personal preferences among competing values to come to a decision regarding the optimal version of common law to adopt for their jurisdiction. Thus, appellate judges may, even after a paradigm shift, continue to resolve disputes and to create common law in a way that satisfies their personal sense of justice and optimal social policy and also continue to present these judgments in their published opinion in a way that obscures the degree of personal instinct and predisposition involved. Given that there is little self-interest-based incentive for appellate judges to openly embrace the paradigm shift from formalism to instrumentalism, there is correspondingly little incentive for them to advocate for the kind of structural and procedural changes in the legal system that would be more compatible with an instrumentalist approach to common law lawmaking.

Broadening the focus of this insight some, one can appreciate that there also exist few incentives for larger institutions in our society to embrace the shift from common law formalism to instrumentalism. While legislative and executive branch actors may occasionally chafe at the limitations that the judicial branch places on their powers, and while they may disagree with a particular version of the common law adopted by the judiciary, the political authority of appellate courts to create common law generates a number of tangible benefits for the other branches of government, both at the state and federal level.

Appellate courts can develop the law through common law lawmaking in ways that may be practically necessary but are mundane in nature, and that offer little or no practical political advantage to elected legislators. The power of appellate courts to create law permits legislators, and to some extent also executive branch actors, to avoid or reduce anticipated political costs by avoiding taking public positions and recording formal votes on especially controversial or problematic matters. In the case of lawmaking in the form of statutory interpretation,[4] appellate lawmaking permits elected politicians to forge agreement in difficult instances through the adoption of vague or ambiguous language in enacted legislation that will inevitably need to be interpreted by the far more politically insulated appellate courts.

In addition, it is well understood that in cases of conflict between law created by the appellate courts and law constitutionally created by the legislature, a legislative enactment preempts the common law and takes precedence. Therefore, the legislature faces essentially no risk that laws made by appellate courts will permanently usurp conflicting preferences of the legislative branch. This means that legislative actors can rely upon the lawmaking power of appellate courts when they perceive an advantage in doing so without the risk of involuntarily ceding meaningful lawmaking power to them.

Given this collection of potential benefits, there is little reason for legislators, or the legislative branch as a whole, to desire or to support greater public understanding that appellate courts are not, in fact, operating in a largely, objective, strictly logical, and value-neutral fashion. In such circumstances, it is little surprise that

[4] See Chapter 10 herein.

legislatures have shown virtually no interest in encouraging appellate courts to be more explicitly instrumentalist in their published opinions or in considering the kind of reforms to appellate court structures, appointments, and procedures that would make them more compatible with instrumentalism.

Finally, the practicing bar has few incentives to take a leadership role in any large-scale transition from formalism to instrumentalism. The mystique that formalism affords to the process of common law lawmaking is a benefit to practicing attorneys to the extent that it suggests that appellate courts depend upon a complicated and highly technical kind of uniquely legal analysis that requires the involvement and active participation of specially educated and formally licensed attorneys (licensed attorneys both representing the parties and also serving as the appellate judges). One could hardly imagine a party to appellate litigation in this country considering representation by anyone other than a licensed attorney, and most likely a licensed attorney who specializes in appellate litigation. This, of course, is a favorable state of affairs for practicing attorneys, especially those who specialize in appellate litigation.

One of the consequences of the shift from formalism to instrumentalism is a significant demystification of the appeals court process. For example, the California Supreme Court opinion in *Tarasoff* is far more accessible to an educated but not legally trained individual than a typical opinion written in formalist terms would be.[5] With greater transparency would come greater client comprehension of the work of their appellant attorneys and, especially with sophisticated corporate clients and relatively technical arguments regarding the practical costs and benefits of different versions of common law doctrine, greater confidence by the client in its own independent evaluation of the quality of the attorney's work. This might well be less attractive to the practicing bar, and thereby act as a disincentive for them to more aggressively embrace and support a transition from formalism to instrumentalism.

Furthermore, appellate advocacy within a formalist framework can be expected to be less expensive, and perhaps very much less expensive, than in an instrumentalist mode. Analysis within a formalist paradigm, and thus advocacy, is largely confined to materials that can be found in a typical law library or database. Not so with instrumentalism, which requires court consideration of likely practical costs and benefits of various possible dispositions of the case and various different versions of the common law in the real world. Since the analysis required of an appellate court under instrumentalism is dramatically more expansive than under formalism, the arguments appropriate to persuade an instrumentalist court will need to be correspondingly more expansive and empirical in nature. The more expansive the scope of analysis and the supporting argumentation, the more expensive the development of those arguments will inevitably be. An environment surrounding appellate advocacy that is both significantly more expensive for the client and significantly

[5] See Chapter 4 herein.

more transparent to the client is hardly a circumstance likely to be welcomed, or pursued, by the appellate bar.

Upon reflection, there may be no specific persons actively involved in the process of common law lawmaking, and no larger institutional interests, that are naturally motivated to advocate for a more explicit acknowledgment and structural accommodation of instrumentalism.

7.7 FORMALISM, INSTRUMENTALISM, AND STARE DECISIS

There is nothing about the difference between formalism and instrumentalism that implicates the long-standing practice of stare decisis. Stare decisis requires subordinate courts in their resolution of current cases to follow previously announced decisions of superior courts within the same court system. Thus, if the facts of a current dispute are the same in all relevant respects as that of a dispute previously resolved in the same court system by a superior court, then the subordinate court deciding the current case is obliged pursuant to the discipline of stare decisis to resolve the current case consistently with the previously decided case.

It can be said that the adherence to stare decisis in a given court system results in that system being more consistent in the judgments and pronouncements that it produces, both across different decision-makers within the system and over time. From a conceptual perspective, decisional consistency across both decision-makers and over time can be thought of as attributes of basic fairness (or due process). Thus, the operation of stare decisis within a court system can be understood to increase the degree to which that system functions in a fair manner.

The dominant practical benefit generated by a court system adhering to the doctrine of stare decisis is reliance. It allows persons in the jurisdiction in some class of cases to accurately predict how a current subordinate court will likely resolve a current or future dispute. This permits such persons to productively arrange their activities and affairs with reasonable reliance on the substance of the common law that will be applied by the courts of the jurisdiction to certain disputes that may arise (those being disputes that have previously been addressed and resolved by appellate courts in that jurisdiction). Much like the beneficial reliance generated by a well-designed law of contracts, the reliance on previously established common law provided by stare decisis can be powerfully productive to persons operating in a given jurisdiction and is, as a result, highly societally valuable.

Because it is often possible to identify one or more differences between a current legal dispute and previously decided disputes, and because it is fundamentally a matter of judgment and not literal fact whether these differences are meaningful enough to appropriately remove the current case from the strict discipline of stare decisis, the operation of the doctrine is in practice more a function of system-wide custom and usage than it is the formal enforcement of the rule per se. Subordinate courts generally appreciate the power and importance of stare decisis and resolve current cases accordingly. If they do not, appellate courts are often waiting for further litigation in the case to bring the matter to them for correction.

The degree to which a court system adheres to the rule and to the spirit of stare decisis, and thus harvests its benefits, is independent of the nature of the jurisprudential approach that courts in that system employ to make new common law. Under instrumentalism, appellate courts in a given court system could do their work by carefully considering the practical costs and benefits of the various plausible versions of a common law rule relating to a current case and also decide not to alter a prior judgment of a superior court with respect to the substance of this rule, or the application of the rule to resolve a given kind of dispute, unless they are convinced that the advantages of deviating from the prior decision outweigh the reliance benefits of adherence. Deciding whether the resolution of a current case should be determined by an application of the doctrine of stare decisis because it is sufficiently similar to a case previously decided by the same court system is one kind of judgment to be made by a court while the decision regarding how to analyze and resolve the case if its resolution is not fixed by the application of stare decisis is another.

To further illustrate the point, note that it would be possible for two different court systems to both be thoroughly instrumentalist in their approach to resolving disputes and making new common law and to also differ very significantly in the degree to which they are inclined to apply the doctrine of stare decisis to new cases. One such court system might have a customary practice of interpreting stare decisis broadly and to thereby decide that a relatively high percentage of new cases coming into the system fall under the doctrine and should, therefore, be resolved consistent with one or more prior decisions. The other court system might customarily interpret stare decisis narrowly and, as a result, routinely decide that only a relatively small percentage of new cases coming into that system fall into its outcome-determining mandate. And yet when both court systems decide in their markedly different ways that a new case is sufficiently novel so that the doctrine of stare decisis does not appropriately apply, they both apply the same thoroughly instrumentalist approach to dealing with those novel cases.

The same dynamic would exist with two different court systems that are both seemingly formalist in their approach or with two different court systems where one is formalist in nature and the other instrumentalist. A court system's orientation toward, and customary practice regarding, the doctrine of stare decisis is independent of that court system's approach to creating new common law. Because the degree to which the common law in a particular jurisdiction is stable over time is a function of that jurisdiction's practice with respect to stare decisis, and because that practice is unconnected to the larger jurisprudential approach that the appellate courts in that jurisdiction adopt, there is no greater or lesser stability of a particular jurisdiction's common law associated with either the formalist or the instrumentalist paradigm.

This important point is sometimes confused or misstated. As a consequence, it has been asserted that formalism necessarily yields a more stable and less volatile common law in a given jurisdiction than does instrumentalism and that this difference should be viewed as a relative advantage for a formalist approach.

For one, this assertion relies upon an implicit rejection of one of the critical insights established by the legal realist critique – that a formalist approach to common law analysis, while pretending to a high degree of logical determinism, did not in fact yield results that were determined by formal logic or any kind of supposedly technical, specialized, uniquely legal analysis. Subordinate courts in a given formalist court system that wish to deviate from previous decisions by superior courts can select as a starting point for analysis a different principle or maxim than did the prior court, or they can interpret the same generic or vague principle or maxim chosen by the prior court in a different, but equally reasonable, way. Because of this indeterminate quality of formalism, there is no reason to expect that common law will necessarily be more stable over time in a formalist jurisdiction than in an instrumentalist one. The critical factor determining the stability of a jurisdiction's common law over time is instead the approach that the court system in that jurisdiction adopts toward the practice of stare decisis.

Second, it is not at all clear that the stability of law over time is an independent virtue such that a jurisdiction should aspire to the most stable law possible. For example, imagine copyright law (or defamation law) adopted and developed in a certain jurisdiction in the early twentieth century. Is there any reason to suppose that the jurisdiction is better served if that copyright law is relatively stable and unchanged after all of the new and often revolutionary communications and content creation technology that was introduced later in that same century, including most especially the internet? While stability supports beneficial reliance, and such reliance generates powerful societal benefits, the rigidity of existing law in the face of dramatic changes in the regulated environment often generates its own powerful costs. Courts should, of course, continually and consciously manage the balance between these conflicting values, but no matter how that process is handled, it is clearly not the case that greater stability in isolation for its own sake is necessarily a greater societal good.

7.8 THE CRITICAL ROLE OF TRANSPARENCY IN APPELLATE COURT OPINIONS

Given the difficulties and costs associated with the instrumentalist approach to common law lawmaking described in Chapter 5, it is useful to remember that the previous formalist paradigm was not toppled by a direct challenge from instrumentalism or the success of some effort to convince the legal community that instrumentalism would be an easier, cheaper, more efficient, or more politically appropriate approach for appellate courts to take in creating common law.

Formalism was debunked by the legal realist movement which, in relevant part, demonstrated that the asserted attributes of formalism, attributes that grounded its claims to be a legitimate means of lawmaking by unelected appellate judges, were simply not true. Legal realism convinced a consensus of the legal community that the choices made by appellate judges operating within the formalist tradition were not, as was professed, logically determined, primarily deductive, and largely value-free. In contrast, the realists showed that appellate judges creating common law in the formalist era necessarily depended upon value-laden choices among various possible outcomes and standards when they chose to adopt one possible version of a common law rule as the law of the jurisdiction over other viable alternatives and possibilities.

Once this realist exposure of formalism was widely accepted as true, the dominant perceived problem with formalist lawmaking became its lack of transparency. Preferences were being made on a discretionary basis by appellate judges when resolving cases and making new common law and those judgments were being disguised and obscured by the formalist manner in which those decisions were being announced and explained in published opinions.

This lack of transparency in the public explanation of common law lawmaking and the resolution of appeals was not necessarily the product of a conscious effort by appellate judges and, thus, not necessarily intentional. It is entirely possible that appellate judges identified their preferred resolution of the case and the version of the common law they thought optimal on an instinctual, perhaps subconscious, basis and then more or less worked backward by choosing a general principle or maxim, or choosing an interpretation of a generic and vague principle or maxim, that would permit them to construct a line of deductive logic that would lead from the broad principle, so selected, to their preferred result. Once constructed in this way, the external presentation can appear to be an almost inevitable and logically fixed analytical path from a well-recognized first principle to the announced specific result. As the judge had no alternative specific and articulated basis for preferring the result to begin with, the formalist construction can come plausibly to feel like the genuine basis of the decision to even the judge himself.

One of the primary purposes of expecting, if not requiring, that appellate courts produce a publicly available published opinion announcing and explaining the decisions that it has made is that such a requirement serves as a constraining discipline on the exercise of formal power by unelected appellate court judges. They may not enjoy an electoral mandate, but instead, appellate judges are expected, unlike elected legislators, to set forth the rationale for their decisions in writing and to publish that explanation for the public. To the extent that the published opinion does not reveal, but instead obscures, the trade-offs, value choices, and social preferences upon which the judicial judgments were actually based, this important function of publishing appellate opinions is thwarted. To the extent that almost any one of a broad and reasonable set of possible outcomes and choices of common law doctrine can be justified by logically connecting it to any one of many equally honored general principles that exist, or by connecting it to a highly generic and abstract truism, the authority-constraining discipline of requiring written published appellate opinions is very much frustrated.

Another important purpose of maintaining a strong custom of appellate courts producing written and published explanations for their decisions is that these published opinions provide to future courts a guide to the analysis upon which the authoring court based its judgments and decisions. This allows future courts to review those prior analytic elements in light of current conditions and better decide the degree of appropriate deference to grant to the prior analysis and the prior judgments. This purpose of published opinions is also badly compromised when the prior published opinion is more constructed formalist veneer than candid explication. Perhaps the prior court assumed a practical consequence of one possible version of a common law rule that was a reasonable empirical expectation at that time, but that would no longer be so under the changed circumstances of the present. Perhaps the prior court relied upon a value or preference that was commonplace at the time but is now generally viewed as anachronistic. A heavily formalistic presentation by appellate courts of their analysis and decision-making largely robs future courts of the opportunity, without engaging in speculation, to identify these aspects of prior court decisions and to adjust the current analysis and current doctrine appropriately.

A third purpose for expecting appellate courts to support an exercise of their formal power with a written published opinion is that it allows the practicing bar, and to some extent the public at large, to judge when an existing common law rule in the jurisdiction is backed by still solid rationales and analysis and can therefore be confidently relied upon. It also, in contrast, allows attorneys and the public to discern when the offered published support for an existing common law rule has grown suspect and weak, thus suggesting that the doctrine may be ripe for challenge and change. Under a formalist paradigm, published rationales for most all of the existing common law in a jurisdiction strive to present the chosen doctrine as logically inevitable and determined. Unless the first principles previously relied upon have meaningfully changed (an unlikely occurrence), these kinds of explanations for appellate court judgments and decisions remain static and rigid over time, and provide neither the practicing bar nor the public with any useful guide in distinguishing among them in terms of their stability as continuing law.

A fourth purpose for expecting appellate courts to produce written published opinions is that a candid explication of a court's reasons for resolving a dispute as it did, and for selecting one possible version of common law doctrine instead of others, is that such an explanation greatly assists practicing attorneys in crafting more potentially persuasive arguments when litigating before these courts. This is not just a private benefit to attorneys. To the extent that attorneys arguing before appellate courts can accurately discern the factors that these courts find most relevant and persuasive with respect to a given issue, or to a broader field of common law, the more effectively these attorneys can fashion and then offer to the courts' arguments that most directly address the issues upon which the courts are most focused, and can thus as a result be most helpful to the court in its deliberations. Relevant and persuasive arguments benefit attorneys and their clients and also powerfully aid the court in its decision-making process.

Formalism frustrates this benefit of the transparency sought by a strong custom of written and published appellate court opinions as well. It is rarely the case that the path of formal logic that leads from the first principle, or the version of the first principle, chosen by the court to the conclusion chosen by the court is the one and only exclusive path of logical analysis that was available, and yet a formalist opinion presents it as such. What is an attorney anticipating arguing before such a court in the future to do with such an opinion? The attorney can see that the expected presentation to the court is one based on formal logic and deduction from supposed first principles. And the attorney can know to construct and offer to the court a chain of alleged formal logic that leads from an asserted first principle to his client's preferred resolution of the case. But on the more critical question of why the court should select one particular logical path over other plausible and equally valid ones, the prior opinion is more or less useless, and the attorney left with little or no guidance. The less guidance that is provided by the prior published opinions, the less genuinely helpful attorneys practicing before appellate courts will be, all to the detriment of the quality of common law lawmaking by appellate courts.

In a formalist world, there is a radical disconnect between the external, public façade of the appellate court process and the actual, internal determinants of appeals court outcomes. Formalist courts set forth their opinions in formalist terms, thus attorneys present their arguments to these courts in formalist terms, and none of the briefs, oral arguments, or published opinions provide much useful guidance to the public as to how the common law that governs them and to which they are subject is made, and why its substance is as it is. The lack of genuine transparency within a formalist paradigm is profound, and the cost, both practical and political, is enormous. Once the legal realist critique exposed that profound lack of transparency, the legal community lost its traditional faith in the formalist paradigm.

It is, however, one thing to expose and unmask an existing paradigm and a different thing altogether to establish a new prevailing paradigm. The legal realist movement and the revolution that it occasioned was not necessarily engaged in that latter project. Instrumentalism came to supplant formalism less as a successful usurper and more as the default occupier of a vacuum. As such, it is not such a surprise that instrumentalism as a prevailing paradigm for common law lawmaking comes with very significant costs and some radical incompatibilities with existing appellate structures, existing appellate procedures, and some basic tenants of a democratic republic. Similarly, as a default occupier of an existing vacuum, instrumentalism has enjoyed few enthusiastic affirmative advocates and supporters.

Instrumentalism taken seriously threatens to disturb some established practices and some powerful and influential players, both individual and institutional. As a result, a concrete, earnest, and sustained effort to transition to the new paradigm by implementing foundational changes to appellate court appointments, structure, and procedure and by altering the public understanding of these courts and the nature of their work has yet to materialize.[6]

[6] It is interesting to note that after these words were initially written and before they were published, President Biden prominently proposed new federal legislation that would formally limit the terms of United States Supreme Justices, and would result in other major changes. See Katie Rogers, *Warning of "Extreme" Agenda, Biden Calls for Supreme Court Overhaul*, N.Y. TIMES, July 29, 2024, at A1.

8

Empirical Instrumentalist Analysis

Understanding the Absence of a Duty to Reasonably Rescue in American Tort Law

Should the tort law of negligence include a formal legal duty for individuals to affirmatively assist a stranger in peril? This is an issue of common law torts that has had to be confronted and resolved by dozens of American appellate courts, and courts in other Western countries, over many years.

This issue is especially interesting in that it presents in as nearly a stark and direct a manner as possible the kind of conflict that can exist between a formalist and an instrumentalist approach to creating common law doctrine. While one can imagine the bare possibility of a formalist analysis that supports the absence of such a legal duty (it would need to start with asserted adherence to a general principle that supports maximum individual liberty and freedom from collective legal obligations), the choice of an abstract analysis starting with generally recognized legal maxims, bromides, and truisms heavily stacks the deck in favor of a conclusion that the law should impose a duty on persons to at least act reasonably on behalf of others when they encounter them in peril.

This is borne out by the appellate opinions and academic commentary that exists in this area of law. For example, a recent law review article on the subject concludes that "A duty to rescue one's fellow human in their hour of greatest vulnerability, where one is found to be at risk of death or injury, is a duty promulgated by the philosophy of natural law."[1]

In sharp contrast, as demonstrated by what follows, an analysis of the issue that is focused upon the likely practical consequences of either the existence or the absence of such a formal legal duty is almost certain to support a decision to not include such a duty as part of a jurisdiction's negligence law. By the illustration that follows, it is made clear that the difference between a formalist and an instrumentalist paradigm of common law lawmaking is not just the surface method of analysis employed or the style of decisional presentation offered in published opinions but it is also the very substance, the actual content, of the common law.

---

[1] Jack Power, *My Brother's Keeper: A Theoretical Justification for a Positive Duty to Rescue under Irish Law*, 27 Trinity College Law Review 265 (2024).

Shortly after noon on January 2, 2007, Wesley Autrey, a fifty-year-old construction worker, was waiting for the subway at 137th Street and Broadway in New York City. He was with his two young daughters, ages four and six. Not far from them on the platform was Cameron Hollopeter, a twenty-year-old film student. Hollopeter suffered a sudden seizure that caused him to collapse, and after unsteadily getting to his feet, he stumbled backward over the edge of the platform onto the tracks below. With the No. 1 train quickly approaching, Autrey jumped down and pressed himself and Hollopeter tightly into a space between the tracks little more than a foot deep. The train, unable to stop, rumbled over Autrey and Hollopeter, mere inches above them, smudging Autrey's knit cap with grease. Both men emerged alive and largely uninjured from the ordeal.

Just two days later in a different borough of the same city during the same noon hour, three-year-old Timothy Addo crawled through the window of his babysitter's apartment in the Bronx and out onto a fire escape. The child climbed down one story and ended up dangling from the metal structure four floors above the sidewalk, rapidly losing his grip. Two lifelong friends – forty-three-year-old Julio Gonzalez and forty-year-old Pedro Nevarez – spotted the child and ran across the street, positioning themselves under the fire escape just as Timothy let loose and fell. The child landed hard on Nevarez's chest, knocking Nevarez onto the sidewalk. Timothy was then caught in the air by Gonzalez who maintained his hold on the forty-five-pound child. Neither man was seriously injured, and Timothy was released from the hospital after being treated for minor scrapes. Later in the day, New York City Police Commissioner Raymond W. Kelly said, "This is a week of heroes here in New York."

It was not nearly the same kind of week in New York City some forty years earlier when the borough of Queens was the setting of what is almost certainly the most notorious incident of callousness in the face of another's mortal peril ever to occur in America. In the very early hours of March 13, 1964, Catherine "Kitty" Genovese was stalked, stabbed, brutally attacked again, and eventually killed by Winston Moseley, a complete stranger to Ms. Genovese. This all took place on the public streets of Queens over a thirty-five-minute period during which at least thirty-eight witnesses heard the twenty-eight-year-old woman desperately scream in fear and for help, but none of them did anything whatsoever to assist her. It is reported that one couple turned out the lights in their apartment and pulled chairs up to the window in order to better observe the drama.

More recently, in May 2006, David Sharp, a thirty-four-year-old veteran mountaineer, had just achieved a lifelong ambition to reach the summit of Mt. Everest when, on his way down, he experienced symptoms of severe oxygen deficiency. He managed to maneuver himself into a shallow snow cave approximately 1,000 feet below the summit adjacent to a well-traveled trail. As Sharp sat cross-legged in the snow cave struggling for his life, more than forty climbers, all sufficiently experienced and physically conditioned to have ascended to 28,000 feet, walked right by him on their way up to the summit. Nearly all of them passed without offering any assistance whatsoever, and none attempted any sort of rescue. A British film crew even shot footage of Sharp as he sat in the snow cave, talking lucidly, saying, "My name is David Sharp. I am with Asian Trekking." One of the mountaineers who passed by Sharp was Mark Inglis, the first double-amputee to climb Everest and the beneficiary of a successful rescue effort that brought him down from New Zealand's highest mountain, Mt. Cook, twenty-four years earlier.

On May 15, 2006, David Sharp died where he sat, not far from the frozen remains of an Indian climber who died in 1997 and whose body Sharp had walked past on his way up to the summit. Sir Edmund Hillary, the legendary mountaineer who, with Tenzing Norgay, reached the summit of Everest for the first time in 1953, openly criticized the climbers who failed to help Sharp: "It was wrong if there was a man suffering altitude problems and huddled under a rock, just to lift your hat, say, 'Good morning' and pass on by. . .. On my expedition there was no way you would have left a man under a rock to die." Ed Viesturs, among the strongest and most accomplished mountain climbers in the world, said, "This isn't the first time this has happened. . .. Passing people who are dying is not uncommon. Unfortunately, there are those who say it's not my problem. I've spent all this money and I'm going to the summit."[2]

Just a few months before his death, as he was preparing to embark on the expedition to Everest, David Sharp sought to console his anxious mother. "'You are never on your own,' he told her. 'There are climbers everywhere.'"[3]

What is the status under American tort law of a failure to reach out and affirmatively aid another in peril? Could a victim, who suffers greater harm because no effort was made to help, successfully sue those who chose to do nothing when reasonable, even easy, opportunities to aid were available? With a few exceptions, the general rule in American tort law is that bystanders will not be liable to a victim for their failure to affirmatively aid. There is, in other words, no general duty to reasonably rescue in American law.

This feature of American tort law differs markedly from the legal treatment of the same issue in other parts of the world where legal obligations to affirmatively aid another in peril are common. It also stands in striking contrast to most conventional views of common decency and morality. Perhaps because of this, the no-duty-to-rescue doctrine has been frequently and widely condemned, with the great majority of the academic literature on the subject recommending abandonment or change. And yet, the doctrine remains a standard part of the common law canon.

It is a long-established feature of American tort law that a person owes no legal duty to affirmatively act to aid a stranger in peril, no matter how reasonable a readily

[2] Pete Thomas, *Morality on a Slippery Slope*, Los Angeles Times, June 1, 2006, at A1.

[3] Ian Herbert, *'On Everest, You Are Never on Your Own', Words of the Climber Left to Die at Summit*, Independent (United Kingdom), May 25, 2006, at 18.

available affirmative act might be. Thus, if I am standing by my car in a fairly steeply sloped parking lot of a shopping center, and I see a heavy metal shopping cart, completely unattended, rolling toward a small and oblivious group of people conversing together some yards downhill, I need not do so much as shout a simple warning in order to avoid subsequent liability for negligence when the cart hits and badly injures some of them.

The overwhelming majority of people in a similar position would have at least called out a warning. A shouted warning would have been nearly free of cost to me and would almost certainly have saved the victims from significant physical injury. Under no recognized approach to determining the reasonableness of a person's judgment would not calling out a warning be deemed acceptable. And yet, in most every jurisdiction in this country, I would face no exposure to negligence law liability for my complete failure to act reasonably in this instance, for in American tort law, I have no legal duty to reasonably act toward a stranger in peril – no duty to affirmatively aid.

There are three basic exceptions to the general no-duty-to-rescue rule that are recognized in a majority of American jurisdictions. One covers situations in which a particular relationship exists between the plaintiff and the defendant. The two relationships most commonly held to fall within this exception are the businessperson–customer relationship and the employer–employee relationship. Thus, if a sales associate working in a department store observes a customer on the sales floor kneel over in apparent pain and fall to the ground, the clerk, representing the department store, could not fail to take any action on behalf of the stricken customer without having that decision potentially second-guessed in a subsequent negligence suit. Similarly, if the sales associate was experiencing medical distress and the manager of the department was observing the scene, the manager would not be protected by the no-duty-to-rescue rule from subsequent negligence liability for a failure to act.

A second well-recognized exception to the general rule applies to circumstances in which the defendant was a cause of the peril faced by the plaintiff. Thus, if the plaintiff's and the defendant's cars collide, and the plaintiff is knocked unconscious, slumped in his driver's seat, while the defendant remains alert and capable, the defendant will owe to the plaintiff a legal duty to take reasonable measures on the plaintiff's behalf.

A third exception to the general no-duty-to-rescue rule is triggered by the defendant voluntarily rendering aid to the plaintiff. Suppose the defendant sees the plaintiff, a stranger, fall to the sidewalk of a public street and lapse into unconsciousness. A small crowd of onlookers gathers around the plaintiff. The defendant says out loud, "I'll go for help," and begins to walk briskly down the street. After turning a corner and moving out of sight of the crowd, the defendant abandons his plan to seek help and instead walks home. In such circumstances, the plaintiff may, through a negligence claim, formally question the reasonableness of the defendant's failure to do more on his behalf.

Despite the existence of these three traditional exceptions, the general no-duty-to-rescue rule remains robust, covering a large number of possible circumstances in which a person's condition may be seriously worsened by another's failure to reasonably help. Why would a regime of negligence law that is willing to scrutinize for reasonableness all manner of human judgments be unwilling to do its usual work in even the most obvious of these no-duty-to-rescue cases? Why not impose upon each of us an obligation to act with at least reasonable care when confronted with another in peril? Why, in the earlier example, impose an obligation to drive to the shopping center with reasonable care, to park with reasonable care, to shop with reasonable care, and to depart with reasonable care, but fail to impose upon me any obligation at all to reasonably call out a warning to the people threatened by the runaway shopping cart?

Surely no satisfying explanation of this feature of tort law resides in the degree to which it gives expression to conventional morality or ethics. The overwhelming majority of us, if asked, would certainly say that the proper, socially acceptable response to a stranger in physical peril is to offer at least reasonable aid. No serious religion or secular system of ethics recommends that its adherents fail to aid another in peril when a reasonable response is available. In fact, a person who fails to act in such a situation could rightly be condemned for such a decision, and every now and then celebrated cases of this sort receive their share of national attention.

How, then, can tort law possibly justify the continued presence of this no-duty-to-rescue rule? The answer lies within a collection of approximately half a dozen basic arguments, some of which carry more weight in the overall scheme than others.

The rationale for the rule begins, interestingly enough, with the same conventional moral wisdom that makes the rule seem so counterintuitive. Namely, that it is an uncontroversial element of generally accepted societal behavior that one should act reasonably to help another facing serious peril; that every individual should at least call out for help if, while walking in the mall, he comes across a person lying on the floor, bleeding, and crying out in pain. So unquestioned is this simple behavioral norm that it is fair to assume that the great majority of people who find themselves in such a situation will, in fact, call out for help, or otherwise act reasonably, to aid the stranger on the floor.

Thus, it should be acknowledged that a no-duty-to-rescue rule – that is, a rule that threatens negligence liability for a defendant failing to reasonably assist a stranger in peril – would generate only a small number of additional rescue efforts than currently exist under the no-duty rule. Because the underlying behavioral norm is so strong and uncontroversial, there can be said to already exist a very high level of uncoerced compliance with the desired behavioral goal. In other words, society already enjoys very high levels of reasonable affirmative responses to others in peril even in the absence of a coercive legal rule.

In this sense, one can look at a duty-to-rescue rule as being a bit like an affirmative legal requirement that parents care for the basic physical needs of their newborn children. No one questions the importance of parents caring for their infant children or the significant social cost that would result if parents failed to do so, but the clear tendency of the overwhelming number of parents to care for their newborns, and to do so even in the absence of a formal legal rule requiring them to, strongly suggests that the existence of such a rule would have little practical effect on overall parenting behavior. It is of little surprise, therefore, that over time the American legal system has not developed a vigorous jurisprudence in this area.

In contrast, there are some behaviors deemed by society as useful and important for individuals to undertake, but in the absence of a coercive legal rule, many citizens may be unwilling to undertake them. This may be the case even in the face of widespread general consensus that these behaviors are socially valuable or even necessary. One example of such a behavior is the payment of taxes to finance the operation of government. In the absence of a coercive legal rule and aggressive enforcement, one would expect a fairly low level of purely voluntary compliance with this behavioral norm, even among those who would acknowledge the validity of the norm itself. Hence, we see the maintenance of a very vigorous jurisprudence in this area of the law.

If one accepts that reasonably responding to another in peril is more like parents caring for their newborn than like paying taxes, one can then conclude that the practical benefit of switching from a no-duty-to-rescue rule to an affirmative duty-to-rescue rule would be quite modest. This is especially true as technological advances, such as mobile telephones, often make a reasonable effort to aid another in peril easy and virtually risk free. Because the vast majority of persons subject to the rule are already thought to be engaging in the desired behavior, only the actions of the uncommon few who refuse to conform to the prevailing societal norm are subject to change. Whatever the cost of this candle, we can say with some confidence that the light that it will produce will be rather dim.

Few overall changes in behavior are likely to result from the adoption of an affirmative duty to rescue. The assertion that high levels of uncoerced reasonable rescue efforts currently exist also allows the behavioral analysis to focus usefully on the predicted actions and reactions of those who would only engage in reasonable rescue efforts in the presence of a coercive legal requirement.

The situation is much like the recurring discussion among law school faculties about which courses in the curriculum should be required of all students prior to graduation. Take, for example, a course like corporation law. There are very interesting arguments, in the abstract, for the value of corporation law as a subject of study and as a necessary or desirable body of predicate knowledge prior to practicing law in the modern world. In an important sense, however, these arguments are somewhat beside the point. The overwhelming majority of students do, in fact, take a course in corporation law and in other foundational subjects such as constitutional law, evidence law, and commercial law before they graduate, even if not formally required. Thus, the more relevant inquiry is less whether such courses are generally valuable or invaluable, but why the small minority of students who choose not to take the course prior to graduation make that decision.

If I were to discover that most of the students who choose not to take corporation law do so because they were undergraduate business majors, held advanced degrees in business management or accounting, or were otherwise exposed to basic corporate law through experience in the securities industry or elsewhere and thus wished to spend their credit hours on a subject with which they were less familiar, I would feel one way about making corporation law a graduation requirement. In contrast, if I came to believe that most of these students avoided the corporation law course out of a generalized distaste for business matters and the fear of having to work with numbers and finance, I would feel quite differently.

Similarly, in predicting the differences in behavior when society applies a no-duty-to-rescue versus an affirmative duty-to-rescue rule, the most useful analysis focuses only on the likely behavior of persons who would behave differently under the two competing rules, i.e., those who would only attempt to rescue because of an affirmative, coercive legal requirement to do so. These persons can be called, for convenience, reluctant rescuers. When thinking about reluctant rescuers, it should be acknowledged that not all persons who would choose not to reasonably aid another in the absence of a coercive legal rule would necessarily respond by engaging in the socially desired behavior when faced with the threat of tort law liability. After all, much more severe consequences now exist for those found guilty of homicide, armed robbery, and other serious crimes, and yet people continue to commit those crimes.

Moreover, situations in which a person comes across an opportunity to reasonably aid another in peril and chooses not to do so rarely present an easy opportunity for the victim to identify the potential defendant and subsequently bring suit. If the driver of the first car standing at the light of an intersection at which a severe collision has just occurred fails to pick up his mobile phone and call for emergency services, who among the potential plaintiffs is likely to ever know? What are the chances of detection and civil prosecution when someone passively watches a shopping cart strike its victims in the parking lot? Thus, the often undetectable nature of possible defendants diminishes further the practical effect of an affirmative duty-to-rescue rule.

Of course, the likelihood of identification as someone who failed to reasonably aid another in peril increases dramatically if there are bystanders other than the victim physically present. Consequently, one might expect those who would otherwise fail to render aid to be more likely to do so when there are other persons present. The relative importance of requiring a reluctant rescuer to act, however, decreases as the number of other people present on the scene and available to render aid to the victim increases. Therefore, it is likely that an affirmative duty to rescue will produce a greater number of additional rescue efforts in just those circumstances in which additional coerced rescue efforts are least needed.

In summary, the practical benefits of an affirmative duty to reasonably rescue in tort law would be quite meager, both because the existing level of uncoerced compliance is quite high and because the percentage of noncompliers likely to change their behavior because of a coercive rule will be small.

To this point in the argument, the focus has been on the minimal nature of the perceived benefits of switching from the current no-duty-to-rescue rule to an affirmative duty-to-rescue rule. As such, the analysis is vulnerable to the following challenge: why not switch to a more morally intuitive and satisfying legal rule, even if such a switch is likely to result in only an insignificant increase in the number of rescue efforts? Is it not better, particularly from a potential victim's point of view, to increase the number of rescue efforts modestly than not at all? After all, an affirmative-duty rule that has only slightly better results than the current no-duty rule is still a superior rule.

To support the no-duty rule in the face of this challenge, the likely costs of an affirmative duty must be identified and shown to outweigh the modest benefits that an affirmative duty promises. This goal can be achieved by shifting the standard by which the superiority of one rule over the other is measured. Thus far, the analysis has proceeded as if the superior rule is the one that results in a greater number of rescue efforts when such efforts are reasonable under the circumstances. This seems eminently sensible, because most of us, if placed in a position of peril, would presumably prefer a greater likelihood of rescue to a smaller one.

It is important to recognize, however, that not all rescue efforts, even efforts deemed reasonable under an affirmative-duty rule, will result in an improvement in the victim's condition. Inevitably, some affirmative attempts by strangers to aid others in peril will cause greater harm than good. The best intentioned rescuer could move the victim of the fresh car accident into a seemingly more comfortable position and, as a consequence, aggravate his injuries. The person seeking to help a stranger in distress on the sidewalk could pick up their mobile phone and, flustered and distracted, badly misidentify to emergency personnel the location of the victim.

The fact that an affirmative duty-to-rescue rule would encourage only reasonable rescue efforts will do nothing to alleviate this problem. The rule, embedded in negligence law, would compel the potential rescuer to affirmatively act only if, and only to the extent that, a reasonably prudent person faced with similar circumstances would act. The incentive to act has its primary effect when the potential rescuer is faced with the possibility of rescue action ex ante. Thus, the rule cannot discriminate between rescue efforts that subsequently benefit the victim and those that go awry.

For example, imagine a defendant who is boating on a lake and comes across a person stranded in the water, clinging desperately to an overturned canoe. An affirmative duty-to-rescue rule in negligence law would expose the defendant to liability if he failed to take reasonable action to aid the other. So, if the defendant could have easily thrown the victim a flotation device and did not, and as a result, the victim suffered greater harm, liability would be likely. If, all things considered, diving into the water to attempt a more vigorous hand-to-hand rescue would have exposed the defendant to unreasonable risk, then the defendant's decision not to do so should trigger no liability.

In neither case, however, should the specific outcome of the defendant's decision to affirmatively aid properly factor into the analysis of whether the decision to rescue was reasonable or not. It is, at least in the abstract, reasonable for the defendant to throw the victim a flotation device whether the victim is effectively spared from drowning or instead the throw is misjudged, strikes the victim on the head, and takes him under. Similarly, the reasonableness of the defendant attempting a rescue by personally diving into the water should be determined independently from the actual outcome of the rescue effort. As a consequence, an affirmative duty to rescue will encourage a greater number of reasonable rescue efforts irrespective of whether or not these additional rescue efforts result in actual benefit to the victim. Inevitably, some additional rescue efforts that, in fact, do the victim no good or result in greater harm to the victim will occur as a result of the adoption of an affirmative-duty rule. Under either an affirmative-duty or a no-duty regime, the actions of a rescuer, once begun, will be subject to a duty of reasonable care, but that is not relevant one way or the other to this aspect of the no-duty-to-rescue analysis.

The standard to determine the superiority of either the no-duty or the affirmative-duty rule should not be the degree to which one rule or the other encourages a greater number of rescue efforts. Instead, the more appropriate measure is the degree to which one rule or the other creates conditions in which the victim's situation is likely to be improved. The superior rule should result not just in more rescue efforts, but in more successful rescue efforts.

From this perspective, at least one more characteristic of rescue situations should be noted. While not always the case, a great many potential rescue situations possess an aspect of exclusivity. That is to say, in a large number of circumstances in which a person in peril needs aid from another, the natural inclination to offer help diminishes significantly once someone else has begun the effort. It is far less likely that a bystander will move to help a stranger lying on the ground in the park in obvious medical distress if he sees that someone else is already kneeling down beside him. A driver is far less likely to pull his car over to the side of the road in response to a recent accident if he will be the third or fourth car to do so.

This natural tendency identifies a potential practical cost of encouraging a greater number of rescue efforts through the adoption of a formal duty to affirmatively aid. The argument goes like this: the only persons whose behavior will be altered in the switch from a no-duty to an affirmative-duty rule are the reluctant rescuers, the individuals who will attempt a rescue effort only under a coercive rule out of fear of their potential liability if they do not. Given their attitude and motivation, such rescuers can be expected, in general, to engage in a lower quality of rescue effort than would a purely altruistic rescuer, who would choose to act on their own under either legal regime. Given the often exclusive nature of rescue situations, the actions of a reluctant rescuer will sometimes preempt, and thereby replace, the actions of an altruistic rescuer. In such situations, the victim will, as a result of the existence of the coercive rule, receive a lower quality of affirmative aid than he otherwise might. This substitution in some situations of a higher quality altruistic rescuer by a lower quality reluctant rescuer represents a cost to victims generated by the adoption of an affirmative duty to aid.

One possible objection to this argument might be that a victim would prefer even a reluctant rescuer to no rescuer at all in those situations in which the only possible rescuer is a reluctant rescuer. While this is almost certainly true, its practical significance may be quite small.

Remember that reluctant rescuers are those individuals who would not act to aid the victim in the absence of a legal requirement, but who would act in the presence of a coercive legal rule. Perhaps some of these individuals would change their behavior out of abstract respect for the law. Assuming that the overwhelming majority of reluctant rescuers change their behavior from fear of liability should they breach the legal duty, it is reasonable to assume that they are more likely to act in those situations in which their exposure to liability would be greatest and, conversely, that they would be least likely to act, even in the presence of a legal duty to do so, in those situations in which they are unlikely ever to be held legally liable for doing nothing. Doing nothing, after all, is the preferred behavior of the reluctant rescuers in the absence of a coercive rule.

In a world in which a duty to affirmatively aid exists, a person could most easily be held liable by the victim for failing to reasonably aid when the defendant's failure occurred in a setting in which other persons were present. Conversely, the risk of eventual liability for failing to reasonably act would presumptively be smallest in those situations in which only the victim and the defendant were present. Thus, a reluctant rescuer, prepared to reasonably aid another only because such action will avoid possible liability, is far more likely to engage in rescue efforts when others are present to observe his failure to do so than in circumstances where no one else is likely to know of his failure to act.

Therefore, the presence of a coercive legal duty to affirmatively aid will most effectively encourage reluctant rescuers to act in those situations in which other people are present, and these are exactly the situations in which the actions of the reluctant rescuer are most likely to supplant more desirable altruistic rescue efforts. It is in those situations in which no one else is present, and the reluctant rescuer's actions are most needed by the victim, that the coercive legal rule generates the weakest incentive for the reluctant rescuer to act.

Thus, while the adoption of an affirmative duty to aid can be expected to increase the overall number of rescue efforts, the additional rescue efforts generated by the duty-to-rescue rule can be expected to be relatively small in number and more likely to occur in those circumstances in which they would impose an undesirable burden on the victim by supplanting higher quality efforts to help.

Another cost associated with the adoption of an affirmative duty to aid can be identified by looking at the effect of such a rule on the majority of persons whose behavior would be unchanged in the shift from a no-duty to an affirmative-duty regime. For these individuals who would shout a warning to those in the path of a runaway shopping cart and otherwise would act reasonably to aid another in peril, the adoption of an affirmative-duty rule marks a subtle, but arguably profound, shift in the social quality of that behavior.

Under the current no-duty doctrine, there is little doubt that those who undertake rescue efforts on behalf of another are doing so voluntarily and altruistically, and they may rightfully enjoy higher self-esteem and greater regard by others as a result. Conversely, if a legal duty to affirmatively aid was adopted, these same behaviors by these same individuals under the same circumstances could be viewed as no more than mere compliance with the legal requirement, engaged in as much out of a desire to avoid subsequent legal liability as from genuine altruism or beneficence. In the eyes of others, and perhaps to some extent to themselves as well, the nature of their act has been transformed from the manifestly honorable to the merely compliant.

This effect can be called a discount of altruism. Assuming that an overwhelming percentage of persons will at least act reasonably on behalf of another in peril in the absence of a coercive legal rule, then the adoption of a coercive duty to act will, in a sense, taint the moral and social quality of socially desirable behavior that would have been engaged in by the vast majority of persons anyway. Such altruistic, praiseworthy behavior will be transformed and diminished to not much more than ordinary obedience to the law and compliance with the minimum social expectation that is articulated by that law. While this may not be a devastating tangible cost of adopting an affirmative duty to act, it is a significant intangible cost and will affect most persons who actually engage in affirmative rescue efforts.

Another cost of an affirmative duty to rescue focuses less on a particular group of actors than on the broader nature of an affirmative duty to act. The argument begins with an appreciation for the fact that the great complex of formal second-guessing that is tort law negligence, unbounded by the prosecutorial discretion that is integral to criminal law, is a rather intrusive system of oversight and regulation. As noted earlier, the implicit burden of reasonable care and the threat of liability for its breach applies to nearly every imaginable action that can proximately cause harm to another.

Now, it is one thing to say to the citizens of a jurisdiction that when you choose to go out in the world and seek your fortune and your pleasure, you must behave with reasonable care toward other persons and their property. It seems reasonably appropriate for society to determine that when individuals venture out to seek their satisfaction, they should be mindful of and should answer for harm that they carelessly inflict on others.

It is entirely and importantly different for society at large to say to an individual that it will not only second-guess the reasonableness of his behavior when he affirmatively moves about in the world, but that it will also, with his assets at risk, second-guess his decision not to act at all. While it may be a fair societal determination to impose a formal duty of reasonable care when one enters the game and chooses to play, it is something else altogether to second-guess the reasonableness of one's decision not to play at all.

It must be remembered here that the affirmative actions taken by a rescuer, reluctant or voluntary, can always be the object of a subsequent negligence claim should those actions go awry and cause greater harm to the plaintiff. Thus, under an affirmative duty-to-rescue rule, reluctant rescuers are forced into action when they otherwise would have done nothing and are then subjected to the second-guessing mechanism of negligence law with respect to the quality of those coerced actions.

In effect, under an affirmative duty to act, there is no space to which a person can retreat and, in exchange for doing nothing at all, in exchange for seeking nothing at all, avoid the otherwise constant gaze of the reasonably prudent person. With an affirmative duty to act, that final refuge will be penetrated. There will exist no sanctuary in which the pervasive duty of reasonable care will not reach. The elimination of that final private space marks a degree of intrusiveness by negligence law that, while perhaps practically modest, is theoretically and symbolically profound. It inevitably involves an undesirable degree of intimate intrusiveness on the autonomy of individual choice and judgment.

It was argued earlier that the proper measure of the superior legal rule regarding rescues should not be the encouragement of the maximum number of rescue efforts or even the maximum number of reasonable rescue efforts. Instead, it should be the creation of conditions that encourage the maximum number of successful outcomes for the victims in peril. Additionally, the superior rule should also encourage the maximum number of successful outcomes for the individual engaging in the rescue effort. In other words, while rescue efforts may go awry and place the victims in greater peril, they may also turn out badly for the rescuers themselves, causing them harm.

It is conventional wisdom in professional lifesaving circles that unless you are well trained and confident of success, you should not jump into an emergency situation in an attempt to save another. Much too often such behavior results in two victims rather than one successful rescue. More generally, it is obvious that an attempt to provide aid to someone in peril could, in a wide range of circumstances, result in injury or death to the rescuer.

This is an inherent risk involved in choosing to provide another with affirmative aid, especially under emergency conditions. It is part of what makes rescue efforts morally praiseworthy and sometimes even heroic. It is a risk that every person who provides aid to another in peril voluntarily assumes under the current no-duty-to-rescue regime.

This risk, however, under an affirmative duty-to-rescue doctrine, will fall upon reluctant rescuers only because of their coerced compliance with the legal rule.

Some of these reluctant rescuers will inevitably be injured in the course of their rescue efforts. Some will die. By definition, no reluctant rescuers will suffer such harm under a no-duty-to-rescue rule, and this difference must be counted as a cost of an affirmative-duty regime.

This concern can be extended one small step further. Criminals sometimes prey upon their victims by posing as someone in need of assistance or emergency aid. For example, a predator could ask for directions and try to draw the victim into his car to point the way on a map. A predator could impersonate a motorist stranded on the shoulder of a remote road next to a disabled automobile. If an affirmative duty-to-rescue doctrine is to have any practical effect at all, its presence should result in a greater number of rescue efforts in such situations than would occur in its absence. In every such case in which the apparent victim in peril is, in fact, a lure for criminal activity and the actual victim-rescuer would not have been drawn in but for the existence of a legal duty to rescue, the resulting harm inflicted upon the victim is another cost of an affirmative-duty rule.

Consider again the infamous Kitty Genovese incident described in this chapter. In the current environment in which no duty to rescue, either civil or criminal, generally exists, an individual who is present when another is in peril and chooses to do nothing may be subject to moral condemnation, but they face no exposure to legal liability. As a result, their willingness to cooperate with police who may be investigating the harm suffered by the victim is not affected by the current status of the legal rule regarding rescues.

All this would change with the adoption of a formal legal duty to rescue. Under such a rule, all individuals who fail to assist at the scene of an accident would face the possibility of liability for their failure to render aid. That is, of course, the intended operation of a duty-to-rescue doctrine. For those who believe that they may have breached this legal duty, such a regime would create a significant disincentive to cooperate with investigations of the incident and with any subsequent prosecutions. The disincentive would be felt both by those who failed to act altogether as well as by those who are concerned that they may not have done enough to satisfy the legal requirement. This deterrent would be generated by the adoption of either a tort law or a criminal law duty to rescue. However, with a criminal law duty to rescue, police and prosecutors would have the option of granting an important witness immunity for the failure to aid sufficiently in exchange for their cooperation with the investigation. No such option would be available with a tort law duty to rescue.

A formal duty to affirmatively aid would also discourage those who initially fail to help another in peril from reconsidering their decision and subsequently acting. Suppose, for example, that a driver on a road late at night in a relatively rural area comes across two badly damaged cars on the shoulder of the road that appear to have just collided. Both cars are badly damaged. A figure is slumped behind the steering wheel of one car. Another person is standing on the shoulder of the road waving for help. Startled by the scene and a little frightened, the driver drives right past without stopping. After driving for another minute or two, he calms down a bit and begins to think about turning around and going back to help.

In the absence of a legal duty to rescue, the ultimate decision will depend upon each individual's own unique personal complex of considerations. If there exists a legal duty to affirmatively aid, however, the potential rescuer must also consider the significantly increased risk of liability for his initial failure to help. By returning, the rescuer becomes known and identified. No matter how grateful the person flagging the driver down might be when he returns, they may feel differently sometime later. How will the person still in their car and slumped behind the wheel react upon hearing that his rescuer initially passed them by? Even by merely picking up a mobile phone and notifying the authorities of the existence and location of the accident scene, the rescuer's identity and failure to stop initially or subsequently turn around will be known. Thus, an affirmative duty to rescue creates barriers for an individual rethinking an initial failure to aid and considering making an effort to provide delayed aid.

And so, the basic rationale supporting the maintenance of a no-duty-to-rescue rule in American tort law involves at least seven main arguments: (1) because of the already high level of uncoerced reasonable rescue efforts, the increase in the number of such attempts that will be produced by adoption of a coercive rule will be quite small; (2) because all of the increase in rescue efforts will come from reluctant rescuers, because the quality of rescue efforts by reluctant rescuers generally will be of lower quality than that of purely voluntary rescuers, and because lower quality coerced rescue attempts will sometimes replace higher quality voluntary rescue efforts, it is not at all clear that a person in peril requiring affirmative aid from another would be better served, as a purely practical matter, by a formal duty to affirmatively aid; (3) the existence of an affirmative duty to aid would discount the obvious altruism of otherwise voluntary rescue efforts; (4) it would be a significant and unwelcome extension of the intrusiveness of negligence law's duty of reasonable care; (5) it would increase the risk that harm will be suffered by those providing rescue efforts; (6) for those who fear that they may have breached an existing duty to rescue, it would create a disincentive to cooperate with the authorities or the plaintiff in subsequent investigations of the incident; and (7) it would deter providing delayed aid.

The existence of an affirmative duty to rescue within tort law would be enforced through a negligence action brought by the victim or the victim's wrongful death beneficiaries against those persons who failed to provide the victim with at least reasonable rescue efforts. In a number of different ways, this would represent a particularly poor context for the operation of the normal second-guessing mechanism of negligence.

One difficulty would involve the formulation, even implicitly, of a consensus regarding the circumstances that should trigger the legal obligation to affirmatively aid. In other words, just what kind of peril faced by another is sufficient to compel one to take affirmative action on their behalf?

There will, of course, be easy cases, such as the person drowning or being attacked on a public street. But there will be an endless series of difficult cases: an adult loudly scolding a young child in public, perhaps using profanity and harsh insults, perhaps also vigorously shaking the child; teenage siblings locked in a physical wrestling match that appears to be intensifying and growing more hostile, either in public or in their own backyard; a nearby passenger on the train who is having her wallet quietly lifted from her bag by the person sitting next to her; a colleague who is the victim of vicious and false rumors at the workplace.

Unlike the typical negligence claim, in which the affirmative action of the defendant invokes the legal obligation to engage in that action reasonably, a breach of a duty to affirmatively aid will require the decision-makers, be it judge or jury, to decide in a wide range of uncertain circumstances whether any legal obligation existed for the defendant to have acted at all. Few clear social conventions exist to guide the formal decision-makers in this task or to inform the public at large about their likely judgments. An enormously wide range of responses to essentially similar situations could be expected both within and across jurisdictions, raising serious due process concerns. Risk-averse individuals might be expected to react to this inevitable uncertainty by affirmatively acting in an ever greater number of questionable circumstances.

Assume a relatively easy and rather common set of facts to which most of society would attach a formal duty to rescue: the defendant is driving on a public road and comes across two cars located on the shoulder, obviously having recently collided with one another. There are a few people located in and around the cars but no other vehicles in sight. Apparently, the defendant is the first person not directly involved in the collision to arrive at the scene.

What would be required of the defendant in such a situation to fulfill a legal duty to reasonably rescue and to avoid liability for a breach of that duty in a subsequent negligence action? Is making a call to official emergency services and notifying them of the existence and location of the accident scene enough? Is it sufficient to wait and make that call at the next pay phone (increasingly unavailable these days) if the defendant does not have a mobile phone in the car? Must the defendant vigorously search for the nearest available pay phone? Should he exceed posted speed limits in doing so?

Before making a call to the authorities, what kind of precautions should the defendant take to ensure that he is correct about the location of the cars and the number and condition of the people on the scene? Should the defendant at least stop or pause briefly at the scene to determine the extent of any critical injuries and the general condition of the victims before determining that a phone call alone is a sufficient reasonable response?

The answers to these questions, all absolutely relevant to the determination of the defendant's actual breach of a duty to reasonably rescue, could be expected to vary significantly depending on slight changes in the factual circumstances. How remote was the location of the accident scene? How heavy or light was the traffic on the road at the time? Did this occur in the middle of the day or late at night? What were the weather conditions? How many people did the defendant see at the scene and in what condition? Were there children, either with or without adults? How old was the defendant and was he alone or with others in his car? Has the defendant ever had any experience or training in rendering emergency aid?

The behavior required of the defendant to satisfy the legal duty and to avoid subsequent liability will vary significantly based on the specific answers to these questions and many others. In making the determination of whether the defendant failed to take sufficient, reasonable affirmative action to aid the victims, the legal decision-maker will most likely not enjoy the benefit of an existing social custom or industry standard with respect to such behavior as is often available in negligence cases. This distinguishes the breach in a duty-to-rescue case from even the most complicated medical malpractice case, where the jury at least has the benefit of extensive expert testimony describing the customary professional standard of care and procedures typically used under circumstances similar to those faced by the defendant.

The determination of what a reasonable affirmative response should be in even the most straightforward factual circumstance is obviously a very complex and subtle social calculation. It does not easily yield clear and objective conclusions. It is fraught with value judgments and beliefs about the appropriate nature of relations and obligations among strangers in a complicated society. It is necessarily rooted in cultural and religious traditions and practices. It is hardly easy work for judges and juries, and the results reached by them over time and across different jurisdictions can be expected to vary significantly and frequently be inconsistent and contradictory.

Even in the small number of cases in which both the need to affirmatively aid and the nature of a reasonable affirmative response are fairly determinable, a claim for a breach of a duty to reasonably rescue is a particularly poor context in which to engage in the usual second-guessing project of negligence.

Unlike the typical negligence case in which the defendant is accused of having engaged in some behavior in an unsafe manner, like failing to adequately maintain the brakes of his car or stocking an insufficient supply of bottled oxygen in a surgical theater, the defendant in a breach-of-duty-to-rescue case is most likely confronted suddenly by the situation of the plaintiff in peril. The circumstances probably call for a very quick assessment by the defendant and an equally quick response to provide the plaintiff with effective assistance, especially if the risk threatening the plaintiff is severe.

A given individual's response when unexpectedly thrust into such a situation is probably determined, in whole or in part, by largely immutable elements of their personality: by their quickness of thought and action, their confidence in the face of pressure to physically perform, their fear of failure, their tendency to freeze when taken by surprise, their natural athleticism and physicality, etc. This is in contrast to the typical negligence action where the defendant's judgment on safety and his willingness to expend resources on adequate precautions in advance of the actual harm-producing circumstance is the focus of the second-guessing inquiry. For example, did the defendant reasonably maintain the brakes on his automobile in the months preceding the actual day that they failed and the car smashed into the rear of the plaintiff's vehicle? What procedures did the hospital have in place to ensure that the operating theaters were adequately stocked with bottled oxygen before and on the day of the surgical procedure?

The incentive that negligence law creates for the public at large to act with reasonable care toward others works best when it reviews the safety judgment exercised by the actor and can be satisfied by considered investment in greater precaution. This incentive is far less likely to be effective when it is directed, as it most often would be in failure to reasonably rescue cases, to the quality of the defendant's reaction to a sudden and highly pressurized situation that demands a rapid physical response. To the extent that a given individual's ability to perform in such circumstances is a function of largely immutable personal characteristics, the threat of legal liability for the failure to react adequately is unlikely to result in much of an increase in the actual quality of such reactions. This is particularly pernicious in a failure to adequately rescue situation where the defendant's decision to act at all, and in a way that is now being evaluated for its adequacy, may well have been influenced, if not coerced, by the very existence of a duty-to-reasonably-rescue rule.

Moreover, the glacially paced, backward-looking, highly formal context of negligence litigation is far better suited to a second-guessing of the defendant's underlying judgment regarding safety and his investment in adequate precautions. While perhaps not perfect, one can imagine a jury taking in the offered evidence and then carefully considering in the leisure and hindsight of its deliberations whether the defendant took reasonable care of his automobile brakes or took reasonable measures to ensure that a sufficient supply of bottled oxygen was present in the operating theater. Far less confidence can be invested in the thought of these same jurors trying to summon the specific empathy to place themselves in the emergency situation faced by the defendant and accurately imagine how they, or a hypothetical reasonable person, would have reacted. The whole of the defendant's encounter with the plaintiff in peril and the defendant's response thereto probably lasted no more than a few minutes. In stark contrast, the jury's review of the defendant's performance will take place years later, in the abstract, and at a very deliberate pace.

Even accepting that the general population should not have a formal duty to rescue, does it make sense to add a fourth exception to the list of established exceptions to the no-duty-to-rescue rule that would cover only individuals specially trained, experienced, or possessing a certification in rendering aid?

One argument in favor of such a doctrine is that because such persons already possess an obligation to affirmatively aid a stranger in peril arising from the ethical mandates of their profession or a requirement of licensure, the adoption of a formal duty to affirmatively aid for such persons would not come with the cost of significantly discounting the altruism of the act because it is required already. Nor would it add any additional level of intrusiveness to the formal duty of reasonable care. Another argument in favor of such a limited duty is that the risk of low-quality rescue efforts would be relatively small, whether the rescue efforts were purely voluntary or coerced. One would, therefore, not expect a meaningful difference, on the whole, in the quality of rescue efforts between voluntary and reluctant rescue efforts that were undertaken by the specially trained. Thus, it could be reasonably asserted that at least three of the arguments that support the no-duty-to-rescue rule with respect to the public at large do not apply, either at all or with nearly the same force, to those who possess special training, experience, or certification in emergency aid.

On the other side of the issue, those with special training could be divided into two groups: those who operate under an independent professional obligation to affirmatively aid and those who do not. For those who possess an obligation not arising from any duty of care in negligence law, the existence of a formal legal duty would be superfluous. Among this group, one would expect the adoption of a legal duty to rescue to generate no more than a trivial number of additional rescue efforts, if it encouraged any additional rescue efforts at all. Thus, the substantive effect of adopting such an affirmative duty would be practically nil, consigning to irrelevance, for the purpose of this analysis, the higher quality of coerced rescue efforts, the lower discount of altruism, and the smaller degree of intrusion that might exist within this group.

Among the other group, those specially trained individuals who do not bear an extralegal obligation to provide affirmative aid to a stranger, it should be conceded that the quality of coerced rescue is likely to be higher than the quality of rescue efforts coerced from reluctant rescuers at large, and probably high enough, given their special training, not to pose any significant problem for those in peril. Despite a higher quality of coerced rescue efforts, however, the number of additional rescue efforts induced by a formal duty imposed upon the specially trained would be quite small and very much smaller than among the population at large. After all, in contrast to the general population, those who possess special training can be supposed to be a self-selected group that voluntarily sought to improve their ability to be of help to others in peril and thus are much more likely to use their heightened skills to provide aid voluntarily. Specially trained and experienced individuals are also far less likely than untrained individuals to panic in the face of an emergency of this sort and are, therefore, less likely to be inhibited by fright or anxiety from helping another in peril.

Moreover, there is no reason to believe that the discounting of altruism and the greater intrusiveness of second-guessing arguments against the adoption of an affirmative duty to rescue would have any less force among this group than they would with respect to the public at large. The same is true with respect to the increased risk of harm to rescuers, the disincentive to cooperate in subsequent investigations, and the deterrence to provide delayed aid arguments.

Further, with respect to specially trained people in either subgroup, a limited affirmative duty designed to pertain only to them would come with its own rather significant costs. For example, how might one functionally define the specialized group to whom the affirmative duty to rescue would apply? How much and what kind of training or experience should be required? How recent should the training or experience be? How close to the focus of the defendant's training should the aid required by the person in peril be in order to invoke the affirmative duty? None of these questions have obvious answers, and the working out of the contours of the rule in each jurisdiction, along with the resulting uncertainty among the specially trained, will consume resources and constitute costs.

Finally, the adoption of a formal legal duty to rescue that applies only to the specially trained will act as a deterrent for some individuals who otherwise might seek, or agree to receive, such special training. Such a deterrent compromises the larger social goal of creating conditions that maximize the possibility of those in peril receiving quality aid and being successfully rescued.

All things considered, the lack of an affirmative duty to rescue applicable only to the specially trained seems, while perhaps not inevitable, at least fully understandable. Yet, simply abandoning the analysis at this point would leave it wanting. Without something more, tort law would simply operate with a no-duty-to-rescue rule that would apply to the regular individual and to the specially trained individual in the same manner. This is arguably unsatisfactory for at least two reasons.

The first is that, at least from the perspective of the person in peril, the affirmative aid of a specially trained individual will probably be far more valuable than the rescue efforts of an untrained and inexperienced person. A tort law regime that treats both of them alike is, therefore, less desirable than one that more vigorously encourages affirmative aid from the specially trained. This is especially true when one continues to consider the quasi-exclusive nature of many rescue situations. Once again, it can be argued that the creation of an incentive for reluctant rescuers to affirmatively aid is less attractive than it may seem due to lower quality reluctant rescue efforts potentially replacing higher quality altruistic rescue efforts. A tort law rule that treats equally the specially trained and the untrained individual can be faulted for failing to minimize these situations in which a lower quality rescue effort by an untrained individual will effectively replace a higher quality rescue effort by a specially trained person. A superior liability regime is one that would generate a stronger incentive for the specially trained to act than it would for an untrained individual.

Second, there is some reason to believe that those individuals who are specially trained in disciplines most likely to be relevant to rescue situations, like physicians, might actually be less willing than untrained individuals to engage in voluntary rescue efforts in the absence of a coercive legal rule. The argument here rests upon the notorious distrust and suspicion that communities of recurring defendants in tort cases, like physicians, have developed regarding the fairness and accuracy of the judgment of courts, and especially juries, in negligence cases. The literature of such professions is replete with complaints about the unfair operation of negligence law, stories of outrageous outcomes in specific cases, and proposals for reform. Specially trained individuals who are regularly exposed to this literature, and who might share many of these same sentiments, may be reluctant to affirmatively aid another when such a situation arises. They may well fear that should things go badly for the victim, the reasonableness of their behavior in the circumstances will not be fairly or accurately judged in any subsequent negligence action.

To the extent that this is true, the existence of such a dynamic would indeed be ironic. Negligence law's efforts to encourage specially trained individuals to affirmatively aid when reasonable and necessary would be compromised, in part, by the mistrust of these very individuals in the fair operation of negligence law itself. In such circumstances, increasing pressure on specially trained individuals by creating a coercive rule that applies only to them is likely to be counterproductive. If they are already more reluctant than they might otherwise be to render aid voluntarily for fear of unfair treatment in a subsequent negligence action, expansion of negligence law's jurisdiction in these situations is hardly likely to help. After all, the regulated individual's distrust of that very system of negligence may be the source of their reluctance to act.

A hypothetical illustration can demonstrate this point. Imagine a commercial airliner on a flight from Hawaii to California located midway across the Pacific Ocean flying at 30,000 feet. A passenger on board the plane begins to experience symptoms of a severe heart attack. His condition is apparently worsening. The stewards rush back to the passenger's seat on the plane and carry him up the center aisle to the front galley where they lay him down. They activate the intercom on the plane, explain the situation, and ask if anyone among the other passengers on board is a physician or possesses any specialized medical training and if they would be willing to come up to the front of the plane and provide emergency aid to the distressed individual. No one responds. Another request, and again no response. The passenger dies before the plane can touch down in California.

Suppose further that some subsequent investigation locates the passenger manifest for the flight and determines that one or more persons on board were in fact fully licensed physicians. A bizarre and unrealistic scenario? As noted at the beginning of this chapter, in May 2006 a climber attempting to descend from the top of Mt. Everest fell into distress not far from the summit and was ignored and abandoned by approximately forty other climbers who walked right past him, most of them twice. While conditions near the summit of Mt. Everest may be uniquely hostile, it is certainly fair to presume that climbers of the caliber and experience necessary to place themselves within 1,000 feet of the world's highest peak are thoroughly trained in at least the rudiments of providing aid to other climbers in distress. And yet, among this exceptionally elite group, not a single one reportedly did anything to help.

Consider then the physicians on board the airplane who chose not to respond to the stewards' calls for help. Should they simply be regarded as moral monsters? What could they possibly say by way of justification for their actions?

Perhaps they could say something like the following: "Yes, I am an experienced and licensed physician; yes, I was on board that plane and heard the request for assistance; and yes, I chose not to respond. Because I am a physician I could see when the passenger was carried up to the front of the plane by my seat that he was in a grave and near terminal condition.

'I knew from my watch that we were nowhere near land and that it was unlikely that this man would survive until touchdown."I suppose I could have gone to the front galley and tried to make him comfortable and perhaps provide some solace, but with only the equipment and medications available on board, I knew that his chances for survival were small and that the odds of saving his life were very slim.'

'What do you think was most likely to happen had I provided him aid and he died before landing as he was almost certain to do? I would find myself, some months down the road, a defendant in a negligence action in which the lawyers for the estate would try to convince a naive and technically ignorant jury that if only I had thought to perform some improbable procedure with the materials at hand, I could have saved the man's life.' And in such circumstances my hard-earned professional reputation, my financial resources, and my liability insurance coverage would all be ultimately exposed to the judgment of those untrained and inexperienced jurors.

'No, I thought to myself. On balance, the meager benefit that I might provide to that unfortunate man is outweighed by the enormous risk to which I would expose myself.'"

To the extent that this imagined justification for inaction is realistic, the existence and operation of negligence law itself can be considered to be operating as a deterrent to the very behavior by the very individuals that we, on behalf of those who are facing such a peril, would most want to encourage. This effect is reinforced by the fact that in most potential rescue situations, unlike the case of the airplane, it is extremely difficult for a potential plaintiff to identify those individuals, specially trained or not, who quietly and anonymously choose not to render any aid. Thus, in most cases, a specially trained individual who decides not to affirmatively aid and thus discretely moves along, or away, faces little risk of identification and subsequent suit.

At this point, common law tort doctrine, exclusively dependent upon the negative reinforcement regime of threatened liability, has exhausted its options. While it would be desirable legally to encourage specially trained individuals to engage in reasonable rescue efforts, the prospects of doing so through the creation of a formal legal duty within negligence law are thin. In fact, as previously discussed, it is indeed possible that the existence of a negligence-based duty of care invoked after the specially trained individual acts deters such rescue efforts.

In the face of this circumstance, tort law has taken an interesting twist. Lacking a negative reinforcement strategy that is likely to succeed, it has instead sought to offer a carrot, though one of a peculiarly tort-like nature. Rather than offering a tangible reward to those who engage in reasonable rescue efforts, as one might expect from a positive reinforcement scheme, tort law promises not to hit them with potential liability quite as hard as it otherwise might. In effect, tort law offers to voluntary rescuers the prospect of having their rescue efforts judged in any subsequent negligence action by a lowered standard of care or even, perhaps, not to have their rescue efforts second-guessed at all.

These carrots are offered to potential rescuers by laws that are commonly referred to as Good Samaritan statutes. As a general matter, Good Samaritan statutes modify the usual duty of care standard ordinarily applied in a negligence action that is based upon a plaintiff's assertion that the careless rescue efforts of the defendant harmed him. These statutes can lower the usual standard in various ways, such as by requiring the court to apply an unmodified reasonable person duty of care to the actions of a specially trained individual or requiring the use of a gross or reckless negligence standard. They can also go even further by eliminating the possibility of a subsequent negligence action altogether.

As to the beneficiaries, Good Samaritan statutes can make these incentives available to all persons who engage in reasonable rescue efforts, or they can instead offer them only to those possessing special training or experience. Moreover, more sophisticated Good Samaritan arrangements can mix and match these options so that persons possessing different levels of training and experience are offered correspondingly different levels of inducement.

Good Samaritan statutes, in general, encourage voluntary rescue efforts by decreasing legal exposure and thus lowering the risk of a voluntary rescue effort. This is especially true in the case of specially trained individuals. By this device, negligence law, in a sense, moves or is pushed out of the way, and we rely upon the strong moral value of voluntarily helping another in peril to take over and produce sufficient reasonable rescue efforts.

Now that Good Samaritan statutes have become common in this country, the adoption of a formal affirmative duty to rescue becomes even more problematic. The practical consequence of a formal duty to rescue combined with a Good Samaritan statute that applies to all rescuers would be to coerce some additional rescues and to then judge the quality of the reluctant rescue effort on a lower than normal standard of care, or to not formally second-guess the quality of the reluctant rescue effort at all. However, an important argument against an affirmative duty to rescue is a concern for lower quality reluctant rescue efforts replacing higher quality voluntary rescue efforts, the consequences of which will only intensify if the reluctant rescuer either faces no liability or his effort is held to a lowered standard by the operation of a Good Samaritan statute.

The foregoing analysis offers a comprehensive justification for the traditional absence in American tort law of a duty to reasonably rescue. The framework for the analysis is not abstractly philosophical, nor is it historical. It does not rely upon theoretical distinctions between commissions and omissions or misfeasance and nonfeasance, nor does it suggest that the rule as it stands is the only logical extension of Locke's or Hume's theory of the individual and the state. It is not at all formalist in nature. It is, instead, fundamentally instrumentalist in nature.

9

Conceptual Instrumentalist Analysis

Understanding the Purpose and Function of Causation in Tort Law

The preceding chapter, Chapter 8, offers a detailed example of one kind of instrumentalist analysis in law – what could be called empirical instrumentalist analysis. Empirical instrumentalist analysis considers the appropriate resolution of a common law issue by trying to identify and weigh all of the meaningful, practical consequences that will be the result of adopting one or another of the plausible versions of legal doctrine available with respect to the issue under inquiry. Such an approach concludes by suggesting that the version of common law that should be adopted is the one that promises the best mix of net benefits over costs.

The starting point for empirical instrumentalist analysis is not an abstract legal principle or maxim, as it is with a formalist approach, but is instead the social purpose or purposes sought to be achieved by the relevant legal doctrine. The primary focus of empirical instrumentalist analysis is not a search for a specific legal doctrine or doctrines that can be said to be deductively required by, or at least logically consistent with, a preexisting complex of accepted first principles, as it is with formalism, but is instead a search for the specific legal doctrine that most effectively advances the social policies that animate the legal issue in question. Empirical instrumentalist analysis considers the likely actual, real-world consequences associated with each plausible version of the legal doctrine under examination.

There is another kind of instrumentalist legal analysis as well. This kind of analysis, much like empirical legal analysis, and unlike formalist analysis, also takes as its starting point the social purpose or purposes sought to be achieved by the legal doctrine under consideration. This analytical approach, however, is then less concerned with practical consequences than it is with the degree to which the doctrinal design in a given area of law may or may not be optimized to achieve the desired social results. This kind of instrumentalist approach can be called conceptual instrumentalist analysis.

Conceptual instrumentalist analysis, like empirical instrumentalist analysis and unlike formalist analysis, views legal doctrine essentially as a tool, or instrument, by which desired social outcomes are sought to be achieved or advanced, and undesirable social outcomes are sought to be minimized or avoided. Its design and content are not fixed and determined by abstract first principles, as it is with formalism. Instead, the structure and specific content of legal doctrine is viewed as malleable and alterable and it should be designed, adopted, and applied by the courts in a fashion calculated to maximally advance the underlying social policies. The prevailing legal doctrine should also be altered by the courts as needed to continue to maximize the social policy benefits that it is intended to achieve.

Empirical instrumentalist analysis focuses on the practical advancement of the underlying social policy. Conceptual instrumentalist analysis focuses on the degree to which the ideas and concepts that constitute the abstract legal doctrine itself operate, both alone and in conjunction with associated legal doctrines, to apply legal tests and requirements in a manner that best achieves the underlying social purpose of the particular doctrine. Empirical instrumentalist analysis asks what kind of legal resolution of a particular issue is most likely to best advance the social interest at stake. Conceptual instrumentalist analysis asks what particular kind of doctrinal design and content will best reflect and implement within the administrative apparatus of the law the general resolution identified as instrumentally optimal.

The presence, and indeed the need, for conceptual instrumentalist analysis demonstrates that it is a misunderstanding to think of formalism as being primarily abstract and conceptual in nature while thinking of instrumentalism as being primarily empirical in nature. As a tool, legal doctrine is composed of ideas, requirements, distinctions, and tests that are themselves concepts and ideas. Viewing legal doctrine primarily as an instrument that should achieve certain desired practical results means having to be able to understand and analyze the design and operation of that doctrine as a conceptual construct and instrument. This is the nature of conceptual instrumentalist analysis.

What follows is an example of conceptual instrumentalist analysis. It seeks to explicate the way in which current tort law doctrine in the area of causation is designed and constructed to maximize the underlying social purposes for including a causation requirement in tort law generally, and especially within the negligence tort.

Causation is a concept of enormous importance in the law. In no area of the law is causation as foundational and omnipresent as in tort law, and in no sphere within tort law is it more prevalent than in its dominant cause of action, negligence. Unsurprisingly, then, the causation requirement in tort law and in negligence has received a great deal of attention and analysis by both courts and commentators. Nevertheless, there remains a striking lack of consensus regarding the causation requirement, ranging from disagreement about the basic rationale for its existence as a part of the negligence claim to the more specific details of its doctrinal organization and articulation.

What follows is an attempt to develop a functional and accessible understanding of the causation requirement in tort law from an instrumentalist perspective; specifically, to explicate its purpose, function, and operation as a requirement of the dominant cause of action in modern tort law – negligence. No claim is made that the account offered herein is the only way of usefully understanding the causation requirement, or that it encompasses and explains every possible valuable insight regarding causation, or even causation in tort law. Instead, what follows is an elucidation of the causation requirement in negligence that seeks to provide courts with a practical understanding of the requirement that can be productively applied to the adjudication of actual negligence actions in the United States and also offers to students and scholars of the subject a theoretical foundation underlying the acknowledged doctrine and leading cases in the area.

In the United States, a prima facie case for the tort of negligence consists of duty, breach, causation, and harm. A claimant seeking to establish negligence liability against another must, at a minimum, prove that: (1) the defendant under an actual prior set of circumstances owed to the plaintiff a legal duty to act with a minimum level of care toward the plaintiff and his or her property; (2) the defendant acted less carefully than the applicable legal duty required; (3) the defendant's behavior that fell below the applicable legal standard was the cause of harm; and (4) actual harm was experienced by the plaintiff.

The third of these four required elements – causation – is conventionally understood to consist of two parts, each of which the plaintiff must independently establish. One part is known as actual cause, actual causation, or cause-in-fact. It requires the plaintiff to prove that the chain of actual, physical causation extended from the defendant's breaching behavior to the harm suffered by the plaintiff and for which the plaintiff is seeking compensation from the defendant by means of the negligence claim. In other words, the plaintiff establishes actual causation by showing that the defendant physically caused the harm suffered by the plaintiff.

This is typically accomplished by the plaintiff satisfying what is known as the "but-for" test of actual causation. This test is satisfied when the plaintiff can prove that but-for the defendant's breaching behavior (the behavior of the defendant used by the plaintiff to establish the second element of the prima facie case for negligence – the breach element) the plaintiff would not have experienced the harm for which the plaintiff is seeking compensation from the defendant. Put slightly differently, the but-for test for actual causation is satisfied in circumstances in which the hypothetical elimination of the defendant's breaching behavior would result in the absence of harm experienced by the plaintiff. Only when the breaching behavior of the defendant was physically necessary in order for harm to be experienced by the plaintiff is the actual cause prong of the causation requirement satisfied.

In addition to actual cause, a plaintiff bringing a negligence claim must also establish what is conventionally known as proximate cause. Proximate cause in this context is established by showing that a reasonable person in the position of the defendant, in similar circumstances, would have foreseen that his or her breaching behavior would result in the kind of harm experienced by the plaintiff. In other words, proximate cause is satisfied when the plaintiff shows that under the specific circumstances of the case, the harm suffered by the plaintiff was reasonably foreseeable given the unreasonably careless actions of the defendant.

At a black letter doctrinal level, the existence of a causation element in the prima facie case of negligence requires the plaintiff to establish that the unreasonably careless behavior of the defendant both actually (physically) caused the harm for which the plaintiff seeks compensation in the negligence action and that such harm was also a reasonably foreseeable consequence of that unreasonably careless behavior under the specific circumstances of the case.

While other social purposes are cited as being served by tort law, there are two generally undisputed, dominant social purposes, or policies, advanced by a properly functioning law of torts, including the negligence tort: (1) to provide an additional source of monetary compensation to injured individuals for recovery and rehabilitation (a compensation goal or policy) and (2) to discourage some harm-producing activities by imposing an involuntary and legally enforced obligation on some harm producers to personally provide that compensation to successful plaintiffs (a deterrence goal or policy). Large swaths of black letter tort doctrine have been rationalized by courts and commentators on the basis that tort law furthers a social policy of appropriate compensation, a social policy of appropriate deterrence, or both.

So pervasive is the understanding that tort law is dominantly about the business of advancing appropriate compensation and appropriate deterrence that it is easy to presume that every standard element of well-established tort law claims, such as negligence, have been crafted over time, and are fundamentally rationalized, on this basis. Part of what makes causation in tort law such a persistently difficult and vexing requirement – to understand, rationalize, and implement – is that it does not conform to this otherwise pervasive attribute of the law of torts. The presence of a causation requirement in negligence cannot be satisfactorily understood or adequately explained by reference to the way in which it advances either a compensation objective or a deterrence objective. In fact, it can be persuasively argued that the presence of a causation requirement in the prima facie case for negligence actually operates to retard the potential for the claim to more robustly advance both compensation and deterrence.

Imagine, for example, a social system based on negligence that does not include any causation requirement. Such a system might offer injured individuals monetary payments calculated to compensate them for certain recognized injuries so long as these claimants could produce adequate proof of their own lack, or relative lack, of culpability in the infliction of the harm for which they are seeking compensation, and also adequate proof of the unreasonably careless behavior of another person in the relevant jurisdiction during a specified period. In such a system, the prima facie application for the receipt of compensation might be: (1) proof of the suffering by the applicant/plaintiff of harm of the right sort (not loss of economic advantage only, not modest and purely emotional distress, not familial or spiritual injury, etc. – just like existing tort law); (2) proof that the applicant/plaintiff was not more than a specified percentage personally responsible for the infliction of that injury (similar to contributory negligence and partial comparative negligence systems), or imposition of a reduction in the compensation awarded based on the applicant's own culpability in the infliction of the harm (similar to pure comparative negligence); and (3) proof that a specified individual (the defendant) acted in an unreasonably careless manner with respect to the kind of harms recognized by the system during some specified period.

Such a system could assess a fine and thus impose legal liability against those defendants who were shown by plaintiffs to have acted unreasonably carelessly; much as modern criminal law systems routinely assess monetary fines against defendants shown to have acted in a proscribed manner irrespective of whether the proscribed behavior in fact resulted in actual harm. These fines would serve as the basic source of funding for the compensatory payments made by the system to successful applicants.

For instance, if a given jurisdiction decided to segregate all, or part, of the money that it collected during a given period as a result of its passive enforcement of traffic laws (speed and red-light cameras, for example) and made that money available as compensation exclusively to those injured on the roads of that same jurisdiction during that same period, such a system would operate in a similar fashion to the one suggested, substituting the state in place of the injured individual as the party establishing the liability of defendants. Such a hypothetical system would further the compensation goal of tort law by offering appropriate resources to injured individuals and would further the deterrence goal by imposing liability on those who have been shown to have acted with unreasonable carelessness, all without any recourse to a requirement that there be any causative link between the specific plaintiff's harm and the unreasonably careless behavior of the defendant.

In fact, such a system would very likely be a more powerful provider of compensation and a more robust generator of deterrence than the traditional negligence tort. Why?

Because this system would offer compensation to plaintiffs who were injured by ways and means that did not involve any unreasonably careless behavior by another and also to plaintiffs who were injured by unreasonably careless persons who are not – as a practical matter – effectively responsive to negligence liability, such as defendants without assets or insurance. These are two classes of innocently injured individuals who are currently excluded from the compensatory benefits of negligence, and who may represent a large number, both absolutely and relatively, of all injured persons in a jurisdiction.

Such a system would generate a far more robust deterrence to engage in unreasonably careless behavior than does negligence because the deterrent effect of such a system would potentially extend to all persons within its jurisdiction who engage in unreasonably careless behavior, not just those persons whose unreasonably careless behavior actually resulted in tangible harm to another. Similar to those injured in the absence of someone else's unreasonable carelessness, those who engage in unreasonably careless behavior in a specific circumstance and do not cause harm to another as a result may represent a large number, both absolutely and relatively, of all persons in a jurisdiction who engage in unreasonably careless behavior.

Note that both the compensatory and the deterrence features of this imagined system are not novel. Many compensation systems that respond to injured or otherwise ailing individuals, such as medical care insurance and workers' compensation, offer compensatory benefits to such individuals without regard to the specific mechanism or cause of the harm. Criminal law has long included the so-called inchoate crimes: behavior that does not result in actual injury to another but that, nevertheless, triggers criminal liability. In fact, the modern development of passive traffic enforcement mechanisms and the many millions of dollars in criminal fines that they generate represent an explosive growth in the societal deterrence of unreasonably careless behavior that does not result in any actual injury.

A social system could feasibly be designed to achieve the attractive benefits of compensation and deterrence provided by negligence without including any requirement that the unreasonably careless behavior of the defendant be shown to have, in any way, been the cause of the plaintiff's harm. Such a system would far more powerfully generate and achieve both compensation and deterrence than does our current negligence tort system. This means that not only can the presence of a causation requirement in negligence not be properly understood and rationalized by means of its contribution to compensation and deterrence, but that the presence of a causation requirement in negligence should also be understood to be at the expense of greater compensation and deterrence. In other words, the causation requirement comes at a cost; namely, the cost of negligence pursuing its two dominant social purposes – compensation and deterrence – less effectively.

If the presence of a causation requirement in negligence cannot be accurately understood by recourse to its contribution to either compensation or deterrence, and if, in fact, the existence of a causation requirement meaningfully limits the compensation and deterrence that is achieved by the negligence tort, then what might satisfactorily explain its existence? Putting aside the more descriptive possibilities of legal custom, specific common law history, and path dependence, what might account, normatively, for the continued presence of a causation requirement in negligence and, to some extent, its existence more generally in the law of tort? What value or values are advanced by a causation requirement that justifies the burden it imposes on the dominant goals of compensation and deterrence?

One answer to these questions is that the presence of a causation requirement in negligence, and to a large extent more generally in tort law, is necessary in order to ensure the existence of a certain, specific kind of fault by the defendant in every instance in which negligence liability is imposed. The causation requirement functions to ensure that the liability generated by the negligence claim is confined to those defendants who are what I will call "genuinely socially responsible" for the plaintiff's harm. Thus, the inclusion of a causation requirement will result in the negligence tort imposing legal liability for the forced compensation of a victim only on those defendants who are found to be at fault for the plaintiff's harm in all of three distinct ways: (1) the defendant is at fault for having engaged in unreasonably careless behavior; (2) the defendant is at fault for having actually caused the plaintiff's harm as a result of that unreasonably careless behavior; and (3) the defendant is at fault for being genuinely socially responsible – for being morally blameworthy – for the harm suffered by the plaintiff. These three kinds of fault are not the same, and the social consequences of conditioning negligence liability on some without the others are potentially profound.

Consider a typical, casual playground pick-up game of basketball. Anyone having much experience with this activity knows the standard of play with regard to the calling of rule violations is "no harm, no foul." That is, no rule violation is to be called unless, at a minimum, the violation had a meaningful negative effect on the other team. If it did not make a significant difference, then it is to be ignored and forgotten, and play should proceed uninterrupted.

The policy underlying such a standard in this activity is fairly straightforward: the primary purpose of the activity is the pleasure of the play itself, including its competitive aspect. The participants are there to play ball – not to engage in a test of rule knowledge and compliance. If an otherwise clear and unambiguous rule violation does not seriously impair the pleasure or the competitive fairness of the ongoing game, then, while no less a violation of the rules, it is not to be enforced. No harm, no foul.

Within such a regulatory framework, there can be said to be two kinds, or levels, of faulty behavior by players. One kind of fault is the violation of an established rule. Thus, a player on offense who stands in the lane for more than three seconds consecutively is at fault for violating a rule of the game. This behavior is, within the context of the game, more blameworthy, and thus the violator is more at fault, than a player who fully conforms to the rules. This kind of fault can be called "behavioral fault." It is, without more, a violation but no harm.

This kind of fault is importantly different, however, especially in the context of a pick-up basketball game, from the kind of fault that attaches to a player who stands in the lane close to the basket for more than three seconds consecutively and then receives a pass, turns, and makes a short shot for a score. This kind of second-level fault can be called "consequential fault." It is a violation resulting in competitive harm, and it, therefore, represents a fair opportunity for calling a rule violation during the pick-up basketball game under the no harm, no foul principle.

Without a causation requirement, the negligence tort would still require the behavioral fault of liable defendants. It does this through the breach element of the prima facie case. One of the purposes of the causation requirement in negligence is the addition of a consequential fault requirement to a behavioral fault requirement. In this way, negligence embraces the same no harm, no foul principle as the pick-up basketball game.

In contrast to the no harm, no foul commitment of tort law, the criminal law will impose formal liability on persons who possess only behavioral fault and not consequential fault. Inchoate crimes such as the various versions of conspiracy, attempt, and solicitation threaten potentially severe criminal sanctions in response to behavior that is deemed antisocial but that has not, in fact, resulted in any actual harm.

Why might tort law adopt such a strikingly different posture than does criminal law with respect to the matter of imposing formal liability in response to only behavioral fault? Why does tort law adhere so closely to a no harm, no foul principle of liability when criminal law so clearly, and increasingly, does not?

One approach to these questions is to consider in more detail a negligence-based compensation system lacking a causation requirement. Persons who have experienced harm not due to their own fault under such a regime would create a significant demand for evidence of unreasonably careless conduct by another of the sort that would qualify them for compensatory benefits. It would likely not take long before a cottage industry developed that would satisfy this demand.[1] In this way, an extensive network of private surveillance and evidence collection would begin to permeate the affected community.[2] Private citizens, either directly or through organized third parties, would have a strong incentive to aggressively monitor the observable behavior of their fellow citizens for admissible evidence of unreasonably careless behavior.

Is such a scenario entirely speculative and imagined? Hardly.[3]

Is it only imaginable in countries outside of the United States? Again, hardly.[4]

1 Rebecca B. Fisher, *The History of American Bounty Hunting as a Study in Stunted Legal Growth*, 33 New York University Review of Law & Social Change 199, 200–04 (2009).

2 Emily Michael Stout, *Bounty Hunters as Evidence Gatherers: Should They Be Considered State Actors under the Fourth Amendment When Working with the Police?*, 65 University of Cincinnati Law Review 665, 666 (1997).

3 Choe Sang-Hun, *Help Wanted: Busybodies with Cameras*, New York Times (Sept. 28, 2011), https://www.nytimes.com/2011/09/29/world/asia/in-south-korea-where-digital-tattling-is-a-growth-industry.html. In South Korea, the government in recent years has established various programs that offer private citizens financial bounties for providing to the government evidence of the commission of mainly minor crimes by their fellow citizens, "some as minor as a motorist tossing a cigarette butt out the window." *Id.* As a result, "snitching for pay has become especially popular" and resulted in large numbers of South Koreans who, encouraged by news reports of individuals who earn tens of thousands of dollars a year reporting crimes, "roam cities secretly videotaping fellow citizens breaking the law, deliver the evidence to government officials and collect the rewards." *Id.* Reportedly, "the phenomenon is large enough that it has spawned a new industry: schools set up to train aspiring paparazzi [as these bounty hunters are typically called]." *Id.*

4 See Michael Wilson, *$87.50 for 3 Minutes: Inside the Hot Market for Videos of Idling*, New York Times (Mar. 19, 2022), https://www.nytimes.com/2022/03/19/nyregion/clean-air-idle-car.html (reporting on New York City's "Citizens Air Complaint Program, a public health

Under the negligence-based compensation system lacking a causation requirement, this citizen-on-citizen monitoring and surveillance activity would be motivated by the prospect of the receipt of compensatory benefits – a sometimes-substantial financial incentive. In addition, each instance of successful evidence collection and submission would result in the imposition of legal liability, sometimes substantial, on the actor so ensnared.

Given these likely consequences, it could be argued that tort law has embraced, and continues to embrace, a no harm, no foul principle of liability out of concern that normal life in the absence of such a limitation on civil liability would become intolerable. Much like the pick-up basketball game, the primary goal is to live (to play), not to enforce the rules and norms of communal life (the game). Monitoring and enforcement of behavioral rules and standards should serve the purposes of enhancing the quality of life in the relevant community; the quality of life should not suffer in service to more aggressive and thorough monitoring and enforcement of those rules and standards.

If this analysis is sound, then why would criminal law not join tort law in embracing and internalizing a no harm, no foul principle of liability? One might argue that the recent development of relatively inexpensive systems of enforcement, such as passive speed and red-light cameras, have introduced a powerful revenue motive for governments to pursue criminal liability in response to citizen behavior that demonstrates behavioral fault but not consequential fault. However, the existence of inchoate crimes, such as conspiracy, attempt, and solicitation, long predate the modern era of highly profitable enforcement of undesirable behavior that, in fact, causes no concrete harm.

One possible answer to the existence of these contrasting approaches lies in the difference between the plaintiffs – the moving parties seeking liability – in the two systems. In tort law, the plaintiff is overwhelmingly a private citizen who is pursuing a tort claim that will potentially generate a personal monetary benefit for that individual. When considering the prospect of seeking tort liability, such an injured individual is not required, and is generally not expected, to take into account larger societal interests and values, such as whether greater overall deterrence for behavior like the defendant's is at the present time societally beneficial, or whether the likely amount of eventual liability imposed on the defendant is reasonably and fairly proportionate to the larger societal culpability of that behavior. A given plaintiff's analysis of whether to bring a tort claim, what specific tort claim to bring, and how

campaign that invites – and pays – people to report trucks that are parked and idling for more than three minutes, one minute if outside a school. Those who report collect 25 percent of any fine against a truck by submitting a video just over three minutes in length that shows the engine is running and the name of the company on the door. The program has vastly increased the number of complaints of idling trucks sent to the city, from just a handful before its creation in 2018 to more than 12,000 last year.").

aggressively to pursue the claim will almost always be economic and individual in nature.

In contrast, the criminal law system has a structural element of public prosecutorial discretion. Overwhelmingly, actual criminal prosecution of behaviorally blameworthy conduct does not commence, or continue, until a public official has reviewed the matter and made an affirmative decision that criminal prosecution is in the best interests of the community. Moreover, enforcement activity in the realm of criminal law typically involves significant triage, whereby limited enforcement resources are allocated on the basis of perceived societal interests.

It is the near omnipresence in the criminal law system of processes by which both enforcement and prosecution resources and activities are deployed on the basis of larger societal interests that makes tolerable the presence of criminal law liability in response to behavior that is antisocial but does not, in fact, cause harm. Tort law, lacking any such mechanism or filter, has developed its in a way that doctrinally excludes civil liability for such behavior.

How does the analysis thus far help in determining the social purpose underlying the causation requirement in negligence?

It allows one to say with some meaning that the causation requirement in negligence exists to ensure that all defendants who are held liable for negligence possessed not just behavioral fault under the circumstances, but also possessed more specific consequential fault for the harm suffered by the plaintiff. In order to be liable for negligence when negligence requires causation, the defendant must at least have acted in a faulty manner (satisfying the breach element), and that breaching behavior must have resulted in actual harm to the plaintiff (satisfying the actual cause requirement). The defendant must have been, in a sense, at least doubly at fault, not just at first-level behavioral fault. In other words, the causation requirement includes in the basic design of the negligence tort a no harm, no foul principle, much like the pick-up basketball game.

Causation in negligence does more, however. The causation requirement not only limits legal liability to those defendants who both fouled and harmed but also limits liability to only those defendants who are thought to be genuinely socially responsible – morally and socially to blame – for the plaintiff being burdened with the harm for which the plaintiff seeks forced compensation by way of the negligence tort.

Requiring genuine social responsibility is not necessary for the feasible operation of a negligence-based compensation system, no more than is requiring causation at all. It is a normative choice, a value judgment. It is the consequence of a decision not to impose the power of the state to force an involuntary transfer of assets from one individual to another through the civil action of negligence unless the target of that power, the defendant, is found to have been genuinely socially responsible for the recipient's, the plaintiff's, harm. It is the consequence of a larger social judgment to apply a notion of just deserts to the formal imposition of negligence liability.

Whether or not such a requirement ever was warranted, and whether it still is, can be the subject of legitimate and rich debate. The claim here is not that negligence must include such a requirement or that society and the individuals within it are better off when negligence does include such a requirement. Instead, the claim is that the existence of the causation requirement that, in fact, exists in negligence (and to some extent more generally in tort law) is best explained and understood as serving the purpose of requiring that all liable defendants be genuinely socially responsible for the plaintiff's harm. In other words, causation, as that doctrine is currently configured, exists in negligence in order to restrict liability generated by that tort to only those defendants who are properly thought to be blamed for the plaintiff's injury, who are genuinely and fully responsible for it.

One test for the likely validity of this claim is the degree to which it explains and gives useful meaning to long-standing, and still current, causation doctrine. To what extent does the law of causation in negligence conform to the purposes of advancing this underlying social value? To the extent that the claim appears valid, it then offers a useful and powerful way to understand, to rationalize, and to implement causation doctrine moving forward.

From the perspective of pursuing the goal of restricting negligence liability to only those genuinely socially at fault for the plaintiff's harm – to those who are appropriately morally blameworthy – the design of causation doctrine can be seen as akin to an attempt to hit and to completely cover a specified target, such as the old boardwalk arcade booths at which a patron tries to completely shoot out a star target with pellets from a BB gun. In this case, the ammunition is the legal liability generated by the negligence tort and the target is those defendants, and only those defendants, who are genuinely socially responsible for the plaintiff's harm. Black letter causation doctrine can be said to be better designed to the extent that the pattern of liability it helps to generate conforms to the intended target, and it can be said to be worse to the extent that the pattern of liability it helps to generate is either overinclusive or underinclusive of that target.

Without the causation requirement, the prima facie case of negligence requires only "behavioral fault." Behavioral fault involves the defendant having acted in a way that violates an existing behavioral norm or rule. The existence of behavioral fault by the defendant in a negligence case is ensured by the satisfaction of the breach element of the prima facie case. There can be no fault by, and no appropriate moral blaming of, the defendant for the harm experienced by the plaintiff if the defendant's behavior, no matter how much it might have been the physical cause of the plaintiff's harm, was itself not blameworthy.

So, causation doctrine operates within negligence in an environment in which one aspect of genuine social responsibility – behavioral fault – is already accounted for, and causation doctrine need not, therefore, cover that contingency.

What remains to be done? At the very least, causation doctrine needs to ensure the existence in every case of what I have called "consequential fault." As discussed previously discussed in this chapter, both behavioral fault (requiring norm-violating behavior by the defendant) and consequential fault (requiring that the defendant's norm-violating behavior be the actual cause of the plaintiff's harm) are required in order to appropriately trigger liability in a system that embraces a no harm, no foul principle.

Ensuring the existence of consequential fault is the primary work of the actual cause prong of the causation requirement. That work is primarily done by the "but-for" test of causation, requiring the plaintiff to establish that the defendant's breaching behavior was part of the chain of actual, physical causation that extended from that breaching behavior to the harm suffered by the plaintiff and for which the plaintiff is seeking compensation from the defendant by means of the negligence claim.

The but-for test of actual cause performs exceptionally well in terms of it including within negligence liability all defendants who are properly thought to be genuinely socially responsible for the plaintiff's harm. It is, in this respect, one of the great products of the common law. Using a straightforward, elegant formulation that is relatively easy for laypersons on juries to understand and employ, the but-for test effectively captures nearly all instances of negligence defendants who would be generally regarded as being socially responsible and, therefore, at fault for the plaintiff's injuries. From the perspective of avoiding mistakes of underinclusiveness, the but-for test should be credited with being excellent.

Excellent, but not perfect. There are two well-known exceptions to the but-for test as the means of determining whether or not actual cause can be established in a negligence action. Both respond to relatively rare instances of underinclusiveness.

The more common of the two exceptions is generally known as concurrent cause. It arises in cases in which there existed more than one sufficient actual cause for the plaintiff's harm. In such cases, the but-for test is overwhelmed by multiple sufficient actual causes and, as a result, excludes as a legal actual cause of the plaintiff's harm the actions of a defendant who is without much question genuinely socially responsible for that harm.

For example, suppose that the plaintiff owns a remote cabin in a forest. Defendant 1 unreasonably carelessly starts a fire in that same forest north of the plaintiff's cabin, and the fire burns toward the south. Defendant 2, independently, unreasonably carelessly starts a fire in the same forest just west of the plaintiff's cabin and that fire burns toward the east. The two separate and independent fires converge at the site of the plaintiff's cabin, and it is burned to the ground.

In such a scenario, without some exception or alteration to the but-for test, the plaintiff would be left with no possibility of recovery through a negligence claim. The plaintiff would be unable, factually, to establish that the actions of either Defendant 1 or Defendant 2 were, separately and independently, a but-for actual cause of the harm. This is the case because, in the complete absence of Defendant 1's carelessness, the plaintiff would have nevertheless suffered the same harm, thus excluding Defendant 1's carelessness as a but-for cause of the harm. The same analysis and conclusion apply to Defendant 2's carelessness in this situation. There being no such thing in law under these circumstances as "Defendant 1 and Defendant 2" together, treated as a single, unified entity against whom the but-for test could be established, the plaintiff is left without a successful negligence claim against either one alone, meaning that the plaintiff is left with no successful negligence claim at all.

In such, and similar, circumstances, courts have labeled the unreasonably careless actions of both Defendant 1 and Defendant 2 as "concurrent causes" and have altered the actual causation instruction provided to the jury from the but-for test to a question of whether the individual defendant's breaching behavior was a "substantial factor," or, in some jurisdictions, a "material element," in the physical infliction of harm on the plaintiff. Such an alteration of the legal test for actual cause would, in a situation such as the one involving the remote cabin in the forest, permit a jury to find that either or both of the Defendants were an actual cause of the harm to the plaintiff's cabin, even though the actions of each Defendant, separately, clearly do not satisfy the usual but-for test of actual cause.

Why would courts, over a long period of time, recognize these concurrent cause cases as requiring some alteration to the usual but-for test for actual cause? What is unacceptably wrong with the result dictated by the use of the usual but-for test of actual causation in these cases?

The answer suggested by the understanding of the causation requirement offered herein is that the unaltered use of the usual but-for test in these cases results in an inappropriate resolution of the negligence claims in as much as it dictates a lack of liability for one or more defendants who are genuinely socially responsible for the plaintiff's harm. In these circumstances, both Defendant 1 and Defendant 2 possess both behavioral fault and consequential fault with respect to the harm suffered by the plaintiff, and as such they are appropriate targets of liability under a no harm, no foul principle. They are arguably genuinely socially responsible for the harm to the plaintiff's cabin. The existence of another, independent, and sufficient cause of the harm (the other fire) is not relevant to the blameworthiness of either defendant. The presence of another independent and sufficient cause is a coincidence in these situations that in itself does not relieve either actor from full moral and social responsibility for the harm. In other words, each defendant is as much at fault (at every level) for this injury despite the other actor's existence and actions.

The fundamental purpose of the causation requirement is the limiting of negligence liability to only those defendants who are genuinely socially responsible for the harm to the plaintiff. One is not genuinely socially responsible if one did not actually cause the harm to occur. In the overwhelming percentage of circumstances, whether a person actually caused harm to another can be determined by asking whether the harm would have nevertheless been experienced by the plaintiff even in the absence of the defendant's behavior. In relatively unusual circumstances, however, the but-for test is overwhelmed by multiple sufficient causes of the plaintiff's harm. In these cases, the but-for test comes out wrong in terms of its fundamental purpose as it identifies certain behavior as not being a legal actual cause of the harm when a jury might well reasonably conclude that the person who engaged in that behavior was genuinely socially responsible for it. In such circumstances, the but-for test, seen through the lens of its underlying function in the negligence tort, is underinclusive and, therefore, not performing its policy function appropriately.

The alternative to the but-for test for actual cause used by courts in cases of concurrent cause – that the defendant's unreasonably careless behavior was a substantial factor, or a material element, in the infliction of harm upon the plaintiff – provides the jury an opportunity to find the defendant liable to the plaintiff for negligence if they believe that the defendant was genuinely socially responsible for the plaintiff's experience of harm, an opportunity not reasonably available to them if they are required to use the but-for test to determine actual cause.

Recognizing that the concurrent cause doctrine and its alternative tests for actual cause function in this manner and for these purposes lead the way to the formulation of an appropriate test, or threshold, to be used by courts in deciding whether or not to declare a given set of circumstances a concurrent cause situation. At present, such a test is strikingly absent in the cases and the academic literature on concurrent causes. A court should determine that a given negligence case is a concurrent cause case, and should provide the jury with an alternative test for actual cause, whenever in the court's judgment: (1) a reasonable application of the but-for test to the facts of the case would result in a determination of no actual cause and (2) a reasonable juror could nevertheless conclude based on the facts that the defendant was genuinely socially responsible for the plaintiff's harm.

A second instance of courts permitting negligence liability to be imposed on a defendant despite the plaintiff's clear inability to satisfy the but-for test of actual cause is illustrated by the famous case of *Summers v. Tice*.[5] In this case, three hunters together went out with shotguns into an open range to hunt quail. At some point during the adventure, one hunter (eventually the plaintiff) became separated and stood uphill from the other two. Sometime thereafter, a quail was flushed and flew between the plaintiff and the two defendants. Both of the defendants shot in the direction of the quail, which was also in the direction of the plaintiff. One shotgun pellet struck the plaintiff in the upper lip, and another stuck him in the eye, though it was the injury to the eye that was the dominant cause of harm. There was, at that time, no means of determining from which of the two shotguns the seriously damaging pellet came, and thus no way of determining which of the defendants was the actual cause of the plaintiff's legally meaningful injuries. The trial court found, and the Supreme Court affirmed, that the defendants acted with

[5] Summers v. Tice, 199 P.2d 1 (Cal. 1948). The doctrine illustrated by this well-known case is sometimes referred to as "alternative liability."

unreasonable carelessness in shooting as they did, and that the plaintiff was not contributorily negligent for his own injury.

Summers v. Tice presents a situation in which two parties (two possible defendants) act in an unreasonably careless manner toward the plaintiff. One of the two parties actually caused meaningful harm to the plaintiff, the other did not, and no one, including the plaintiff and the two possible defendants, will ever know who, among the two defendants is the actual harm-producer.

Similar to concurrent cause cases, though in a different way, *Summers v. Tice* presents the injured plaintiff with a fatal obstacle to establishing the actual cause prong of the causation requirement, and thus prevents the plaintiff from satisfying the prima facie case for negligence. In a case like *Summers v. Tice*, the probability of either defendant having actually caused harm to the plaintiff is exactly 50 percent. The plaintiff bears the burden of establishing every element of the negligence prima facie case to a preponderance of the evidence, which, absent whatever else it might require, requires that the plaintiff establish each element as being at least more likely than not – a threshold which, by definition, a 50 percent probability cannot meet.

Also similar to concurrent cause cases, *Summers v. Tice* presents a situation wherein a plaintiff cannot establish the actual cause requirement against a defendant who is genuinely socially responsible for the plaintiff's injury. In this way, both kinds of cases feature a malfunction of the proper purpose underlying the causation requirement in which its normal operation results in the impossibility of liability being imposed on a party who has acted with unreasonable carelessness and, in so doing, caused the plaintiff harm for which the defendant was genuinely socially responsible.

Unlike concurrent cause cases, however, the situation illustrated by *Summers v. Tice* cannot be satisfactorily handled by offering the jury an alternative test for actual cause, such as substantial factor or a material element. The problem posed by *Summers v. Tice* is, in a sense, more difficult than that. The plaintiff in a case similar to *Summers v. Tice* simply cannot establish that either defendant was any part of the actual chain of events that resulted in the plaintiff's injury – any part of the actual cause – by more than a 50 percent probability, which, as noted in this chapter, is too small a probability to meet the preponderance of the evidence standard. Neither defendant can be shown to have been more than 50 percent likely to have been the but-for actual cause of the plaintiff's injury, a substantial factor in the infliction of that injury, a material element in the actual cause of that injury, or having had any part whatsoever to play in the actual infliction of the harm.

As such, an alteration of the but-for test for actual cause will not suffice. A court can only provide the plaintiff relief from a situation similar to *Summers v. Tice* by granting the plaintiff a presumption of the satisfaction of the actual cause prong of the causation requirement, or provide the plaintiff no relief at all. This alternative is strong remedial relief in as much as it operates as an exception to the basic legal requirement that the plaintiff bear the burden of proof for every element of the prima facie case, including the actual cause requirement.

The analysis of the causation requirement in negligence offered herein provides a sophisticated and powerful understanding of the traditional willingness of courts in cases similar to *Summers v. Tice* and its progeny to provide plaintiffs with this extraordinary remedy, and the long-standing decision of the Restatements to endorse those decisions.

To begin, what is the argument forwarded by defendants in cases similar to *Summers v. Tice* to urge courts not to create an exception to the normal operation of the actual cause doctrine, and to thereby allow that normal operation to prevent the plaintiff from satisfying the prima facie case for negligence against either defendant? The basic thrust of this argument is that allowing the plaintiff to hold these defendants liable under these circumstances would represent an exception to, and thus in a sense a violation and compromise of the policies underlying, the long-standing rule that imposes on the plaintiff the burden of proof to establish every required element of the prima facie case of negligence, including the prima facie requirement of actual cause. There are important policies and values that support the placement of the burden of proof on the plaintiff, and there should exist important countervailing policies and values that are served whenever an exception to that rule is recognized and implemented.

Moreover, providing the plaintiff in cases similar to *Summers v. Tice* an opportunity to satisfy the actual cause requirement when it cannot be done under the normal operation of the doctrine will result in both defendants being held liable. This means that with respect to one of the two defendants, the case will unquestionably come out wrong; one defendant will be held liable when they did not, in fact, cause the harm in question to the plaintiff. Such a result violates the basic no harm, no foul principle embedded in the causation requirement and, thus, in the negligence tort, with respect to that defendant. It is an obvious, fully foreseeable, and unjust consequence of providing the plaintiff with an exception to the normal burden of proving actual cause to a preponderance of the evidence.

How can plaintiffs in these cases possibly justify this kind of outcome: the intentional, cold-eyed imposition of negligence liability on a party who is known not to have caused the plaintiff the harm for which that party is being held liable (even if no one knows which party that is)? Such an outcome not only carves out for the plaintiff an exception to the usual rules regarding the burden of proof, but it also carves out an exception to the requirement that negligence liability (and to a large extent tort law liability generally) be contingent upon the defendant having actually caused the harm to the plaintiff for which the defendant is being held liable. This is not an instance of traditional strict liability – liability with causation but without fault – it is instead liability with fault but without causation. How can this be justified?

As with the presentation by the defendants, the argument by the plaintiffs in support of an extraordinary remedy in these circumstances begins by stressing that the failure to impose such an exception will also result in the foreseeable, and thus intentional, and equally cold-eyed resolution of the negligence claim against one of the defendants in the wrong way. One of these defendants did, in fact, act in an unreasonably careless manner and as a result actually caused tangible harm to the plaintiff. Every purpose and policy of tort law dictates the imposition of liability upon that defendant to the compensatory benefit of the plaintiff. In other words, there is more than one kind of mistake that can be made in the resolution of these cases: (1) the imposition of liability when it is not appropriately justified and (2) the failure to impose liability when it is fully justified. Part of what makes situations similar to *Summers v. Tice* so endlessly interesting to students and scholars of tort law is that they present a circumstance in which either one or the other of the mistakes must be made.

Given the inevitability of at least one bad outcome no matter how courts choose to resolve the issue of actual cause in this class of cases, are there reasons to prefer one kind of mistake over the other? Plaintiffs could argue that there are.

What are the more specific tort law policy costs and benefits attached to each possible resolution of these kinds of cases? If the plaintiff is granted relief by the court from the actual cause dilemma, then both defendants will be held liable. This outcome will, with respect to one of the two defendants, violate the no harm, no foul principle of actual cause (and negligence), and thereby violate the norm that negligence liability should only be imposed when the defendant was genuinely socially responsible for the harm inflicted upon the plaintiff. However, while one of the two defendants did not possess consequential fault for the plaintiff's injuries, they did possess behavioral fault in as much as they acted in an unreasonably careless manner. Thus, this resolution of the claim, while in violation of the no harm, no foul principle, does result in deterrence of the defendant's unreasonably careless behavior. It also serves the basic compensation goal of tort law by providing the plaintiff with an additional source of assets for recovery and rehabilitation.

Put a different way, it could be argued that by granting the plaintiff in these kinds of cases a presumption of the satisfaction of the actual cause requirement of the prima facie case, courts can advance, even with respect to the defendant who did not in fact cause any harm, both an appropriate deterrence objective and an appropriate compensation objective. However, achieving such objectives will come at the cost of violating the no harm, no foul principle of negligence liability. In addition, the court gets it entirely correct with respect to the defendant who did in fact cause the plaintiff injury by his unreasonably careless act.

What is the contrasting account of costs and benefits if the court instead denies the plaintiff any relief on the actual cause requirement and neither defendant is held liable? With respect to the defendant who did in fact cause the harm, the court gets it entirely wrong and thereby forgoes an appropriate opportunity for deterrence and compensation. Additionally, the outcome also violates, in the negative, the no harm, no foul principle. With respect to the defendant who did not cause harm, an appropriate opportunity for deterrence and compensation is missed, though the no harm, no foul principle is appropriately honored.

Given the choice set forth in these terms, it seems less surprising, and less extraordinary, that courts in the *Summers v. Tice* line of authority have chosen to grant plaintiffs the necessary relief with respect to actual cause.

This way of analyzing and understanding the actual cause requirement of negligence offers courts confronting similar *Summers v. Tice* type problems in the future at least two kinds of guidance. One is that the extraordinary relief granted in *Summers v. Tice* is harder to justify if both of the defendants who are held liable as a result have not engaged in unreasonably careless behavior (i.e., do not possess behavioral fault). In such circumstances, holding the defendant liable who did not actually cause the harm serves no appropriate deterrence purpose whatsoever. Holding that defendant liable thereby shifts from providing a partial deterrence benefit (in the *Summers v. Tice* situation) to providing no deterrence benefit at all, and thus, must be viewed as involving pure cost (or error) from a deterrence perspective.

Secondly, the extraordinary relief granted in *Summers v. Tice* is harder to justify if there are more than two defendants involved and still just one possible source of actual harm. This is the case because in such circumstances, the benefit of resolving the case correctly with respect to one of the defendants comes at the cost of getting it wrong with respect to more than just one of the others. The more defendants there are who could not have actually caused the harm compared with the number of sources of possible harm, the less attractive relief for the plaintiff becomes.

This understanding of the *Summers v. Tice* line of cases would, correctly as it has turned out thus far, have been helpful in dampening unwarranted optimism for the long-term prospects of market share liability when it emerged in the 1980s. A variation on both the basic facts and the result in *Summers v. Tice*, market share liability cases often involve at least one of the attributes identified in the foregoing analysis as being problematic to the granting of special relief to the plaintiff: more defendants (often many more) than possible sources of actual harm.

The understanding of actual causation offered herein would also counsel caution regarding attempts to refine or recast the but-for test of actual cause in ways that significantly complicate the matter without providing sufficient corresponding benefits in terms of improving or refining the ability of the test to accurately identify genuine social responsibility by the defendant. Complication is a real and quite tangible cost in this context, one that is tempting to ignore or to discount from an academic perspective. A doctrine like actual cause and a test like but-for causation must be used by lay persons serving on juries, and it is simply impractical (and unrealistic) to expect that courts will provide jury members with a separate training session or seminar so that they might understand a complicated approach to the actual cause requirement of the negligence claim. Moreover, it is often the goal of such efforts to improve the actual cause test from a scientific or a philosophical perspective, which misses the primary function of that test in the context of the negligence tort, which is to provide a first-level measure of the defendant's genuine social responsibility for the harm inflicted upon the plaintiff.

While the but-for test for actual cause does a generally excellent job of including within negligence liability all of those defendants who are genuinely socially responsible for the harm experienced by the plaintiff, it performs far less well in terms of its overinclusiveness. If taken literally, which is what the jury instruction typically charges triers of fact to do, the but-for test for actual cause includes within its scope a great many possible defendants who may have engaged in unreasonably careless behavior but who would not be thought to be genuinely socially responsible for the plaintiff's injuries.

One classic statement of this circumstance appears in the famous case of *Palsgraf v. Long Island Railroad Company*: "A boy throws a stone into a pond. The ripples spread. The water level rises. The history of that pond is altered for all eternity. It will be altered by other causes also. Yet it will be forever the resultant of all causes combined. Each one will have an influence. How great only omniscience can say. You may speak of a chain, or if you please, a net. An analogy is of little aid. Each cause brings about future events. Without each the future would not be the same."[6]

A virtually endless number of prior behaviors by others are literally but-for required in order for the defendant in a particular negligence case to even have physically been at a specific place at a specific time so that his or her unreasonably careless behavior would result in harm to the plaintiff. Without some additional formal limitation in the prima facie case, all of these persons who engaged in behavior that could be characterized as being in some way unreasonably careless would be potentially subject to liability to the plaintiff for negligence.

Imagine, for example, a very simple negligence case in which the plaintiff claims that the defendant carelessly failed to apply the brakes of his or her car in time and, as a result, collided with the rear of the plaintiff's car while the plaintiff was legally stopped at a red light. Without much doubt, the plaintiff could establish actual cause against the defendant (Defendant 1) in these circumstances. Assume, however, that Defendant 1 is without assets or adequate insurance coverage or is otherwise not responsive to suit or judgment.

Plaintiff then develops evidence establishing that a different person (Defendant 2) was on that same day driving carelessly on a different road on which Defendant 1 also drove before turning onto the road on which the collision with the plaintiff occurred. Defendant 2's unreasonably careless driving created a disturbance among drivers on that road which in turn caused traffic to dramatically slow in front of Defendant 1. But-for Defendant 2's careless driving, Defendant 1 would not have been situated behind the plaintiff's car at all and, thus, no collision with the

6 Palsgraf v. Long Island RR Co., 162 N.E. 99, 103 (N.Y. 1928).

plaintiff's car would have taken place, and no harm would have been experienced by the plaintiff.

Rather clearly, Defendant 2's unreasonably careless driving is literally a but-for cause of the injury to the plaintiff, and it also satisfies the duty and breach elements of the prima facie case for negligence. Equally clearly, Defendant 2 should not be held liable to the plaintiff under any system of liability that preconditions the imposition of liability on the defendant having been genuinely socially responsible for the plaintiff's harm. While Defendant 2's unreasonably careless behavior was literally and physically necessary in order for the plaintiff to have been harmed in this particular way, no one would seriously assert that Defendant 2 was genuinely socially responsible – was morally at fault – for the specific injuries suffered by the plaintiff. Moreover, the behavior of persons in a community, including highly productive behavior, might well be paralyzed if a system existed that imposed formal legal liability on them for careless behavior that somehow resulted in harm to another that far down the line of actual causation.

Note that the preceding example includes behavior by Defendant 2 that is still relatively close in time and not far on a chain of physical causation from the infliction of injury on the plaintiff. The same analysis, however, would apply if Defendant 2 were a neighbor of Defendant 1 who, coming home late and inebriated the night before, unreasonably carelessly parked his car blocking Defendant 1's driveway. The next morning, Defendant 1 is forced to rouse Defendant 2 and request that Defendant 2 move the car before Defendant 1 can drive to work. This makes Defendant 1 late, frustrated, perhaps preoccupied, and physically places him behind the plaintiff that morning when Defendant 1 otherwise would not have been. Again, Defendant 2 is a clear but-for cause; and yet just as clearly, few would seriously assert that Defendant 2 is genuinely socially responsible for the plaintiff's injuries. Examples could be offered that extend Defendant 2's behavior even further away in time and further back in the chain of actual cause from the plaintiff's injury.

A system that requires genuine social responsibility for the imposition of formal negligence liability cannot, as a design matter, leave unaltered a prima facie case for negligence that requires only duty, breach, actual cause, and harm. Such a system would generate liability that includes very large numbers of defendants who were not arguably morally at fault for the plaintiff's specific harm – the harm for which the defendant is required by law to compensate the plaintiff. Such a system would, in other words, be massively overinclusive.

The specific function of the proximate cause prong of the causation requirement in negligence is to limit, or to tailor, the scope of liability ultimately generated by the negligence tort so that only those defendants who are genuinely socially responsible for the plaintiff's harm are held liable. It has no other function, and its long-time presence in the prima facie case of negligence can be satisfactorily explained in no other way.

While the design and policy purpose of the proximate cause requirement can be accurately identified, the practical task remains difficult. At a black letter, doctrinal level, the key concept employed by proximate cause doctrine is foreseeability. The central notion is that a person is not genuinely socially responsible for a given consequence – is not morally at fault for that result – if the result could not be reasonably foreseen by the actor under the circumstances at the time the triggering behavior was engaged in. One cannot be fairly blamed for having caused a result if that result was not reasonably foreseeable to the actor, even if the actor was one of the actual causes of the harm. This is, as a general matter, a rather impressive attempt to capture the essence of our collective consensus sense of moral responsibility in a single, simple concept usable by laypersons who serve on juries.

For example, imagine two friends deciding together where to go out for dinner. Person 1 prefers a certain restaurant while the other, Person 2, prefers another establishment. Ultimately, after some debate, the two friends drive to the restaurant preferred by Person 1. When they return to the car in the parking lot after the meal, they find it badly damaged, with no witnesses or messages present to explain how or why. While Person 1 is clearly a but-for actual cause of this unhappy consequence, in that it would not have occurred had the friends not gone to the restaurant that Person 1 preferred, Person 1 cannot reasonably be said to be genuinely at fault for the harm to the car because Person 1 could not have reasonably foreseen that going to that restaurant might result in such damage.

Unless the risk of the harm that actually occurred is reasonably part of the calculus concerning the actor's (the defendant's in a negligence claim) judgment and behavior, the actor cannot appropriately be blamed, socially or morally, for that resultant harm, even if the resultant harm would not have occurred but-for the actor's behavior. Harm in such circumstances is, in common parlance, a pure accident, implying that no one is to blame for it.

Similar to the but-for test and actual cause, foreseeability as a measure of proximate cause is elegant, in that it is simple and can be quickly and reasonably well understood by persons serving on juries. Unlike the but-for test, however, which yields largely determinate results, reasonable foreseeability, when applied to a range of normal, common circumstances, often yields uncertain and indeterminate results. It is, in fact, among the most uncertain, unpredictable, and indeterminate doctrines in all of tort law.

For example, consider the hypothetical situation described in this chapter, in which Defendant 1 fails to apply the brakes on his car in time and, as a result, collides with the car directly in front of him at a red light, a car owned by the plaintiff. There is little doubt that the collision with the plaintiff's car, the one right in front, is a reasonably foreseeable consequence of failing to apply the brakes. What if the collision with that car causes it to move forward and collide with a third car, a car directly in front of the plaintiff's car? Is such harm reasonably foreseeable to the defendant? What if the third car, when struck, moves forward into the intersection and is struck by a car moving on the cross street? Is that harm reasonably foreseeable to the defendant? What if the driver in the third car, when struck, reflexively activates the horn on the car, which in turn startles a driver on the intersecting road who swerves into an adjacent lane and thereby strikes yet another car? And on and on. While easy agreement and consensus are likely achievable in obvious cases on both ends of the spectrum, there are a very large number of conventional circumstances in which juries can be expected to be uncertain, and perhaps in disagreement, regarding the question of reasonable foreseeability.

Apart from the frequent indeterminacy of reasonable foreseeability itself, the underlying concept of genuine social responsibility – genuine social fault – is likely a subtle and multi-factor judgment that is only loosely captured by a simple reasonable foreseeability test, and it likely shifts and changes over time and across different jurisdictions. For instance, it is probably the case that many persons' sense of a given defendant's genuine social responsibility for particular harm that was actually caused by the defendant's conduct is to some extent a function of the degree of blameworthiness, or unreasonableness, of the defendant's harm-producing conduct. In the aforementioned example, it is more likely that Defendant 1 will be deemed to be genuinely socially responsible for some of the more remote harm (e.g., the collisions involving the third car) if the reason for Defendant 1's failure to apply the brakes was a high level of voluntary inebriation as contrasted with a sudden distraction from a nearby vehicle, even though the foreseeability of harm is the same in both instances. One's sense of another's blameworthiness for subsequent harm most likely expands and contracts with the degree of blameworthiness of the other's harm-producing behavior, though this factor is not captured by the black letter approach to proximate cause nor the conventional proximate cause jury instruction, both of which focus only on reasonable foreseeability.

Understanding that the function of a proximate cause requirement in negligence is the limiting of negligence liability to only those defendants' who are genuinely socially responsible for the plaintiff's harm provides a powerful perspective from which to make sense of the traditional instances in which courts take the proximate cause judgment away from juries and instead decide the issue as a matter of law. These are particular circumstances in which the proximate cause issue is determined by a preexisting rule of law and not by the discretion of jurors.

From the perspective of the account of the causation requirement offered herein, one would expect that taking away discretion from the trier of fact and resolving the proximate cause issue by preexisting rule would make sense in circumstances in which there is a substantial risk that the outcome of a literal, empirically focused foreseeability test will fail to accurately identify genuine social responsibility by the defendant. In the same way that the concurrent cause and *Summers v. Tice* exceptions to the but-for test for actual cause are needed to respond to instances of underinclusiveness, exceptions to the usual practice of having foreseeability determined by the trier of fact are needed to respond to instances of underinclusiveness of the reasonable foreseeability test for proximate cause.

One such instance applies to cases in which the defendant's unreasonably careless behavior results in the plaintiff being the later victim of subsequent medical malpractice. The relevant issue in these cases is whether the defendant's unreasonably careless behavior is a proximate cause of the additional harm suffered by the plaintiff as a result of the subsequent medical malpractice. Understandably, many courts confronted with this issue express the view that the defendant is genuinely socially responsible – is fully morally at fault – for the subsequent harm suffered by a plaintiff from medical malpractice to which the plaintiff was subjected only as a result of the defendant's unreasonably careless behavior. And yet from an empirical perspective, in the overwhelming percentage of cases, the likelihood of a given person (a victim of prior negligence or not) experiencing unreasonably careless medical treatment is far lower than 50 percent, especially since this rule applies without exception to malpractice engaged in by established medical providers, such as hospitals. From an empirical perspective, it is difficult to impossible for a decision maker to reasonably conclude that the occurrence of an event far, far less than 50 percent likely to happen was reasonably foreseeable by the defendant.

The dissonance in these cases between the likely outcome of the conventional treatment of proximate cause by way of the reasonable foreseeability test – a conclusion of no proximate cause – and the existence of genuine social responsibility by the defendant mandates that in order to align the outcome of the negligence claim with the underlying policy that socially justifies the doctrine, courts must apply an exception that removes discretion from the jury and dictates a finding that the defendant was a proximate cause of the harm suffered by the plaintiff as a result of subsequent medical malpractice. A similar analysis makes policy sense of, and thus rationalizes, the other recognized instances of proximate cause as a matter of law.

One implication of the foregoing analysis is that judges should bring to bear the foregoing understanding of proximate cause as a doctrinal mechanism for limiting negligence liability to those defendants who are deemed to be genuinely socially responsible for the plaintiff's harm when making decisions on what evidence and arguments should be made available to jurors in negligence cases. Issues of materiality, relevance, competency, and ultimate admissibility of evidence regarding proximate cause should be considered in light of an awareness that the fundamental task in the resolution of proximate cause is a determination of the defendant's genuine social responsibility and not a literal, empirical analysis of the reasonable foreseeability of the defendant under the specific factual circumstances of the case.

A second implication of the foregoing analysis is that judges should bring to bear the foregoing understanding of proximate cause when deciding motions that require a trier of law to determine what a reasonable trier of fact could or could not decide on the issue of proximate cause. Though recognized exceptions have been created and exist in response to some instances of dissonance between empirically reasonable foreseeability and genuine social responsibility, such exceptions are unlikely to adequately cover all such instances that may arise in the wide range of factual circumstances that confront courts in negligence cases. Judges should be sensitive to the possibility of the existence of such dissonance and should decide motions for summary judgment and directed verdict in such cases accordingly.

Third, it may improve the accuracy of jury judgments in close cases of proximate cause to include in model jury instructions on the issue more explicit explanation that the ultimate purpose of applying a reasonable foreseeability test to the facts of the case is to identify the existence, or lack, of genuine social responsibility by the defendant for the plaintiff's harm. Jury instructions that only set forth the reasonable foreseeability test without broader context, as most do, invite jurors to adopt an overtly literal, overly empirical approach to the proximate cause requirement and thereby insufficiently recognize that the black letter reasonable foreseeability test is less the sought after objective itself than it is an imperfect, surrogate measure of genuine social responsibility.

10

The Paradigm Shift from Formalism to Instrumentalism and Constitutional Law

One commonly recognized distinction in the law, especially with regard to the work of appellate courts, is a difference between common law adjudication and statutory interpretation. At its simplest level, the common law is binding law that has been recognized and is applied by courts to authoritatively resolve disputes that has not been promulgated by any other authoritative source. Statutory interpretation involves courts resolving disputes by the direct application of a statute, regulation, or treaty provision that has been enacted by a lawmaking source other than the appellate courts themselves.

When engaging in statutory interpretation, an appeals court has resources to work with and factors to consider that it does not have when the court is engaging in the creation or the development of common law. The court has the express language of the statute to contend with. It also has the meaning and interpretation of that language that might have been intended by the legislative body that enacted it. Neither factor is present in a pure common law case like *Tarasoff*.[1] Thus, the jurisprudence of statutory interpretation and common law creation has tended to diverge. For example, the concepts of formalism and instrumentalism are not very prominent in discussions and analyses of statutory interpretation by courts.

Like a great many distinctions in the law, however, the distinction between the making of common law by appellate courts and the activity of statutory interpretation can be reasonably clear on the extremes and not clear at all in the middle. In the case of the California Supreme Court deciding in *Tarasoff* whether a professional therapist should bear a legal duty to warn potential victims of physical violence threatened by a patient of the therapist, this was an issue of first impression that arose within California's common law of negligence and was neither raised nor resolved by the existence of any statute or regulation. When resolving this issue, the California Supreme Court was clearly engaging in the making, and in the refinement, of California common law and was not required to determine the meaning or the application of any statute or regulation.

[1] See Chapter 4 herein.

In contrast, imagine a case in which an appeals court is required to decide whether a person qualifies for a driver's license in a state in which the applicable state statute provides that "the minimum age at which a person is eligible to receive a license to operate a motor vehicle is sixteen." Suppose a particular person cannot produce an official U.S. birth certificate or produces a birth certificate from a foreign country deemed to be administratively unreliable in such matters. Deciding whether this person qualified for a driver's license would pretty clearly involve an act of statutory interpretation by the court. Even though the court in such a case would literally be creating new law for the jurisdiction that did not exist before, the issue that the court was required to resolve only arose because of the existence of a statute and the case raised a relatively minor point regarding the application of the statute to an unusual circumstance. It would be, as a matter of modern usage, misleading to say that the court, in resolving that case, was engaging in the creation, or the development, of common law for the jurisdiction.

Now imagine, in a classic example, that an appellate court is required to decide a case that involves the application of a state statute that prohibits "the presence of a vehicle" in a particular place, such as a public park.[2] While the statute rather clearly prohibits the operation of a standard automobile in the park, does it also prohibit the operation of a motorcycle, a bicycle, a recumbent bike, a mobility scooter, a child's full-sized wheeled wagon, or the use of high-speed roller skates? Does it prohibit the static display of an old Western stagecoach, a military tank, or an airplane?

Similar to the driver's license example discussed in this chapter, this issue arises because of the existence of a statute, and it requires a discretionary judgment regarding the application of the statute to particular factual circumstances. In that sense, and according to modern usage, one would say that the court, in this case, was also engaging in the judicial activity of statutory interpretation. However, it is fairly clear that the kind of statutory interpretation engaged in by the court in the vehicle example is meaningfully different than in the driver's license example is as much as the court in the vehicle example is required to make new law on its own to a greater extent, and in a broader fashion, than in the driver's license example. It may not conventionally be called common law lawmaking, but the vehicle case certainly involves more necessary lawmaking by the court than does the driver's license case.

There is yet another hypothetical situation to consider. In this fourth circumstance, imagine that the relevant state statute provides that a person is only eligible to receive a driver's license in the state when, according to the relevant statute, "they have demonstrated a level of seriousness and maturity appropriate to the responsibility of operating a motor vehicle."

When a person brings a legal action challenging the denial of a driver's license and claiming that the denying authority misinterpreted the statute, in what kind of

[2] H. L. A. Hart, *Positivism and the Separation of Law and Morality*, 71 Harvard Law Review 593, 607 (1958).

activity is the court engaged? In some important respects, the court is engaged in statutory interpretation. In other respects, however, the degree of new lawmaking from scratch that this instance of statutory interpretation requires of the court, and the vagueness of the direction provided by the language of the statute, makes the task look and feel much more like classic common law lawmaking, and makes far more relevant considerations of formalism and instrumentalism, as in typical instances of pure appellate court lawmaking.

One useful insight here is that lawmaking by way of express statutes and regulations, in a system like ours in which the legislative or executive branch enacts these statutes and the judicial branch subsequently interprets and applies them, is by its nature a process of shared governance between the branches. A more detailed and specific statute allocates more lawmaking to the legislature while a more vague, ambiguous, or open-ended statute allocates more lawmaking authority and responsibility to the courts. At some point along the continuum, courts dealing with highly abstract, unspecific, or exceptionally vague statutory terms are involved in essentially the same judicial activity as they are in classic common law cases like *Tarasoff*.

That brings us to the United States Supreme Court (hereinafter the "Supreme Court"). Some of what the Supreme Court does is relatively standard judicial interpretation of federal statutes. For example, in the case of *Lozman v. City of Riviera Beach, Florida*, the Supreme Court was required to interpret the meaning of the word "vessel" in a federal statute, similar to the "vehicle" example discussed in this chapter.[3]

Some of what the Supreme Court does, though it represents only a modest percentage of the Court's work, is to review and create federal common law, much like the *Tarasoff* case. For example, in the case of *Air and Liquid Systems Corp. v. DeVries*, the Supreme Court was required to create new federal common law in the area of products liability. This particular issue arose in a maritime context in which the federal court system is granted exclusive jurisdiction, thus the need for relatively rare federal common law.[4]

Of course, a very significant part of the Supreme Court's work involves the interpretation and application of the United States Constitution. Some provisions of the federal constitution are similar to the sixteen-year-old's driver's license hypothetical situation discussed in this chapter and place the Court in a position to engage in more or less standard statutory analysis. An example is Article II, Section 1, Clause 5, which provides that "No Person except a natural born Citizen, or a Citizen of the United States, at the time of the Adoption of this Constitution, shall be eligible to the Office of President; neither shall any Person be eligible to that

[3] Lozman v. City of Riviera Beach, Florida, 568 U.S. 115 (2013).

[4] Air and Liquid Systems Corp. v. DeVries, 586 U.S. 446 (2019); see Marin R. Scordato, *The Curious Case of Tort Liability for a Defective Product that the Defendant Did Not Make, Sell, or Distribute*, 88 Missouri Law Review 135 (2023).

Office who shall not have attained to the Age of thirty five Years, and been fourteen Years a Resident within the United States."

Other federal constitutional provisions, including many of the most prominent and foundational, are strikingly less specific and markedly more abstract than the aforementioned presidential eligibility clause. For example, Amendment I of the U.S. Constitution (the First Amendment) reads in full as follows: "Congress shall make no law respecting an establishment of religion, or prohibiting the free exercise thereof; or abridging the freedom of speech, or of the press; or the right of the people peaceably to assemble, and to petition the government for a redress of grievances."

While the existence of the constitutional text pretty clearly requires the Supreme Court to determine the constitutionality of state action, in part, based on the degree to which that action, for example, "abridges the freedom of speech," the text provides almost no other meaningful substantive guidance regarding what either "abridging" or "the freedom of speech" means or how it should be interpreted and applied. To the extent that the Court is working with source material that is explicit written text adopted by a legal authority in an appropriate manner, one could say that judicial application of the First Amendment is an act of constitutional analysis akin to statutory interpretation. But in the case of language as abstract and non-specific as the First Amendment, as well as many other similar federal constitutional provisions, such a characterization is misleading.

As a functional matter of jurisprudence, it is arguably more coherent and accurate to understand the First Amendment as directing the federal courts to work on the development of a common law of speech protective constitutional doctrine, much like a state court system may at one time have decided that it needed to develop an appropriate common law legally enforcing some promises, or responding to intentionally caused personal injury with the imposition of legal liability, before the specifics of those bodies of common law had been worked out. From this perspective, constitutional law doctrine in some areas is more accurately and more productively understood as being a kind of common law, and its creation is more a matter of common law lawmaking than an instance of judicial statutory interpretation.

It is in this way that the paradigms of formalism and instrumentalism come into play in the realm of constitutional adjudication. In much the same way that the appellate court creation of common law generally can be seen as being more or less formalist and more or less instrumentalist in nature, the creation of constitutional law in many areas can usefully be seen through the same lens. Correspondingly, the paradigm shift that has taken place in common law jurisprudence over the twentieth century has had its effect on constitutional lawmaking as well.

In fact, perhaps because the Court often confronts constitutional issues that have a high social profile and that generate intense levels of controversy and political passion, the implications of the paradigm shift from formalism to instrumentalism with respect to the perceived value-laden exercise of political power by individuals who have never been directly elected to their life-tenured positions, and never will be, has probably fallen most heavily on the Supreme Court.

In 2018, during his confirmation hearings, now Justice Brett Kavanaugh said in his opening statement that "A good judge must be an umpire – a neutral and impartial arbiter who favors no litigant or policy." Again, as late as May of 2024, at a judicial conference, Justice Kavanaugh was reported as saying "Chief Justice Roberts famously said judges are like umpires" and then calling the phrase "four of the most important words ever uttered."[5]

This kind of self-presentation by appellate judges harkens back to the heyday of formalism and suggests that they perform a predominately objective and technical function, much like an umpire judging balls and strikes, fair and foul balls, and calling runners safe or out in a baseball game. There may occasionally be close calls and the need to exercise discretion, and not everyone will agree with all the calls that are made, but the fundamental nature of what judges, like umpires, do is to apply relatively clear standards to specific factual situations and then determine which way the call should go.

This conception of the work of appellate judges generally has not survived the paradigm shift from formalism to instrumentalism within the legal community itself, and if conventional popular media coverage of the Supreme Court and its constitutional work over at least the last five years is a reliable indicator, it no longer survives in the mind and imagination of the public at large. That Supreme Court justices bring personal preferences, values, perspectives, and political ideological beliefs and commitments to bear on their professional work is no longer just suggested or asserted but is now fully assumed in the popular news media coverage of the Court.

In a sense, the United States Supreme Court has borne the greatest public brunt of the undemocratic implications of the paradigm shift from formalism to instrumentalism. The movement to advance some version of originalism as a legitimate means of constitutional interpretation can be seen in this light as being primarily an attempt to salvage some vestige of a perceived objective basis for constitutional adjudication in the face of the dramatic change over the last twenty or thirty years in the public understanding of the thoroughly value-laden nature of judicial determinations of constitutionality and the development of constitutional law.

Far from merely calling individual balls and strikes, the task of deciding in a principled way whether a wide variety of state action violates federal constitutional provisions regarding, for example, free speech is a judicial project that requires the cumulative construction over time of a well-developed and coherent body of constitutional free speech doctrine that is very much in its nature like the judicial development over time of an area of non-constitutional common law like torts. And just like tort law, a body of constitutional doctrine, like free speech law, can be

[5] Adam Liptak, *Justice Kavanaugh on the Presidency, the Court and Taylor Swift*, New York Times, May 10, 2024.

presented by deciding judges (or justices) in their published opinions as being justified and rationalized on more of a formalist or more of an instrumentalist basis. In this way, it is meaningful to talk about formalist and instrumentalist constitutional analysis and to consider a possible shift in that prevailing paradigm much as with common law generally.

What would instrumentalist constitutional analysis look like? What follows is a detailed example of instrumentalist constitutional analysis in the area of free speech. It specifically focuses on the long-standing First Amendment doctrine of prior restraint. Rather than seeking justification for the existence of, and the appropriate substance of, the doctrine of prior restraint through the abstract manipulation of larger, broader constitutional principles and precepts, or by the construction of deductive chains of reasoning, the following analysis instead examines the degree to which various versions of the doctrine can be fairly expected to actually advance core free speech policies and objectives in the real world. In that sense it is instrumentalist, and not formalist, in nature.

Since the 1931 release of the Supreme Court's opinion in *Near v. Minnesota*, the doctrine of prior restraint has been an essential element of First Amendment jurisprudence.[6] On its face, the doctrine requires that any government action which operates as a prior restraint on speech be subjected to strict judicial scrutiny. So strict is the scrutiny applied under the doctrine that the Supreme Court has never upheld a law that it has characterized as a prior restraint on pure speech.

Despite the frequency with which the doctrine of prior restraint is cited in court opinions and the level of general recognition it has achieved, relevant case law does not provide a concise and logically coherent definition of a prior restraint on speech. Moreover, the Supreme Court, in the years since *Near*, has affixed the prior restraint label to an exceptionally diverse group of laws, regulations, and government actions. Upon inspection, these laws, regulations, and actions appear to have little in common other than the fact that the Court has deemed them deserving of strict judicial scrutiny. As a result, the term "prior restraint" has become largely a legal misnomer, and the doctrine a source of confusion and controversy. The confusion associated with the doctrine of prior restraint results not only from its inconsistent application by the courts but, more importantly, from the incoherence that plagues the conceptual distinction at the root of the doctrine – the distinction between prior restraints and subsequent sanctions.

The distinction between laws that impose a prior restraint on speech and those that constitute a subsequent sanction can be traced to the eighteenth century. In his *Commentaries on the Laws of England*, Sir William Blackstone wrote:

[6] Near v. Minnesota, 283 U.S. 697 (1931).

> The liberty of the press is indeed essential to the nature of a free state; but this consists in laying no previous restraints upon publications, and not in freedom from censure for criminal matter when published. Every freeman has an undoubted right to lay what sentiments he pleases before the public; to forbid this is to destroy the freedom of the press; but if he publishes what is improper, mischievous, or illegal, he must take the consequences of his own temerity.[7]

In the United States, the first and most frequently cited case in prior restraint jurisprudence is *Near v. Minnesota*.[8] In *Near*, decided in the summer of 1931, the United States Supreme Court confronted a judicial injunction prohibiting the continued publication of a vehemently anti-Semitic newspaper. A state district court issued the injunction pursuant to a Minnesota statute that provided for the enjoining as a public nuisance of a "malicious, scandalous and defamatory newspaper, magazine or other periodical."[9] The Supreme Court of Minnesota had affirmed the district court's judgment. In a five-to-four decision, the United States Supreme Court held both the injunction and the statute to be prior restraints on speech in violation of the First Amendment of the United States Constitution. Citing Blackstone as a historical precedent, the *Near* Court formally introduced into American case law the concept of prior restraint as a separate and significant category of First Amendment analysis. According to the Court: "The question is whether a statute authorizing such proceedings in restraint of publication is consistent with the conception of the liberty of the press as historically conceived and guaranteed. In determining the extent of the constitutional protection, it has been generally, if not universally, considered that it is the chief purpose of the guaranty to prevent previous restraints upon publication."[10]

The Supreme Court has consistently reaffirmed the importance of the concept and the category of prior restraint in the resolution of First Amendment issues in a variety of cases since *Near*. Reviewing these cases in 1976, the Court wrote:

> The Court has interpreted these [First Amendment] guarantees to afford special protection against orders that prohibit the publication or broadcast of particular information or commentary – orders that impose a "previous" or "prior" restraint on speech.... The thread running through all these cases is that prior restraints on speech and publication are the most serious and the least tolerable infringement on First Amendment rights.[11]

Given this characterization of prior restraints, one might expect that special care would have been devoted to developing a formal definition of a prior restraint on

[7] 4 W. BLACKSTONE, COMMENTARIES *151–52.
[8] Near, *supra* note 6.
[9] *Id.* at 701–02.
[10] *Id.* at 713.
[11] Nebraska Press Ass'n v. Stuart, 427 U.S. 308, 311–12 (1977).

speech. Nonetheless, neither the Supreme Court nor the lower federal courts thus far have developed such a definition.

Without an explicit judicial definition of a prior restraint, one naturally looks for an implicit definition in the pattern of court decisions in the area. In the cases decided since *Near*, however, the Supreme Court has applied the doctrine of prior restraint to a broad array of government activities. These various activities include: judicial injunctions;[12] systems of administrative preclearance that require a government license or permit prior to publication;[13] a state tax on the gross receipts of newspapers having greater than a specified circulation;[14] a use tax on the cost of paper and ink products required for newspaper publication;[15] a license fee applied to vendors of religious literature;[16] the refusal by a city to rent its municipal theater for a production of the musical *Hair*;[17] a statute prohibiting the publication of the names of juvenile offenders without the permission of the juvenile court;[18] a zoning ordinance limiting the geographic concentration of theaters showing X-rated films;[19] the creation of a commission whose primary purpose was to identify for the public, and for government prosecutors, books and magazines having the tendency to corrupt the morals of youth;[20] and a city ordinance granting the mayor authority to approve or deny applications for annual permits to place newspaper vending machines on public property.[21]

It is difficult to identify any pattern or common characteristics shared by these formally recognized prior restraints, especially so since none involve suppression of speech prior to its expression. In fact, so many types of government activities have, at one time or another, been characterized as a prior restraint on speech that few courts or commentators have even attempted to develop a descriptive theory of the courts' activity in this area. Indeed, some legal scholars have openly acknowledged the conceptual confusion that currently plagues the doctrine.[22] In his treatise on constitutional law, Professor Laurence Tribe has written:

> Indeed, the doctrine [of prior restraint] has been used to invalidate such a variety of restrictions on speech, under such a wide range of conditions, that some scholars have questioned the conceptual clarity of the term. There is much to this criticism, for the Court has often used the cry of "prior restraint" not as an independent

[12] Oklahoma Publishing Co. v. District Court, 430 U.S. 308, 311–12 (1977).
[13] Shuttlesworth v. Birmingham, 394 U.S. 147, 159 (1969).
[14] Grosjean v. American Press Co., 297 U.S. 233, 350–51 (1936).
[15] Minneapolis Star & Tribune Co. v. Minnesota Comm'r of Revenue, 460 U.S. 575, 592–93 (1983).
[16] Murdock v. Pennsylvania, 319 U.S. 105, 117 (1943).
[17] Southeastern Promotions, Ltd. v. Conrad, 420 U.S. 546, 564 (1975).
[18] Smith v. Daily Mail Publishing Co., 443 U.S. 97, 105–06 (1979).
[19] Young v. American Mini Theaters, Inc., 427 U.S. 50, 72–73 (1976).
[20] Bantam Books, Inc. v. Sullivan, 372 U.S. 58, 71 (1963).
[21] City of Lakewood v. Plain Dealer Publishing Co., 486 U.S. 750, 772 (1988).
[22] See, for example, John Jeffries, *Rethinking Prior Restraint*, 92 YALE LAW JOURNAL 409 (1983).

> analytical framework but rather to signal conclusions that it has reached on other grounds.[23]

For all this, the doctrine of prior restraint continues to thrive and to exert its influence on the resolution of contemporary First Amendment issues.

The fundamental problem with the contemporary doctrine of prior restraint is that the distinction upon which the doctrine rests – the distinction between prior restraints and subsequent sanctions – lacks sufficient substance to support a categorical legal rule. The distinction, as developed thus far, fails to provide a means of identifying a category of potentially speech-suppressive government activities that is in any way meaningful for First Amendment purposes. As a result, the prior restraint doctrine lacks the reliability and predictability of application necessary to support constitutionally protected speech. It is, in effect, a distinction without a difference.

Consider, for example, the definition of a prior restraint offered by Professor Thomas Emerson in his classic 1955 article on the subject: "The concept of prior restraint, roughly speaking, deals with official restrictions imposed upon speech or other forms of expression in advance of actual publication."[24] The definition offered by Professors Rotunda, Nowak, and Young in their treatise on constitutional law is similar: "[A]ny governmental order which restricts or prohibits speech prior to its publication constitutes a prior restraint."[25]

The essential problem with these definitions is that once the interpretation of terms such as "restraint," "restrict," or "prohibit" moves beyond the strictly literal, the definition loses the power to exclude most positive laws from its scope. It, therefore, loses its ability to serve as the basis for a meaningful doctrinal distinction. This is the case because nearly all laws, by their nature and purpose, are designed to influence human behavior prior to its actual occurrence. Since the general decline in the acceptance of the concept of natural law, positive laws and regulations have been rationalized primarily on the basis of their ability to reduce the future occurrence of societally disfavored behavior.

After-the-act sanctions are employed in the law largely to restrain members of the regulated community from engaging in the proscribed acts again in the future. In a world in which laws are viewed primarily from this instrumentalist perspective, society views virtually all laws as prior restraints on behavior. Thus, from this perspective, it is clear that a substantive distinction cannot logically be maintained between some laws that operate as prior restraints on speech and others that operate as subsequent sanctions when in fact all of the laws in question do not impose upon potential speakers a legal sanction until the speaker actually has communicated the offending speech.

[23] L. Tribe, American Constitutional Law, Sections 12–34, at 1040 (2d ed. 1988).

[24] Thomas Emerson, *The Doctrine of Prior Restraint*, 20 Law & Contemporary Problems 648 (1955).

[25] 3 R. Rotunda, J. Nowak & J. Young, Treatise on Constitutional Law, Substance and Procedure, Section 20.16 at 72 (3d ed. 1986).

Given the inconsistency inherent in the current distinction between prior restraints and subsequent sanctions, it is difficult to understand how the doctrine of prior restraint has survived intact for so long. Perhaps it has survived because it is perceived as a speech-protective doctrine in a period characterized by expanded protection of speech by the courts. Perhaps it has provided a useful means to facially resolve cases which involve free speech issues that the courts have not wished to confront directly. Regardless of the reasons, it is clear that one crucial element in the survival of the prior restraint doctrine has been the willingness of many courts, and many commentators, to finesse the definitional inconsistency embedded in the modern version of the prior restraint/subsequent sanction distinction.

This finesse is usually accomplished through a two-step strategy. The first step begins by asserting that laws traditionally labeled as prior restraints share one or more constitutionally undesirable characteristics and that the presence of these characteristics justifies subjecting the laws to especially strict judicial scrutiny. The second step of the analysis solves the definitional problem by asserting that all laws possessing the identified undesirable characteristics are, as a result, prior restraints. One reason that this finesse has been so effective is that once a law is determined to be a prior restraint by virtue of possessing certain constitutionally undesirable characteristics, then it is a relatively easy matter to justify the larger legal doctrine mandating that all prior restraints be subject to strict, and usually fatal, judicial scrutiny.

Despite the practical success this definitional strategy has enjoyed, it possesses two serious flaws. The first involves the questionable nature of its major premise, that the undesirable attributes used to define the prior restraint category are, in fact, characteristic of those laws that traditionally have been labeled as prior restraints. The second flaw, following from the first, is that the prior restraint/subsequent sanction distinction, as currently defined, is almost perversely counterintuitive. It uses a category label that possesses a common-sense meaning in our language and yet defines the population of the category without reference to the common-sense meaning of that label. By adopting this distinction as its substantive base, the doctrine of prior restraint becomes little more than a label attached to a legal conclusion already reached; a veil behind which independent, and frequently unnamed, factors are considered and weighed. The result is a doctrine profoundly misleading and ripe for misuse.

The first step in the current definitional approach to the doctrine of prior restraint is the identification of certain undesirable attributes alleged to be characteristic of prior restraints. These identified attributes generally gravitate toward one of two major themes.

The first theme around which the asserted attributes of prior restraints cluster involves alleged differences in the effect that prior restraints and subsequent sanctions have on potential speech. The thrust of this argument is set forth succinctly in the Supreme Court's opinion in *Nebraska Press Association v. Stuart*: "If it can be said that a threat of criminal or civil sanctions after publication 'chills' speech, prior restraint 'freezes' it at least for the time."[26] Professors Rotunda, Nowak, and Young's treatise on constitutional law is one of many secondary sources that embraces, and more explicitly articulates, this same basic point: "[T]he 'marketplace' theory of speech supports the distinction between prior restraint and subsequent punishment. While subsequent punishment may deter some speakers, at least the ideas or speech at issue can be placed before the public. Prior restraint limits public debate and knowledge more severely."[27] The basic argument, echoed in the lower courts and by many commentators, is that prior restraints pose a greater practical deterrent to constitutionally protected speech than do subsequent sanctions.

For the purpose of examining this argument, suppose that the deterrent effect of a particular law or regulation can be expressed as a function of the regulated community's perception of the negative value of the sanction imposed in response to a violation of the law discounted by the perceived probability that the sanction will, in fact, be imposed in response to a given violation. Under this model, a law, or other government action, can influence the likelihood that a given behavior will occur by altering the regulated community's perception of either the unattractiveness of the sanction or the likelihood that the sanction will be imposed in response to a given occurrence of the disfavored behavior. It, therefore, follows that in order to claim successfully that prior restraints result in greater overall suppression of speech than do subsequent sanctions, it is necessary to establish that prior restraints have a systematically different impact on either the perceived unattractiveness of the threatened sanction or on the perceived probability that the threatened sanction will be invoked in response to a given violation of the law.

With respect to the first factor in this calculation, there is no apparent logical or practically necessary correlation between the severity of the sanction imposed in response to a violation of the law and the law's status as either a prior restraint or a subsequent sanction. In other words, there is no reason why laws classified as prior restraints should consistently impose upon violators more severe sanctions than all other laws. For example, speakers found liable for defamation, unquestionably a subsequent sanction, often have faced judgments in the multimillion- and multi-hundred-thousand-dollar range. It is difficult to imagine that sanctions imposed in response to the violation of speech-related injunctions ever reach such levels. In fact, instead of prior restraints consistently carrying with them more severe sanctions, the opposite may be true. As Professor Vincent Blasi has observed, "[S]anctions for the violation of injunctions and permit ordinances tend to be light in comparison with those commonly administered under the subsequent punishment regimes."[28]

[26] Nebraska Press Association v. Stuart, 427 U.S. 539, 559 (1976) paraphrasing A. BICKEL, THE MORALITY OF CONSENT 61 (1975).

[27] ROTUNDA ET AL., *supra* note 25, at 68.

[28] Vincent Blasi, *Toward a Theory of Prior Restraint: The Central Linkage*, 66 MINNESOTA LAW REVIEW 27 (1981).

It is a bit more difficult to evaluate the second factor in the calculation, whether prior restraints systematically influence the perceived probability of a legal sanction being imposed in response to a violation of the law. In his treatise on constitutional law, Professor Laurence Tribe has written: "[I]t might well remain the case that prepublication restraints, especially those affirmatively singling out the would-be disseminator, would deter far more protected conduct than criminal statutes ordinarily would. The latter is essentially a mute, impersonal threat; being told personally not to publish is apt to cause more second thoughts, no matter what defenses are ultimately available."[29]

Professor Tribe suggests that threats of legal sanction that are specific and personal in nature create stronger deterrents with respect to the targeted behavior than do more passive and impersonal threats. The conclusion he wishes to draw from this suggestion is that traditional prior restraints, such as judicial injunctions and denials of license applications, cause members of the regulated community to perceive the probability of eventual imposition of the threatened legal sanction as significantly higher than in the case of similar laws in the form of subsequent sanctions.

At least two points are worth noting in response to Professor Tribe's suggestion. The first is a matter of perspective. While it may be true that the deterrent effect on any given individual in the regulated community will differ depending on whether that individual is subject to specific, personal threats rather than uniform, impersonal ones, it does not necessarily follow that general use of the former in place of the latter would, on the whole, result in a larger net deterrent effect throughout the regulated community. This is the case because uniform, impersonal threats, while they may have less of a deterrent effect on any given individual, will have some influence on every individual in the regulated community. In contrast, specific, personal threats, while perhaps more potent with respect to each targeted individual, are limited in their scope, by definition, to one, or at the most to a very few, such individuals. The overall societal impact of such specific, personal threats, given the large number of individuals in society, is quite small.

One response to this argument might be that particular instances of a specific, personal threat, if publicized sufficiently, could serve as admonitory examples and thus be responsible for an overall societal deterrent much greater than one might otherwise predict. The problem with this response is that the same logic could be applied as easily and accurately to prosecutions of individual violations of a law involving a uniform and impersonal subsequent sanction. Taken as a whole, therefore, there appears to exist no persuasive reason to believe that prior restraints, when viewed from an overall societal perspective, will alter the regulated community's perception of the likelihood of a legal sanction being imposed in response to the utterance of prohibited speech to any greater degree than will laws using subsequent sanctions.

29 TRIBE, *supra* note 23, Sections 12–35, at 1042n.2.

In evaluating the relative strength and acceptability of deterrents likely to be produced by either prior restraints or subsequent sanctions, it is important to keep in mind that the kind of deterrents that are socially undesirable are those that discourage constitutionally protected speech. There is no jurisprudential reason to formally disfavor effective deterrents against speech deemed constitutionally unprotected by the courts. Therefore, even if one could establish convincingly that prior restraints generate more potent deterrents to speech than do subsequent sanctions, this point would have little constitutional relevance unless one also could establish that these more potent deterrents extend beyond the boundaries of unprotected speech into the realm of constitutionally protected speech.

Given the fact, as noted by Professor Tribe, that prior restraints tend to be more personalized and situation specific in nature than do subsequent sanctions, one might reasonably assume that deterrents generated by legal regulation in the form of prior restraints would be more carefully tailored and specifically focused than deterrents generated by laws in the form of subsequent sanctions. Consequently, prior restraints as a class would be less likely to extend their reach into the domain of constitutionally protected speech than would subsequent sanctions. From this perspective, then, it might appear that the current doctrine of prior restraint has it exactly backward. Subsequent sanctions, being more uniform and impersonal in nature than prior restraints, would appear to pose a significantly greater risk of deterring constitutionally protected speech. Thus, subsequent sanctions should be disfavored more vigorously than prior restraints as a form of speech regulation.

As the preceding analysis indicates, there is little support for the notion that traditional prior restraints are associated with more severe punishment than are subsequent sanctions. Similarly, there is little reason to think that the community as a whole will perceive the possibility of a legal sanction actually being imposed as being systematically greater in the case of prior restraints than in the case of subsequent sanctions. Moreover, there is good reason to suspect that subsequent sanctions will generate a chilling effect that reaches substantially more constitutionally protected speech than will laws in the form of prior restraints. Taken as a whole, this analysis strongly suggests that laws traditionally characterized as prior restraints are no more likely to produce a greater or more effective chilling effect on constitutionally protected speech than laws traditionally characterized as subsequent sanctions.

Notwithstanding this conclusion, both case law and scholarly literature present a number of arguments identifying attributes of traditional prior restraints that allegedly cause the implementation of such laws to extend their reach, and thus their deterrent effect, beyond the realm of constitutionally unprotected speech. These arguments typically focus on the operational characteristics of prior restraints, reflecting the second of the two general themes that characterize attempts to rationalize the current distinction between prior restraints and subsequent sanctions. Because the majority of these arguments have focused on systems of administrative preclearance and licensing, they will be examined in this context.

The major arguments advanced in this area are: (1) systems of administrative review and licensing are capable of subjecting a wider spectrum of speech to official scrutiny than are laws in the form of subsequent sanctions; (2) decisions to suppress speech are more easily made in the context of administrative review and licensing systems; and (3) administrative review and licensing systems both attract and reward persons who are disposed more favorably to speech suppression than the average citizen.

The argument frequently is made that: "A system of prior restraint normally brings within the complex of government machinery a far greater amount of communication than a system of subsequent punishment."[30] If taken literally, this argument asserts that it is possible to design systems of administrative preclearance and licensing that subject more speech to legal sanctions than do some laws in the form of subsequent sanctions. This seems clearly true. This interpretation, however, leaves open the prospect that laws may be designed in the form of subsequent sanctions that could screen a much broader range of expression than would carefully tailored systems of administrative preclearance. Since the logic of the argument leaves both of these possibilities equally open, it provides no basis upon which to formally favor either prior restraints or subsequent sanctions as a form of speech regulation.

Viewed in another light, the preceding passage could be interpreted as asserting that systems of administrative review and licensing, in general, will be designed to screen more speech than will laws in the form of subsequent sanctions. Without supporting evidence, however, this assertion is little more than subjective conjecture. Why should systems of administrative preclearance be designed to screen more speech than currently is screened by subsequent sanctions? Would it be practically possible to design a system of administrative preclearance that effectively could screen more speech than currently is screened by subsequent sanctions?

In answering these questions, it is important to remember that there currently exist laws in the form of subsequent sanctions, such as defamation and privacy torts, that make all speech subject to possible legal action and review. All speech is potentially subject to a civil action based on defamation, false light invasion of privacy, public disclosure of private facts, and appropriation. Not all speech will satisfy the requisite elements of these torts and thus generate legal liability for the speaker, but all speech will be "screened" in the sense that it has the potential to generate legal liability for the speaker should the requisite elements be present. It is difficult to imagine a workable system of administrative preclearance that could possibly require official licensing of a similarly broad spectrum of speech. This suggests that the conjecture upon which the aforementioned argument is based is not only questionable but very likely false.

30 Emerson, *supra* note 24, at 656.

Another important aspect of the larger analysis worth noting again in this context is the issue of constitutional relevance. Even if it could be shown that systems of administrative review are likely to be designed to screen more speech than will laws utilizing subsequent sanctions, this fact would be relevant for First Amendment purposes only if it could also be shown that such systems are, as a result, likely to screen more constitutionally protected speech.

In considering this issue, one could argue plausibly that systems of administrative preclearance, irrespective of their scope, are much less likely to impose legal burdens on constitutionally protected speech than are laws in the form of subsequent sanctions. This argument is based on the recognition that laws in the form of subsequent sanctions that provide for the possibility of civil liability as a result of the speech, such as defamation and privacy torts, allocate the power to initiate legal proceedings to the personally aggrieved subjects of the targeted speech. These are the very persons most likely to become aware of the speech in question and who are the most emotionally affected. These persons stand to benefit financially if subsequent sanctions in the form of civil liability are imposed. Thus, this group will be highly motivated to seek the imposition of all possible legal sanctions against the speaker. As between the aggrieved subject of the speech and a relatively impersonal government employee, it is not at all clear that more speech would be screened, in the aggregate, by a group of the latter than by a society full of the former. Nor is it clear that more constitutional mistakes, such as the legal prosecution of speech eventually found to be constitutionally protected, would be made by the latter than by the former. In fact, intuition suggests just the opposite.

In summary, the argument that systems of administrative review and licensing should be constitutionally disfavored because they are capable of subjecting a wider spectrum of speech to official scrutiny should be rejected. The argument ultimately rests upon an assertion that is either trivial in nature or likely false. Moreover, even if true, the argument carries little constitutional significance unless it also can be established that systems of administrative review and licensing are more likely than other laws to disfavor constitutionally protected speech. As the preceding argument has shown, however, there are reasons to believe that just the opposite is the case.

With regard to ease of suppression, the following argument is made:

> A government official thinks longer and harder before deciding to undertake the serious task of subsequent punishment – the expenditure of time, funds, energy, and personnel that will be necessary. Under a system of prior restraints, he can reach the result by a simple stroke of the pen.... For these and similar reasons, a decision to suppress in advance is usually more readily reached, on the same facts, than a decision to punish after the event.[31]

The thrust of this argument is that under a system of administrative preclearance, regulation of speech can be accomplished at far less cost to the government than it

[31] *Id.* at 657.

can under laws using subsequent sanctions. Much like the argument considered under the preceding discussion on breadth of coverage, this argument implicitly adopts as its analytical model the worst possible, and least likely, version of a system of administrative preclearance, asserting as it does that suppression of speech can be accomplished by a government official operating in a system of administrative preclearance "by a simple stroke of the pen."

For this argument to provide serious support to the prior restraint doctrine, which subjects all instances of administrative preclearance to exceptionally strict judicial scrutiny, it should be necessary to establish that nearly all practicable systems of administrative preclearance allow effective suppression of speech at significantly less cost to the government than prosecutions under laws using subsequent sanctions.

One factor weighing heavily against successfully establishing such a proposition is that systems of administrative preclearance regulating activities other than speech require formal procedures for information gathering and adjudication far more sophisticated and burdensome for the government than a solitary decision by an autonomous executive official. For example, the licensing and oversight of nuclear facilities, the testing and approval of new drugs, the issuance of patents, and even the procurement of military supplies and equipment are all areas in which the government's administrative activity must conform to specific guidelines that require adherence to burdensome and often expensive procedures. In fact, though it may be somewhat surprising given the conventional rhetoric surrounding the doctrine of prior restraint, it is also true that speech communicated by means of radio or television has, for more than fifty years, been subject to a sophisticated and procedurally complex system of administrative review and licensing.

The import of this is not that systems of administrative review and licensing are appropriate means by which to regulate speech simply because such systems currently exist. Rather, it is that legislatures have demonstrated their capacity to design systems of administrative preclearance and licensing that require of government officials far more than a single stroke of the pen to prohibit or approve proposed behavior. Moreover, a well-developed body of law regarding judicial review of administrative action is currently in place. Further, and often underplayed in analyses of the prior restraint doctrine, is the fact that constitutional law doctrines exist that are independent of the prior restraint doctrine that place significant limits on the design, scope, and operation of systems of administrative preclearance. Most notable in this regard are the doctrines of overbreadth and vagueness.

Given this current state of affairs, it does not seem persuasive to suggest that systems of administrative preclearance involving speech somehow systematically will fall outside of this existing structure and will be designed to require only a minimum of government effort to effect suppression. In other words, there is no reason to believe that prior restraint in the form of administrative preclearance will permit regulation of speech at an unusually low cost to the government.

An even more serious problem for the ease of suppression argument is that while the creation and maintenance of such systems frequently involve substantial government resources, subsequent sanctions are, by comparison, a tremendous bargain. This is because existing laws in the form of subsequent sanctions provide for civil liability in response to pure speech. Such laws, including most notably the defamation cause of action, generate powerful deterrents to speech without expending any government resources at all, save for the dispute resolution resources of the judiciary. Consequently, one can accurately say that there are laws in the form of subsequent sanctions, not just imagined but currently in force, that routinely lead to the prosecution of pure speech at virtually no marginal cost to the government. In this environment, it is not possible to support a doctrine that views such laws as relatively benign and that subjects all systems of administrative preclearance to especially strict judicial scrutiny on the basis that all, or even the majority of, such systems present the government with the opportunity to regulate speech at significantly less cost than do subsequent sanctions.

Finally, it should be noted again that First Amendment concerns regarding the relative ease of suppression of one scheme of regulation over another are only constitutionally relevant if it can be established that the more efficient schemes of regulation consistently tend to suppress speech that is constitutionally protected. In the absence of such a tendency, greater efficiency generally should be regarded as an attractive attribute of a given system of legal regulation.

Taking this line of reasoning one step further, one might argue that claims of greater efficiency with respect to systems of administrative preclearance may be irrelevant in any case. To the extent it can be shown that such laws consistently suppress constitutionally protected speech, their constitutional status under the First Amendment should be more properly analyzed and determined under the established doctrine of overbreadth. In this context, the question of whether such laws are or are not prior restraints is irrelevant. The attempt to characterize laws as prior restraints based on the likelihood of such laws being applied to constitutionally protected behavior results in little more than the recharacterization of the doctrine of overbreadth as the doctrine of prior restraint.

In suggesting that systems of prior restraint will likely attract participants with a propensity to suppress, it is commonly asserted that: "Most important, administrative preclearance requires a bureaucracy of censorship. Persons who choose to fill this role may well have psychological tendencies to overstate the need for suppression. Whether or not this is so, there are powerful institutional pressures to justify one's job, and ultimately one's own importance, by exaggerating the evils which suppression seeks to avoid."[32]

[32] Jeffries, *supra* note 22, at 422.

This third line of argument is particularly interesting because its message has been echoed by many commentators. For example, in addition to the quoted passage in the previous paragraph Professor Thomas Emerson has written:

> Perhaps the most significant feature of systems of prior restraint is that they contain within themselves forces which drive irresistibly toward unintelligent, overzealous, and usually absurd administration. One factor is the ability and personality of the licensor or censor. . . . No adequate study seems to have been made of the psychology of licensers, censors, security officials, and their kind, but common experience is sufficient to show that their attitudes, drives, emotions, and impulses all tend to carry them to excesses.[33]

Professor Martin Redish has written: "Nonjudicial administrative regulators of expression exist for the sole purpose of regulating; this is their raison d'etre. They simultaneously perform the functions of prosecutor and adjudicator and, if only subconsciously, will likely feel the obligation to justify their existence by finding some expression constitutionally subject to regulation."[34] The Supreme Court has also echoed this theme: "Because the censor's business is to censor, there inheres the danger that he may well be less responsive than a court – part of an independent branch of government – to the constitutionally protected interests in free expression."[35]

Given the frequency with which this argument is advanced, it is surprising to note in these presentations a complete absence of supporting empirical evidence. After all, without empirical support, or at least the development of a more sophisticated a priori argument, the basic thrust of this argument amounts to little more than an expression of distrust of governmental administrators as decision-makers, or, as the argument is sometimes phrased, a strong preference for judicial decision-makers. Preference becomes prejudice, however, in the absence of supporting evidence. Moreover, given that the persons advancing this argument are themselves judges and law professors, the expression of such a strong preference for legally trained decision-makers can be seen as somewhat parochial.

As Professor Howard Hunter has observed, a formal preference for judicial decision-makers in matters of speech regulation is ironic given the actual history of judicial suppression of speech, especially in those instances in which judges perceive free speech rights as being in conflict with the operation of a fair trial. This is, of course, a setting in which the judges' own bureaucratic interests are most clearly at stake. Professor Hunter writes:

> [T]he sixth amendment "fair trial" cases have produced a flurry of "gag orders," courtroom closures, and other limitations on both access to trials and dissemination of information about them. . . . Analysis of recent actions in this area demonstrates

[33] Emerson, *supra* note 24, at 658.

[34] Martin Redish, *The Proper Role of the Prior Restraint Doctrine in First Amendment Theory*, 70 Virginia Law Review 53, 76–77 (1984).

[35] Freedman v. Maryland, 380 U.S. 51, 57–58 (1965).

> that (1) the denial of access to information, to a place, or to an event such as a trial is an extraordinarily effective method of restricting the dissemination of information; and (2) except as limited by the Supreme Court, trial judges have been almost frenetic in their rush to issue orders denying access.[36]

Instead of intuition suggesting that judges should be the preferred decision-makers in matters of speech regulation, it may well be that administrative officials, operating under a system of administrative preclearance and possessing a desire to promote and maintain broad popular support for the particular bureaucracy in which they work, will be relatively more risk-averse in their decision-making. Thus, administrative officials may be relatively less prone to suppression of speech than judicial officers, who, after all, enjoy a much greater degree of formal insulation from popular opinion and from the legislature.

It should also be noted in this context that the decision with respect to the existence and size of a speaker's liability under many laws in the form of subsequent sanctions, such as defamation laws, frequently rests with a jury. There is little reason to believe that juries will be more tolerant, and some reason to believe that they will be far less tolerant, of unpopular speech and unpopular speakers than will officials operating within a system of administrative preclearance. In any case, in the absence of empirical support in one direction or the other, intuitive preferences for judicial decision makers, no matter how frequently sounded, constitute an insufficient foundation upon which to construct basic constitutional doctrine.

This third line of argument regarding an alleged greater propensity for systems of administrative preclearance to suppress speech possesses still another problem. Imagine a regular system of administrative preclearance and licensing that is clearly constitutional but for its possible characterization as a prior restraint. A government official operating within such a system has, in effect, the power to create a legal climate in which a sanction may be imposed legitimately on a speaker if the disapproved or unlicensed speech is in fact expressed. This is, in essence, no different from the power that now resides in and is exercised by all state legislatures, as well as Congress, when enacting legislation in the form of subsequent sanctions. In either case, nonjudicial decision makers are primarily responsible both for identifying the disfavored speech and for establishing the range of appropriate legal sanctions. Assuming the existence of no other constitutional defect in the regulatory scheme, there seems to be no special reason to object to the legislative branch delegating this power, under proper guidelines, to the executive branch. Legislatures, after all, have delegated such authority for decades. Precisely this situation exists at present, and has existed for more than fifty years without successful constitutional challenge, in the regulation of radio and television broadcasts. Given the continued vitality of this regulatory structure, it makes little sense to assert that

[36] Howard Hunter, *Toward a Better Understanding of the Prior Restraint Doctrine: A Reply to Professor Mayton*, 67 CORNELL LAW REVIEW 283, 287–92, 288–89 (1982).

significant regulatory discretion in the hands of administrative officials could possibly serve as the basis for a definition of presumptively unconstitutional prior restraints on speech.

This basic characterization of the work of officials operating within a system of administrative preclearance can also serve to refute attempts to distinguish prior restraints from subsequent sanctions on the basis of what has been called "adjudication in the abstract." In his 1981 article on the subject of prior restraint, Professor Vincent Blasi writes:

> One phenomenon common to licensing systems and injunctions governed by the collateral bar rule is what might be termed adjudication in the abstract. Under both systems, the final authoritative judicial decision regarding the legal status of a disputed communication takes place before the moment of initial dissemination. That typically is not true under the subsequent punishment regimes. When adjudication precedes initial dissemination, the communication cannot be judged by its actual consequences or public reception. The adjudicative assessment of speech value versus social harm must be made in the abstract, based on speculation or generalizations embodied in presumptions.[37]

If by the phrase "the final authoritative judicial decision regarding the legal status of a disputed communication," Professor Blasi is referring to the point at which someone formally determines, as a fact-finding matter, that a particular hypothetical instance of speech will, if expressed, violate the prohibitions of a preexisting statute, then adjudication in the abstract and its corresponding problems will arise in the case of judicial injunctions and systems of administrative preclearance to a greater degree than in the case of laws in the form of subsequent sanctions only to the extent that such laws define the targeted speech in terms of the harm that the speech inflicts. An example of such a law is defamation, which defines the kind of speech giving rise to legal liability on the basis of whether the speech can be shown to have injured the reputation of another. When applying such a law in a given case, judges and juries have the ability to work with established historical facts, including after-the-fact assessments of the actual harm caused by the targeted speech, in determining whether or not to impose legal liability.

Not all laws using subsequent sanctions take this approach, however; some define the targeted speech without any reference to the actual harm caused by the speech. A common example of such laws are those sometimes referred to as the "Son of Sam" statutes. These laws, existing in at least thirty-six states and in federal law, generally require a person convicted of a crime to forfeit the proceeds earned from the sale of rights to a reenactment or depiction of that crime, regardless of whether the sale of such rights can be shown to have generated injury or harm. When dealing with such a statute, or with any law that does not define the targeted speech

[37] Blasi, *supra* note 28, at 11, 49.

by reference to the harm generated by that speech, courts do not have the benefit of after-the-fact assessments of the actual harm caused by the targeted speech in determining whether to impose legal liability. This is true not because such assessments are inherently unavailable but because such assessments are, pursuant to the terms of the law, legally irrelevant to the issue of liability.

From a more general perspective, it is clear that to the extent laws utilizing subsequent sanctions define the targeted speech without reference to the harm actually inflicted by the speech, legislatures enact such laws through a process of prior adjudication that is as fully abstract and "based upon speculation or generalization embodied in presumptions" as the kind of prospective judgments made by judges issuing injunctions and executive officials operating within a system of administrative preclearance. Given the continued existence of just such laws, it is not descriptively accurate to distinguish between prior restraints and subsequent sanctions on the basis of the existence of adjudication in the abstract.

One final point. Imagine again a regular system of administrative preclearance and licensing of certain speech that is unquestionably constitutional but for its possible characterization as a prior restraint. It might well be that an administrative official operating within such a system will possess the practical power, if not the formal authority, to initiate legal proceedings once it has been shown that the unapproved or unlicensed speech has been expressed. The discretion exercised by an administrative official in such a situation is no different from the discretion now exercised by a prosecutor, who is also a government official, when deciding whether to initiate legal proceedings with respect to a possible violation of a criminal statute in the form of a subsequent sanction. The administrative official's discretion is also not remarkably different from that exercised by a private citizen deciding whether to initiate legal proceedings with respect to a perceived cause of action under civil law.

Because none of the three decision-makers in these typical situations is a judicial officer, it makes little sense to adopt or maintain an interpretation of the prior restraint doctrine, assertedly based on the comparative constitutional undesirability of nonjudicial decision-makers, that characterizes the first situation as a prior restraint, thus subjecting it to especially strict scrutiny, while at the same time characterizing the latter two situations as examples of relatively nonproblematic subsequent sanctions.

In fact, all of the problems identified by the proponents of this third line of argument regarding officials operating within systems of administrative preclearance would apply equally to settings in which administrative officials, such as government prosecutors and other officials, participate in decisions regarding the initiation of formal legal proceedings against suspected violators of laws that exclusively utilize subsequent sanctions. Due to the obvious similarity, at least in this context, between administrative officials exercising discretion within a system of administrative preclearance and administrative officials exercising discretion with respect to the prosecution of suspected violators of laws using subsequent sanctions, the perceived deficiencies of administrative officials as decision-makers, even if accepted as true, hardly serve as a rational basis to distinguish between prior restraints and subsequent sanctions.

If the aforementioned argument is accepted, then the definitional strategy that has become so much a part of the conventional wisdom surrounding the doctrine of prior restraint is exposed as being essentially circular in nature. The strategy involves replacing a doctrine that purportedly disfavors prior restraints with a doctrine that instead disfavors laws possessing one or more particular attributes, regardless of whether the identified attributes are uniquely, or even predominantly, characteristic of traditional prior restraints. By using the presence of certain undesirable characteristics as criteria for defining the disfavored category of prior restraint, the doctrine becomes internally self-justifying and therefore, from a legal point of view, tautological.

So long as the members of the disfavored category of prior restraints are chosen because they possess certain undesirable characteristics, then the prior restraint doctrine itself, which mandates that all members of the prior restraint category be subjected to strict judicial scrutiny, will always be facially rational. The problem is that the doctrine, when developed in this way, adds nothing substantive to legal analysis. Its application to a given set of facts does not resolve the issue of a particular law's constitutional status in one way or the other. The prior restraint doctrine does not serve to uncover or illuminate constitutionally relevant factors that may be present in a challenged law or regulation. Instead, all of the serious substantive analysis takes place when deciding whether a particular law is or is not a prior restraint.

The difference between a genuinely substantive doctrine of prior restraint and the current version of the doctrine is the difference between having substantive reasons for disfavoring members of an independently definable category and determining the members of a category exclusively by reference to the substantive reasons for disfavoring them. This latter approach is meaningful only to the extent that a high correlation exists between the population of the suspect category as determined by its overt definition or label and the population of the suspect category as determined by the presence in its members of the factors cited for disfavoring the category.

As a simple example of this point, suppose that there existed in a hypothetical pond fish of many colors and a variety of flavors. Over time, it is determined that the unappealing taste of yellow-colored fish makes them barely edible. Thereafter, it becomes a standard rule among fishermen in the relevant community not to keep for human consumption any yellow fish that are caught. This is an example of the first aforementioned categorizing strategy. The label given to the disfavored category, in this case "yellow," is independently determinable and it correlates highly with an important characteristic shared by the members of the category as so defined; in this case, their unappetizing taste.

Now suppose that the initial unhappy experience of consuming yellow fish led instead to a general rule among fishermen that no brightly colored fish should be caught for human consumption. Over time, the fishermen become more sophisticated in their approach, and they recognize that many brightly colored fish are, in fact, edible and delicious, while a number of dark-colored fish are not good to eat. Nonetheless, the term "bright" continues to be used to connote unappetizing fish, and the general rule among fishermen remains that "bright" fish should not be caught for human consumption, even though the generally accepted definition of that word among fishermen includes some fish that are in fact brightly colored and some fish that are unquestionably dark colored.

This is an example of the second aforementioned categorizing strategy. To preserve a generally accepted categorical rule, in this case, the general rule that brightly colored fish should not be caught for human consumption, the facial category label is maintained, but the members of the category increasingly are defined not by reference to the label. Instead, they are defined by reference to whether they deserve the result that the categorical rule dictates. In this case, unappetizing fish should not be kept for human consumption, and that result effectively is reached by using the categorical rule so long as only unappetizing fish are described as being "bright," regardless of their actual coloring.

In this kind of categorizing scheme, the factors used by the fishermen to determine which fish are and which are not appetizing are not revealed by looking only to the generally accepted categorical rule and its label. The categorical rule uses the term "bright" as little more than a linguistic surrogate for the substantive factors, or patterns of behavior, that are, in fact, employed to determine the desirability of the fish for human consumption.

This kind of categorical rule may be workable when employed within a relatively small and stable community of users. Such users may be able to determine to a reasonable degree of certainty the current definition of the category label by frequent exposure to the actual operation of the rule. Even in a large and diverse community, the use of this kind of categorical scheme may be effective, and perhaps necessary, in those cases in which it is not practically possible to explicitly articulate the bases upon which the relevant categorical decisions are made. For example, it is difficult to articulate, at least in any generic way, the specific factors that a jury uses to determine whether a defendant in a tort suit was at fault for causing harm to the plaintiff. For the purpose of formulating a general categorical rule, we often use the term "negligent." Thus, we say that the tort defendant will be made to pay the plaintiff if the jury finds the defendant to have been negligent. Largely because "negligent" is an unusual word that possesses little or no meaning in our language outside of the context of legal fault and responsibility, its use as a part of a general categorical rule regarding tort liability strongly indicates to an untutored member of the community that the term may carry with it in practice an unfamiliar or nonobvious meaning.

From this perspective, the worst of all possible categorical rules to be employed in a large and pluralistic community would be one that uses as its category label a term possessing some independent meaning in the language and at the same time interprets the term for purposes of the rule in a nonobvious or counterintuitive manner. The use of such a categorical rule can be deeply destructive, encouraging the uninitiated to incorrectly apply the result that the rule dictates. Consider, for example, the novice members of the fishing community, producers and consumers alike. They may have learned the categorical rule but are unaware of the special meaning that the term "bright" has acquired over time. Such persons will inevitably reject a lot of good-tasting brightly colored fish and retain, and consume, many unappetizing dark ones.

In attempting to maintain the viability of the prior restraint doctrine, courts and legal commentators have transformed it into this kind of a rule. The category label "prior restraint" has been retained, but the category has been defined in ways that bear no reasonable relation to the common sense meaning of the category label. In fact, the category has been defined so that the only common thread between members of the category is that they have been deemed to possess certain characteristics that make them deserving of the result that the rule dictates. Worse still, the traditional stalwart members of the category of prior restraint – judicial injunctions and systems of administrative preclearance – do not themselves reliably and consistently possess the characteristics now thought to define the category.

Given the highly problematic nature of the current version of the prior restraint doctrine, one question that naturally arises is whether it would not be best simply to retire it. One prominent legal scholar, Professor John Jeffries, has examined the Supreme Court's activity in the area of prior restraints and has reached this conclusion:

> In sum, therefore, I suggest that in confronting these and similar questions the conventional doctrine of prior restraint be laid to one side. In my judgment, that doctrine is so far removed from its historic function, so variously invoked and discrepantly applied, and so often deflective of sound understanding, that it no longer warrants use as an independent category of First Amendment analysis.[38]

Although Professor Jeffries' work in this area is largely unassailable, and although the foregoing analysis demonstrates the difficulty involved in developing an operationally meaningful distinction between prior restraints and subsequent sanctions, there may remain an appropriate place in First Amendment jurisprudence for a doctrine subjecting government actions resulting in a prior restraint on speech to strict constitutional scrutiny. Preserving such a role for the doctrine of prior restraint, however, requires rather radical surgery. It will require that the concept of prior restraint be taken literally.

The key to placing the prior restraint doctrine on sounder conceptual footing is a realignment of the legal definition of "prior restraint" with the common-sense

[38] Jeffries, *supra* note 22, at 437.

meaning of the phrase. To that end, both the doctrinal and the operational definitions of "prior restraint" would need to be revised to include all government actions, and only those government actions, that result in the physical interception and suppression of speech prior to its public expression. "Physical interception and suppression of speech" should mean literally the effective prevention by the government, either through confiscation or by any other physical means, of any speaker's attempt to communicate an idea, thought, or opinion to the public at large. The prior restraint doctrine then would operate to characterize all such government action as a presumptively unconstitutional violation of the First Amendment.

Excluded from the scope of this proposed definition of prior restraint are schemes of government regulation that do not impose sanctions on a speaker until the offending communication, has in fact taken place. Therefore, judicial injunctions prohibiting speech that are not violated until the prohibited communication occurs and systems of administrative preclearance that encourage compliance by the threat of subsequent punishment would not come within the purview of this proposed definition. This does not mean that government activities of this sort would, or should, be viewed as being constitutionally acceptable under the First Amendment. It simply means that the resolution of questions regarding the constitutionality of such activities would no longer involve an invocation or application of the prior restraint doctrine.

This proposed revision of the prior restraint doctrine possesses a number of attractive features that the current version lacks. From a doctrinal point of view, it presents a relatively coherent, generally understandable, and largely predictable definition of a prior restraint on speech. The development of such a definition would enable potential speakers to predict with greater accuracy whether a particular governmental sanction ultimately will be deemed unconstitutional as a prior restraint. Only this kind of predictability in the content and application of First Amendment standards creates a meaningful legal sanctuary in which free speech can flourish. Similarly, a more direct and understandable definition of prior restraint will serve as a more powerful and effective guide to legislatures as they enact new, and amend old, laws relating to speech.

In addition, this proposed version of the prior restraint doctrine is more rational from a policy point of view with respect to the critical distinction between prior restraints and subsequent sanctions. Once it is determined that the phrase "prior restraint" should include within its scope only those governmental actions in fact resulting in the physical prevention of speech prior to its public expression, then it is clear that prior restraints, as a class, pose a greater practical deterrent to constitutionally protected speech than do all other laws. This is the case because actual physical restraint is a far more effective form of speech suppression than almost any scheme of threatened legal sanction that is not imposed until after the public expression of the prohibited speech.

Moreover, and most significantly from the perspective of preventing the chilling of constitutionally protected speech, every instance of a literal prior restraint will, by definition, involve the actual suppression of speech. This is not the case with respect to laws that have been determined to come within the scope of the current doctrine of prior restraint, nor is it the case with respect to laws utilizing subsequent sanctions. Judicial injunctions are sometimes not obeyed. Speakers may, on occasion, communicate information without first having obtained the required license. In either case, the speech that is targeted by the legal regulation may be well chilled, but it will not necessarily be frozen. Precisely the same analysis applies when the applicable legal regulation is a law using subsequent sanctions.

Under the proposed revision of the prior restraint doctrine, however, every instance of a prior restraint will result in the suppression of speech. The important, and necessary, consequence of this fact is that every constitutional mistake made in the implementation of a literal prior restraint will involve the actual suppression of constitutionally protected speech. This is not the case with respect to the current doctrine of prior restraint, nor is it the case with respect to laws utilizing subsequent sanctions. This disparity fully justifies creating a formal legal distinction between literal prior restraints and all other laws and makes sense of the application of especially strict judicial scrutiny to all instances of literal prior restraints. In other words, it is primarily because literal prior restraints on speech significantly increase the practical stakes involved that it becomes possible to argue persuasively that such laws should be separately identified and subjected to strict judicial scrutiny through the operation of an independent constitutional doctrine.

Perhaps most importantly, the adoption of this proposed version of the prior restraint doctrine, due to its greater clarity, would result in stronger constitutional protection against government suppression of speech prior to its public expression. The practical value of this protection, to the extent that it now exists, is severely compromised by the confusion and indeterminacy that characterize the current prior restraint doctrine. It is important that constitutional protection against government activity that involves the physical suppression of speech prior to its public expression be clear and unambiguous because the practical consequence of such activity is that the targeted speech does not enter the public domain. When speech that the government attempts to suppress does not enter the public domain, the opportunity for democratic public oversight of, and reaction to, the speech-suppressive activities of the government is severely restricted, if not completely foreclosed.

A corollary to this argument, advanced by Professor Martin Redish, is that judicial use of the prior restraint doctrine to resolve First Amendment issues has, in some cases, turned the Supreme Court's focus away from more fundamental First Amendment concerns and thus created an unnecessary chilling effect on constitutionally protected speech. For example, in those cases in which government conduct violates the First Amendment even if not found to be a prior restraint on speech, the Court's reliance on the prior restraint doctrine to invalidate the conduct leaves open the possibility that this same speech-suppressive activity might be found constitutional if sufficiently redesigned and recast in the form of a subsequent sanction. Legislatures may respond to this possibility by authorizing similar government conduct in the form of laws using subsequent sanctions. Persons wishing to publish material that is the object of such laws certainly will think twice before relying upon a judicial finding of unconstitutionality.

It is also important in this context to note that adopting the proposed version of the prior restraint doctrine does not mean that judicial injunctions against speech or systems of administrative preclearance should be free of strict scrutiny under a First Amendment analysis. It means instead that the specific attributes of individual judicial injunctions and particular systems of administrative preclearance more properly should be understood and analyzed through the perspective of other constitutional doctrines, most notably the doctrine of overbreadth, rather than through the disorienting and ultimately irrational perspective of the prior restraint doctrine.

Further, acceptance of the more literal version of the prior restraint doctrine might well facilitate the development within First Amendment jurisprudence of a doctrine that would characterize as presumptively unconstitutional judicial injunctions and systems of administrative preclearance of speech that can be shown to actually possess one or more of the particular operational characteristics and undesirable attributes now thought to define the entire category of prior restraints. In other words, the adoption of a more literal version of the prior restraint doctrine could be the catalyst for the development of a more direct and relevant First Amendment jurisprudence dealing with judicial injunctions and systems of administrative preclearance.

A doctrine dealing directly with systems of administrative preclearance, for example, could be based upon the potential for such systems to: (1) permit the denial of a permit or a license without sufficient investigatory procedures or adequate judicial review; (2) place an unacceptable burden of initiative on potential speakers; or (3) delay or disrupt the timing of speech. Because these potentially speech-suppressive problems are not necessarily associated with government efforts to physically suppress speech prior to its public expression, it is appropriate, and conducive to much greater clarity in First Amendment analysis, that such a doctrine develops independently from the doctrine of prior restraint.

11

The Nature of Legal Scholarship in the Postrealist Era

With formal apprenticeships having largely become a relic of the past, the passing of legal culture to the next generation of lawyers, at least in the first few critical years of their assimilation into the profession, now takes place overwhelmingly at professional graduate schools of law. While the culture of law schools may not exert a continuing influence on mature practitioners, it does have a profound effect on the way that nearly every practicing attorney initially understands the nature and function of law. In at least this way, the concepts of law and the legal system that are in vogue among legal academics at any given time exert a powerful influence on the evolution of legal culture and on the way in which nearly every practicing attorney initially understands the nature and function of law.

Felix Frankfurter, a professor of law at Harvard Law School and subsequently an Associate Justice of the United States Supreme Court, wrote "[i]n the last analysis, the law is what the lawyers are. And the law and the lawyers are what the law schools make them."[1] Anthony Kronman, Sterling Professor and the fourteenth Dean at Yale Law School, has written, "However diverse their professional experiences may be in other respects . . . lawyers still share at least one thing in common: they have all been law students at one time or another, and it is as students that their professional habits first take shape."[2]

When I began the full-time teaching of law in the mid-1980s, one of the prevalent values among law school faculty was the desire to demonstrate to students that law could not be understood in a satisfying way as a system of definite rules that could be mechanistically applied to factual situations and thereby yield definitive results. It was thought to be important to make sure students understood that legally operative language was rarely self-defining, that ambiguity was frequently present,

[1] Rand Jack & Dana Crowley Jack, Moral Vision and Professional Decisions: The Changing Values of Women and Men Lawyers 156 (1989) (quoting Letter from Professor Felix Frankfurter to Julius Rosenwald (May 13, 1927)).

[2] Anthony T. Kronman, The Lost Lawyer: Failing Ideals of the Legal Profession 109 (1993).

and that value-laden choices could not be avoided in the process of interpreting and applying legal standards.

The mark of a sophisticated approach to legal analysis, either in print or in the classroom, was the eagerness with which one looked behind the surface of legal doctrine and sought to understand its deeper meaning by reference to the social purposes that it was intended to serve. The telltale sign of an outdated approach was a preoccupation with formal precedent and an insistence on deriving general principles from prior decisions that were then applied in a supposedly logically deductive fashion to resolve new problems. The most respected scholars and teachers were those whose primary focus was on the social purposes underlying the doctrine and who taught their students to habitually answer the question, "what does this doctrine mean?" by asking the question, "what set of social policies does this doctrine seek to advance?"

This was a time when both "Critical Legal Studies" and "Law and Economics" were vibrant and ascendant, and there nevertheless remained enough stalwart traditionalists to decry both movements. Different law schools were prominently aligned with one approach or the other. Passionate arguments frequently flared among adherents of different movements and among writers within a given movement. Eminent members of the legal academy publicly suggested that faculty members who embraced certain ideas about the nature of law did not belong in a law school classroom.

The feeling was everywhere in the air that big ideas were in play. The stakes were thought to be high. A newly published article by a prominent member of one movement or another was quickly sought out and examined to see in what way the analysis, and the debate, had been advanced. It was, in many ways, a great time to be a law professor. In the years since, things have settled down considerably.

Critical Legal Studies, as a separate school of thought, has all but vanished. Today, employing some of the concepts of economics to explain the operation and effect of legal doctrine hardly serves as an announcement of your allegiance to a distinct intellectual movement. Law schools appear to be far more concerned with their annual ranking in *U.S. News and World Report*, and with the growth of their endowments, than in doing intellectual battle over the proper understanding of the nature of law. Unconcealed and unapologetic careerism, both at the individual faculty and the larger institutional level, feels pervasive.

Looking back, it seems to me that an important part of what animated that period was its relative proximity to the seismic shift in the conventional understanding of the nature of the common law and appellate legal processes that was the legal realist-led paradigm shift from formalism to instrumentalism. It is the purpose of this chapter to consider some of the consequences for legal scholarship of this shift from formalism to instrumentalism.

As an activity that seeks to understand the nature and operation of law, and to communicate that understanding to others, legal scholarship can be expected to be profoundly affected by this paradigm shift. It is also an activity that is engaged in by a segment of the legal community, namely law professors, who have been among the most receptive to the shift and who have most eagerly pursued the paths that the new paradigm has offered. Moreover, as aforementioned, it is an activity that takes place primarily in law schools, and as such, it exerts an important influence on the view of law first encountered by the next generation of attorneys.

What is it that legal scholarship attempts to do? What work does it perform? For the purposes of this chapter, three distinct functions of legal scholarship can be identified. The first is to describe the history and the current state, and to monitor the future development, of legal doctrine. This could be called a primarily descriptive function. The second is to evaluate the degree to which existing doctrine, and proposed new doctrine, expresses and advances the optimal set of legal principles in a given area and to suggest possible improvements. This can be called a primarily normative function. The third is to serve the needs of the practicing bar and the legal academic profession. This can be called a primarily service function.

In a formalist environment, these three functions operate in close harmony. The classic legal analytical skill of inducing general principles of law from the resolution of discrete cases, and the deductive application of general principles to the resolution of new cases, is the fundamental unifying intellectual competence. It is thought to be principally practiced by the courts, especially the appellate courts, and it is generally described and explained in descriptive legal scholarship. It is critiqued and refined in normative scholarship. It is modeled for the practicing bar in publications, and it is taught to law students in law school courses.

One of the defining conceptions of the formalist paradigm is the central role occupied by traditional legal analysis. Given this centrality, the role of a law professor is characterized in large part by an expertise in this distinctively legal analytical skill. This expertise is brought to bear in understanding and describing the work of appellate courts, in critiquing that work, in offering suggestions for improvement, and in conveying this essential skill to succeeding generations of lawyers.

Under this conception, the professional role of law professor is largely coherent and consistent. They have developed a level of expertise and a facility in fundamental legal analysis that is brought to bear and expressed in their scholarship, teaching, and service to the practicing bar. Their authority to credibly engage in each of these activities arises from their possession of this essential expertise.

While the standard portfolio of professional activities engaged in by professors of law has changed very little over the last 100 years, the understanding of the nature of these various activities has undergone a profound transformation in the shift from formalism to instrumentalism. At the core of these changes is the deep loss of faith in the independence and determinacy of legal analysis occasioned by the success of the legal realist critique. This was accompanied by a consequent decline in the previously held consensus that general rules of law, and many of the specific results in discrete cases generated by the application of those general rules, were the logically mandated product of largely objective legal analysis.

For example: "The difficulty ... is that there will always be a point at which an extension of the logic of any constitutional principle of decision will run into the similarly extended logic of competing principles";[3] and "Even if one were to accept the existence of 'reasoned elaboration,' 'neutral principles,' or 'objective interpretation,' judges would still need guidelines to know how to choose between any number of possible competing principles ascertainable from different interpretations of the constitution, legislation and prior court decisions."[4]

This essential change in the perception of the nature of legal analysis, and thus also the status of its products, has been reflected, but by no means widely publicly acknowledged, by the courts. Despite the realist revolution and its full acceptance by most law professors, a large number of published trial court memoranda and appellate court opinions in this country continue to present themselves in traditional formalist terms. While, perhaps, not as aggressively deterministic in tone as in eighteenth century and the early part of the twentieth century, the current written and published products of our courts continue to offer their holdings as the result of a distinctive legal analysis and not an explicit balancing of social costs and benefits. This fact can easily be lost on modern law students, and some faculty as well, because the relatively small number of published appellate court opinions that do engage in open instrumentalist analysis are often widely noted, frequently celebrated, and become perennial inclusions in law school casebooks.

Of course, judges issuing binding and authoritative judgments in actual cases face powerful practical incentives to present their decisions in largely formalist terms. They may be justifiably concerned that an explicitly instrumentalist presentation of their analysis and conclusions would risk a lessening in the respect granted to their decisions by the parties in the instant case. Moreover, they may fear that an explicit and widespread embrace by the courts of the instrumentalist paradigm would eventually result in a serious questioning of, and ultimate challenge to, the legitimacy of their authority.[5]

In contrast, law professors, at least as legal scholars, face no such practical impediments to embracing the greater accuracy of the realist account and the instrumentalist paradigm that flows from it, and they have done so with vigor. This, however, has created an interesting and potentially troublesome situation for legal scholarship. Now legal scholars are addressing, as both realists and

3 Addison Mueller & Murray L. Schwartz, *The Principle of Neutral Principles*, 7 UCLA Law Review 571, 586 (1960).

4 Gary Minda, Postmodern Legal Movements: Law and Jurisprudence at Century's End 41–42 (1995).

5 See Chapter 6, Section 6.6 herein.

instrumentalists, legal texts, at least those produced by courts, which offer a predominately formalist perspective. A critical distance now exists between the approach to legal issues adopted by the legal scholar and the approach presented by the courts, a distance that did not exist under the formalist paradigm, even when the scholar may have disagreed with the specific conclusion reached by a particular court.

What, then, becomes of descriptive legal scholarship in this postrealist world? One type of descriptive legal scholarship that remains largely unaffected by this change is a kind of first-order, or primary, descriptive scholarship that attempts to more or less uncritically report on the results of appellate court cases and the substance of statutes and regulations. This kind of descriptive scholarship typically sets forth the facts, the holdings, and the court's analysis of a case, or of a series of cases in a given subject area, without attempting to offer an independent explanation of why the courts decided the cases as they did.

This kind of first-order descriptive legal scholarship can be conducted largely in the same way under either a formalist or an instrumentalist paradigm. One important difference, however, is in the degree of relative prestige that it is likely to be accorded. In a formalist world, such scholarship is thought to not only be recording the published public rationale that a court provides for its decision but also be describing the critical chain of analysis and reasoning that the court employed and that is likely to be a powerful guide to predicting decisions by other courts in this area in the future.

In a postrealist world, however, the formalistic analysis that a court provides for its holding is understood to frequently be an inadequate explanation for the court's decision to embrace one logically possible conclusion over others. At the heart of realism lies the recognition that many, if not most, interesting cases cannot be definitively resolved through the purely logical application of existing precedent and generally accepted legal principles. Therefore, in an instrumentalist world, a class of descriptive legal scholarship that primarily summarizes – and perhaps even attempts to systematize – the courts' own formalist justifications for their holdings in a particular area almost necessarily fails to provide a satisfying account of the underlying jurisprudential dynamics.

Thus, we have the inexorable logic of the sharp decline in prestige accorded to this kind of first-order descriptive scholarship in the current postrealist environment. When I began teaching law full time in the mid-1980s, the authors of the major treatises in the great areas of common law – Prosser, Corbin, Williston, and Wigmore, for example – were still venerated. That is no longer the case. Now, almost anyone who tries their hand at serious legal scholarship knows that, short of "incompetent," the worst thing that can be said of their work is that it is "merely descriptive."

Thus, descriptive legal scholarship in the postrealist era is pushed to engage in what could be called second-order descriptive scholarship. Here, the scholar may begin with a first-order description of the cases in a given area, but then they must go on to try to provide an account of what is really motivating the design and development of legal doctrine in this area.

However, legal scholarship that does little more than simply demonstrate that a court's formalist explanation for its holdings in a given case fails to provide an adequate account of its actual decisions and judgments can expect a rather cool reception. Such scholarship, while consistent with the prevailing instrumentalist paradigm, simply lacks a receptive audience. For legal academics, the basic realist critique of traditional formalism is well-accepted and well-known. The majority of active law professors have been exposed to repeated demonstrations of the critique of formalist texts in a variety of subject areas while in law school. To publish yet another illustration of the point in the context of a newly issued opinion, or a series of opinions, is hardly revelatory, and is unlikely to be enthusiastically received. After all, how many times can a legal scholar perform essentially the same realist critique of case after case in a given substantive area of law before the work becomes stale?

Even in the law school classroom, the repeated demonstration of the underlying indeterminacy of formalist explanations for court decisions brings rapidly diminishing returns, and for an interesting reason. In their role as a teacher and in their work with the practicing bar, a law professor faces very real pressure to maintain and to reinforce a legitimizing attitude toward the law. After all, law is an active professional discipline that continues to be conducted in largely traditional formalist terms, despite the larger intellectual revolution produced by the realists. This is especially true in trial and appellate court practice.

A perusal of briefs submitted to appellate courts quickly makes it clear that the current dominant presentation to appellate courts, both state and federal, continues to involve the invocation of statute or case precedent using more or less traditional legal analysis and standard logic to persuade the court to adopt the party's preferred outcome. Again, the tone of these presentations may be less severely deterministic than they were, and more of them may explicitly advance instrumentalist arguments. However, the great majority of them are unmistakably rooted in an implicitly formalistic conception of the appellate process.

Because the practice of law, especially before courts and other tribunals, is an active practical discipline that continues in large part to operate, at least on the surface, in a traditional formalist mode, and because law schools are involved in expensive professional education that promises students preparation to successfully engage in that professional practice, enormous implicit pressure exists to present the substance of legal doctrine to students, especially in core law school courses, from a largely formalist perspective. Thus, while a law professor would certainly want to expose their students to the realist perspective and to illustrate it in one or two actual cases, it is simply not, in this environment, a very effective presentation to students learning a legal subject for the first time to continue time after time to subject the appellate cases in the casebook to one variation or another of the standard realist critique.

Once the point is made and illustrated a time or two that courts are frequently disingenuous in the deterministic manner in which they explicitly justify their holdings, there is not much more to say. One can introduce and explicate what is obviously the professor's own understanding of the social choices presented in the field, and then compare and contrast competing views while marching through existing legal doctrine announced by appellate court decisions that have already been exposed as somewhat disingenuous. This is hardly an uplifting intellectual experience for students encountering the study of law for the first time.

For example, let's assume that a scholar of corporate law was convinced from their years of study that the mechanisms that generate legal doctrine in that area had been substantially captured by corporate management interests and that nearly all of the current rules, from the business judgment rule to the waivability of the duty of loyalty to the regulation of executive compensation, reflect a grossly unfair favoring of management interests over the interests of every other corporate constituency. While it would certainly be appropriate for the scholar to introduce this idea to the students in their introductory corporation law course, it would be tedious indeed for all of the doctrinal material to be presented exclusively from this perspective.

It would be not only tedious but also ineffective since one of the obligations of the professor teaching such a course within the context of professional education is to prepare the students to operate effectively in the current legal environment. This includes helping law students to become conversant with the conventional wisdom and the body of generally accepted principles and arguments currently at play in the field, even if the professor is personally convinced that much of it serves as a kind of legitimizing myth.

This would be somewhat analogous to a professor of medicine in a traditional university medical school who became persuaded over time that a combination of unorthodox alternative therapies, such as homeopathy, herbal treatments, and massage, was a far more effective response to a variety of illnesses than those offered by traditional scientific medicine. This faculty member might pursue these beliefs in their research and their writing, and they could well turn out to be objectively correct in many respects, but they should not be featuring these alternative theories in their course in internal medicine to medical students. They need not pretend to their students that they have full faith in the current conventional understanding and techniques of internal medicine, but they are nevertheless obliged to competently and thoroughly expose their students to them. This is part of the nature of professional education and the role of a teacher in a professional school.

It can be seen, then, that when legal scholars engage in the act of describing legal processes and the substance of legal doctrine, which activity takes place primarily when they teach law students in law school, they do so within a context of professional education that more or less compels them to present the procedures and the doctrine as coherent, rational, and largely aligned with the conventionally understood public good, or at least seeking in good faith to achieve a reasonable version of that public good. They face this pressure year after year, semester after semester, in every core law school course that they teach. Moreover, as aforementioned, continued repetitions of the basic realist critique contained in their scholarship, or repeated illustrations of it on newly produced appellate court cases, is unlikely to generate much positive response. This powerful dynamic exists completely irrespective of whether or not such a view of the law and legal processes is an accurate and true account.

Thus, one can come to appreciate that the shift from a generally accepted formalist paradigm to the current postrealist instrumentalist paradigm has created a subtle but profound separation between the law professor's role as a legal scholar and their role as a law school instructor and service provider to the bar. In the former role, the scholar seeks to understand the nature of law and legal processes and to state what is true as they see it. In the latter two roles, they are often obliged to abandon the more cynical or radical aspects of their understanding in an effort to help students and practitioners work effectively within the existing faiths and conventional understandings of the current system.

This tension comes most clearly to bear in the case of first-order descriptive legal scholarship. While not much respected by other legal scholars who have absorbed the realist critique and thus do not see a summary of courts' own words as adequately explanatory, this kind of formalist work is still quite valuable to students and to practicing members of the profession who must, regardless of their personal views, successfully navigate in these waters.

This tension is also prevalent in another particular kind of second-order descriptive legal scholarship. This is the kind of descriptive scholarship that seeks to accurately describe what it is that is motivating the choice of legal doctrine without the uncritical reliance on the published words of the decision-makers, and without necessarily accepting that the motivating factors are tied to the furtherance of public values and the public good. Take, for example, a legal scholar who is interested in finding out why a certain provision exists as it does in the Internal Revenue Code. After substantial research, they are convinced that the provision in question was included in the Act by its sponsors in large part because it would generate substantial benefits for the timber industry and that the senator from a large timber-producing state absolutely insisted on its inclusion as a condition of their critically needed support for the bill. Is this the kind of descriptive analysis of the provision that would be highly valued if offered by a legal scholar in a published article? Most likely not. Such an explanation for the existence of the provision, even if entirely realistic and accurate, is simply not particularly relevant to, nor very useful in, the practice of the profession of law.

To further illustrate this point, imagine an entire treatise on tax law that painstakingly traces similar practical political reasons for the existence of the various provisions in the Internal Revenue Code. Such a book might make for interesting background reading, but it would be of very little sustained usefulness to a practicing attorney, a law student, or even a legal scholar. It is certainly not what most persons seeking out a treatise on tax law would be looking for.

As these examples illustrate, it should be understood that legal scholarship, even predominately descriptive legal scholarship, is not seeking the kind of disinterested objective description of reality that one might associate with a natural science such as physics or chemistry. I do not mean by this that there are sociological forces within the community of legal scholars that influence the award of benefits and the allocation of grant funding so that at a given time some ideas and theories may be advantaged over others, as might well occur in the fields of physics or chemistry. I mean instead that broad vistas of the accurate description of the making of law and its implementation are simply of little value within the realm of legal scholarship, as is illustrated by the aforementioned tax treatise illustration.

Legal scholarship operates within the context of an active and practical complex of social systems in which authoritative law is created, maintained, and applied to discrete cases with outcomes that have serious consequences for individuals. There are, as with any such complex social system, important conventions and shared understandings that play an important role in making the system operate reasonably well: existing law is largely coherent and rational; on the whole, it seeks to further important social values; and those who administer the law and make critical decisions are, overwhelmingly, striving to be fair and impartial and are competent at performing the function. Descriptive legal scholarship, no matter how accurate and true, that constantly challenges and contests these working assumptions is simply not very useful, and it is, as a practical matter, neither much valued nor much present in our current environment.

As a final illustration of this point, imagine that a series of newspaper articles reveal convincingly that a large percentage of the trial and appellate judges currently working in a given city regularly accept bribes from lawyers practicing before them and regularly respond to the receipt of these bribes by ruling in these lawyers' favor. What could reasonably be done with this in the realm of legal scholarship? An article detailing the various ways in which attorneys who are so inclined are able to identify judges who may be receptive to bribes and the methods by which the bribes can be successfully covertly transferred and the corresponding benefits assured? An article suggesting ways in which opposing counsel might come to suspect that the judge in their case is being bribed by opposing counsel? A scrupulous review of the existing precedent in that jurisdiction that could be the product of this tainted process? Not likely. The only plausible bit of legal scholarship that is likely to emerge from such revelations is an article outlining the various rules of judicial conduct and criminal law that are likely to have been violated by this conduct and the professional disciplinary and criminal procedures that will come into play in their enforcement.

This same response by legal scholars could be expected, and can be observed, to reports of significant misconduct by legislators in the crafting of statutory law. One can read a great deal of legal scholarship focused on statutory acts, statutory schemes, and various theories of statutory interpretation without encountering any sustained attention to the role of sophisticated lobbyists, special interests, logrolling, or earmarking in the formation of that legislation, or the implications of such routine legislative influences on the possible interpretation of the resulting law. Descriptive legal scholarship, at least thus far, is work that overwhelmingly seeks to explain and to understand the law from the perspective, and within the working context, of the legal profession.

Given these various tensions, one can see that a different kind of second-level descriptive scholarship can be imagined that might satisfy both the intellectual demands of realism and the more practical demands of students, attorneys, and judges. Moreover, this kind of descriptive legal scholarship would fit perfectly within the traditional jurisdiction of the legal scholar. Such second-level descriptive scholarship would attempt to depict existing doctrinal law in a given area as the expression of an underlying, even if unarticulated, set of social goals or principles.

Thus, for example, the common law rules regarding the tort law cause of action of negligence are described as being designed to encourage efficient, but not excessive, levels of precautionary investment. Traditional contract doctrine is described as being designed to maximize beneficial reliance. Property law doctrines dealing with private nuisance are described as being designed to place the burden of precaution upon the least cost avoider.

This kind of second-level descriptive legal scholarship masterfully combines an implicit rejection of precedent-based logical formalism in a way that satisfies the demands of realism with a wholehearted embrace of the ultimate rationality, coherence, and purposefulness of the law that is more or less demanded by the legal scholar's professional role. The product of such an approach can be enormously complicated and sophisticated. It can also avoid almost all taint of cynicism regarding the legal system and it can promise to its readers a potentially powerful guide to the likely future judgments of appellate courts.

In addition, such an approach to legal scholarship typically substitutes some set of general standards – efficiency, economic productivity, deterrence, compensation, risk spreading, beneficial reliance – for the traditional legal maxims and generalized statements of legal principle of the formalist paradigm, and then works out an explanation for the broad array of doctrine in a particular subject area by deductive reasoning from these new first principles. In this way, legal scholarship of this sort enjoys the satisfying appearance of objectivity and logical inevitability that was thought to be the hallmark of formalism in its heyday while still appearing to be consistent with postrealist perspectives. It is little wonder then that such scholarship has flourished, and perhaps can fairly be said to have dominated the field, during the last quarter of the twentieth century and at least the first quarter of the twenty-first.

Descriptive scholarship of this sort makes a most remarkable claim. It purports to discover retrospectively the real, genuine, internal calculus of decision-making employed by courts in creating and refining common law over hundreds of years, when the courts that actually produced this vast body of doctrine were required to explain their decision-making process in writing and made relatively scant, if any, mention of the general standards and principles that it is suggested they were pursuing all along. The existence of unconscious processes of this sort exerting such a strong and systematic influence upon a particular individual's outward behavior may seem plausible after Freud, and one can also imagine a specific public decision-maker being less than fully candid about the reasons for coming to a given conclusion, but the claim is quite hard to accept when it is generally applied to the professional work of thousands of appellate court judges operating largely independently over hundreds of years.

Furthermore, as a descriptive effort, it is difficult to know just how the claims of such legal scholarship could be definitively refuted. It hardly seems fair to such work to say that it is somehow wrong and discredited because not all of the traditional legal doctrine in a given area conforms to the suggested general principles. Surely it still remains a remarkable thing to be shown just how much of the common law of torts, contracts, and property conforms to the expectations and predictions of law and economics, even if every last doctrine, or even some significant segments of a particular body of law, does not do so.

But to judge this kind of work as important and valuable on this basis, as it unquestionably is, is to acknowledge that it is not descriptive analysis in the usual, traditional academic sense. Unlike an attempt, say, to describe a natural phenomenon, the failure of this kind of legal scholarship to explain the presence of three or four visible characteristics and to be unable to precisely predict the response of the object of study to certain stimuli is apparently not fatal to its perceived value as a descriptive thesis.

This kind of second-order descriptive legal scholarship does not claim to offer a complete and accurate explanation for the common law in any given substantive area, and thus its failure to fully account for all aspects of the doctrine under examination, or to predict all future movements in the law, should not significantly diminish its importance or its value. It is not, then, like a descriptive account of the physical communication among bees in a hive, or the movement of stars and planets. There is not really an expectation that further research and discovery will result in the refinement of a unified set of principles that can fully account for all of the law of contract, or torts, or property. Nor is there really any prospect of additional data being revealed that will somehow definitively refute these kinds of descriptive theories. That traditional tort law doctrine can be characterized as advancing values such as economic efficiency, risk spreading, or corrective justice is interesting and important even if it is thought that such descriptions do not fully and completely account for all of the existing doctrine.

If attempts to describe the law in this way are not like descriptive efforts in the natural sciences, where the basic measure of success is the degree to which the explanation accounts for observable features and predicts future action, then how should they be viewed? On what basis can they be evaluated? How should one determine if a descriptive theory of this sort is improved by a suggested refinement?

There are at least two possibilities that can serve as instructive examples. One is non-empirical descriptive work in sociology and psychology. Here, as in law, academics look at complex human phenomena and attempt to describe or to characterize them in a meaningful way. The work is intended to offer important insights and perspectives on the subject but does not set forth a verifiable, or refutable, descriptive account. The work of Sigmund Freud, for example, is incredibly powerful and has been enormously influential irrespective of whether it is, in modern scientific terms, strictly accurate and true. The same can be said for the work of Carl Jung. Which is the superior account? By what criteria should one go about answering that question? Given the ways in which both thinkers have enriched the culture and added to our insights into human psychology, does this question have any real practical meaning?

Another, not inconsistent, but perhaps more controversial approach to examining this kind of second-order legal scholarship is to treat it as being analogous to the academic discipline of literary criticism. Both disciplines look at a large written canon and seek to comment insightfully upon it. Neither necessarily believes that only the conscious intentions of the individual authors of the work should control its appropriate interpretation. The identification and explication of overarching or underlying themes in the canon is highly valued. Counterintuitive and novel insights and perspectives, if plausible, are also valued highly. Creativity and elegance of expression matter. The degree to which a descriptive theory or insight can thoroughly account for every aspect of the texts under consideration matters little. Empirical verifiability is more or less irrelevant.

Like non-empirical work in psychology and sociology, and academic work in literary criticism, the quality and value of second-order descriptive legal scholarship will inevitably be determined by a consensus of opinion in the relevant community. Beyond the very fundamentals, such as logical consistency and clarity of expression, the value of scholarship of this sort is in the degree to which it is considered interesting and insightful – values that are both highly contingent and perspective-dependent. One can consequently expect trends and countertrends, movements and countermovements. Rarely, if ever, will work that is considered truly important come from an unexpected source. Much of the basis for the evaluation of such work will necessarily be aesthetic.

Given this, and given the larger legal culture within which legal scholarship is produced and consumed, one would expect that over time, a strong preference would develop for descriptive scholarship that seeks to show that long-standing legal doctrine can be understood to implicitly embrace and to promote important social values. For the same reasons, work that seeks to demonstrate that a certain legal doctrine, or a doctrinal area, is logically incoherent, or often inappropriately applied, or applied in a manner that is inconsistent with its stated rationale, is not likely to be highly valued, at least not for long.

In tort law, for instance, different values will likely be placed on two different articles addressing the special limited duty rules of negligence applicable to the owners and occupiers of land. An article that seeks to show that these rules advance efficient use of real property would be thought to be a more sophisticated and significant contribution than an article that describes the rules as an incoherent mess whose primary effect is to favor the economic interests of relatively wealthy landowners over those who are physically injured on their land. Similarly, an article or book that claims to identify previously undiscovered underlying principles that unify and make sense of the United States Supreme Court's jurisprudence regarding the dormant commerce clause would likely be more highly valued than a similar work whose main purpose was to demonstrate that the existing cases lack convincing rationale and cannot be logically reconciled.

Perhaps this difference in the prestige accorded to the first kind of descriptive legal scholarship over the second results from a widely held belief that the former is simply more likely to be true than the latter, that long-standing common law doctrine most likely makes good sense at some level, and that the search for those underlying principles – even when they are not articulated by the appellate courts themselves – is a more valuable scholarly activity than a purely negative critique of the doctrine. While possible, it could be noted that such a bias is not normally thought to be a virtue in other areas of academic work. For example, research into the efficacy and side effects of a new medicine should not be considered more of a contribution to the literature if the results confirm the value of the drug than if the research uncovers previously unknown harmful side effects and problematic interactions with other drugs.

Interestingly, one can see a similar bias in the field of literature. Work that attempts to uncover and explain previously unrecognized levels of meaning and sophistication in the works of a celebrated author, like Shakespeare, is quite likely to be viewed as more valuable than work whose thesis is that the author's use of symbolic images is, in fact, far less coherent and rich than is generally supposed. Similarly, one can suspect that both Freud and Jung have had a more powerful and lasting impact on the broader culture than B. F. Skinner has had, in part because their depictions of human nature are so much more attractive and appealing than the ones offered by behaviorism – this, despite the fact that Skinner's work has yielded far more in the way of empirically verifiable predictions and results.

In the field of legal scholarship, the value of descriptive academic work to judges, practicing attorneys, and law students is simply much greater if it helps them to better understand, rationalize, and manipulate existing legal doctrine than if it describes that same doctrine as a product of flawed logic, an inconsistent line of cases, or extra-judicial social influences. This difference in the relative value of the work to the bench, the bar, and law students is largely independent of whether the one account or the other is actually more convincing, or more accurate. Because the necessary currency of the realm of daily practice before courts is the fundamental rationality and reasonableness of existing legal doctrine, sophisticated descriptive legal scholarship that produces the consequence of legitimizing and rationalizing existing law is considered more valuable and is thus likely to garner greater prestige and professional rewards for its author than more critical work, irrespective of the likely underlying accuracy of the description.

Second-order descriptive legal scholarship of the sort aforementioned is likely to share one further characteristic with the field of academic literary studies, which is a tendency toward increasing narrowness and hyperspecialization over time. After all, the canon that is the subject of study in each field, while not static, is relatively stable and, to some degree, fixed. It has been the object of scrutiny and examination in professional academic work for a long time. Significant additions to the existing body of published material in each area are, therefore, most likely to be found in smaller and smaller niches.

For a scholar working in descriptive legal scholarship, identification of a reasonably meaningful topic that has not enjoyed sustained attention in the existing literature is no easy task. Inevitably, that opening is more likely to be found in a quite narrow or a highly specialized approach to the subject. For instance, imagine the enormous difficulty faced by a current English graduate student who is told that their dissertation must be on some aspect of the work of Shakespeare. The same would hold true for a legal scholar who is hypothetically told that their next professional article must be on the doctrine of consideration in the law of contract.

A number of consequences flow from this ever-greater narrowing of the focus and perspective of much of descriptive legal scholarship. One consequence is that, over time, significant energy is sapped from the enterprise. From an academic perspective, we are now here at the end of the first quarter of the twenty-first century, nearly a century into the paradigm shift from formalism to instrumentalism occasioned by realism. The basic realist critique has been by now frequently stated and restated and has been applied to a wide variety of legal fields and materials. The most likely instrumentalist accounts of nearly every area of legal doctrine have been developed and reviewed and challenged. This is not to say that more interesting and productive work in these areas is not to be expected, but it does mean that the great majority of the work now being done is primarily in the fine stitching.

Perhaps as a result, a kind of cold-eyed careerism seems to be pervasive in the legal academy, with the greatest excitement and tumult being reserved for the annual publication of law school rankings in *U.S. News and World Report* News and the ever-increasing lateral movement of individual faculty members among the more elite institutions. It has been some time since a book or a law review article has been excitedly passed from hand to hand and treated as virtually required reading among law professors not working in that same subject area. Although political affiliations may still matter, it appears that no one with the right credentials and a sufficiently long list of publications is any longer in danger of not being hired because of their jurisprudential commitments.

A second likely consequence of this narrowing of field and focus in descriptive legal scholarship is a reduction in the attention that this work attracts in the larger culture and an attendant reduction in its general influence. The notice and description of recently published academic work in medicine, genetics, finance, and psychology is commonplace in the popular press and broadcast media. Not nearly so much, if at all, with legal scholarship, despite the law being, at least on its face, a far more practical and accessible subject. This is also the case despite lawyers and legal processes being the focus of countless dramatic programs on television and the consistent and sustained coverage that specific legal cases receive in broadcast and print news.

This current relative lack of influence, perhaps even relevance, of descriptive legal scholarship in the larger culture may well extend to the practicing parts of the legal community itself. Very recently, a group of federal judges speaking at a symposium made it quite clear that they find very little value in current legal scholarship. An account of the conference in *The New York Times* included the following:

> "I haven't opened up a law review in years," said Chief Judge Dennis G. Jacobs of the federal appeals court in New York. "No one speaks of them. No one relies on them." In a cheerfully dismissive presentation, Judge Jacobs and six of his colleagues on the United States Court of Appeals for the Second Circuit said in a lecture hall jammed with law professors at the Benjamin N. Cardozo School of Law this month that their scholarship no longer had any impact on the courts.[6]

This narrowness and specialization of descriptive legal scholarship also causes greater conflict between a law professor's role as a legal scholar and their role as a teacher of law students. In core law school courses, students are generally introduced to the subject matter of the course, led through a broad survey of the legal doctrine in the area, and exposed to at least the conventional understandings, theories, controversies, and open questions in the field. The approach to the material that is likely to be most effective in performing this teaching function is not likely to be fertile ground for productive professional scholarship, and vice versa. Put slightly differently, the legal scholar who would be understandably dismayed to be told that their next article must be focused on the doctrine of consideration nevertheless must guide their first-year law of contract students to a full understanding of that doctrine and must do so semester after semester, year after year.

A further effect of the continuous flow of published insight and commentary on the same basic body of materials and the consequent difficulty of identifying

[6] Adam Liptak, *When Rendering Decisions, Judges Are Finding Law Reviews Irrelevant*, New York Times, Mar. 19, 2007, at A8.

promising ground for new work is that scholars facing such a situation are likely to aggressively search for ways of expanding the definition of the field. During the last quarter of the twentieth century and into the early part of the twenty-first, there has been a virtual explosion in interest and resources devoted to international and comparative aspects of the law. The same has occurred in the area of interdisciplinary work. While neither of these phenomena can reasonably be said to have been caused by the pressure of scholarly demands, both trends are entirely consistent with a strong, professionally generated need to expand the field of scholarly inquiry.

Another strategy that legal scholars can employ to find fresh topics for study is to move quickly to examine any newly produced legal materials. It is now rare for as many as six months to pass before formal scholarly analysis has begun to appear regarding any significant decision issued by the United States Supreme Court. Editors of law reviews have noted that the submission cycle following the issuance of a highly anticipated Supreme Court opinion will inevitably include dozens and dozens of articles discussing that case.

On the whole, this rapid responsiveness to new legal developments can be thought to be a positive feature of legal scholarship. Some less attractive features, however, can also be identified. One is that the rapid response to, for instance, a new Supreme Court case can be thought to largely occupy the field. Aside from a scholar who possesses an already well-established reputation and can enjoy the luxury of extended reflection, the great majority of law professors know that they must quickly produce an article discussing that case. If their article is not included in the next submission cycle, they run the risk that law review editors will have already seen the earlier submissions, will have either chosen one themselves or assumed that other reviews have, and will view the case as having already received sufficient treatment. This dynamic is likely to result in less thoughtful and less insightful published commentary on many of the most important legal cases than might otherwise have been produced, an ironic result given that few people look to law reviews for breaking legal news.

A second, even less attractive, feature of an environment that encourages an aggressive competitive leap by scholars to rapidly analyze and discuss important new legal developments is that this pressure, combined with the natural incentive to enhance the apparent significance of the article, will cause scholars who are examining a new phenomenon or development to make more of it than perhaps it is. Consequently, under such conditions, one might expect major trends to be spotted, highlighted, and advanced on a rather modest, perhaps even inadequate, basis. Thus, one sees the rapid rise and eventual decline in the visibility of doctrines that, with greater reflection, may not have possessed that much potential from the start. Just in the area of tort law, both market share liability and hedonic damages come to mind as examples.

Does the picture for legal scholarship brighten when one turns from a consideration of descriptive scholarship to an examination of normative legal scholarship?

Normative scholarship is meant here to describe legal scholarship that purports to evaluate the relative quality or attractiveness of a legal doctrine or that advances a preferred legal treatment of a given problem or issue. Of course, a given work of legal scholarship may combine elements of the descriptive and the normative in the same way that it may combine first-order description with second-order description, but the distinction remains meaningful.

Under a formalist paradigm, there is not much difference in the basic analytical approach that a scholar would be expected to take when engaging in either descriptive or normative work. Both would be grounded on an application of traditional, precedent-based, facially logical legal analysis. For example, a legal scholar working in the formalist tradition who is examining a particular appellate court opinion might begin by describing the formalist analysis set forth by the court. They might then evaluate the soundness of the court's analysis and critique it, offering suggestions for improvement in the future treatment of the issue. The primary tool employed by this scholar in pursuing this work, either the description of the court's analysis or their own evaluation of it, is traditional legal analysis, looking primarily to existing precedent and principle and applying inductive and deductive logic to generate conclusions.

Because the essential intellectual skill used in this work is traditional legal analysis, it seems both appropriate and inevitable that it be the professional work of law professors. This is the central intellectual skill that they were taught as students in law school and that they now teach their students in law school courses. The universe of materials required by the legal scholar working within a formalist paradigm is all more or less readily available in the law library.

This basic approach to normative work is substantially the same for that class of postrealist scholarship that functionally substitutes a defined set of abstract values and goals for formalist precedent and principle as previously described. The scholar starts with the assumption that a fundamental goal of legal doctrine in a given area is, or should be, the pursuit of certain conditions, such as the maximizing of efficiency in a way that will support increased economic productivity. Or the scholar begins with the assumption that the law should seek to achieve fundamental fairness, or social justice, or to maximize human dignity, defined in a particular way. The evaluation of existing legal doctrine is then based on an analysis of how well it performs the defined function, and suggestions for change are all based on ways in which it could more effectively achieve the identified goals.

So long as the set of values that are used to substitute for precedent and conventional legal principle are sufficiently abstract, this kind of analysis can look very much like traditional formalism. It is distinctive enough, and sufficiently engaged in the analysis of primary legal materials, to feel that it rightly belongs in the province of legal scholars. The definition and refinement of the substitute values used in this type of work are typically borrowed from other academic disciplines, such as economics or moral or political philosophy, and are not traditionally part of a lawyer's education, but most of what is borrowed is abstract in nature and reasonably accessible. Still, as with traditional formalism, the materials required by a legal scholar doing this kind of work are all more or less readily available inside the law library, or not far from it.

It is when one steps away from these highly abstract, quasi-formalist approaches to legal scholarship, however, that things quickly get much more problematic. Once the realist critique effectively exposed and debunked the logical determinism of formalism, at least for most academics, the question as to what the basis should be for an appellate court choosing one possible version of a legal doctrine over another was effectively reopened. For example, on what rationale should a court decide that a therapist either does or does not have a formal legal duty to warn another of the possible danger posed by a patient?[7] On what analysis should a court determine that the tort law of that jurisdiction either does or does not include a duty to affirmatively aid?[8]

The alternative to formalism that has thus far been accepted by most of the legal community in this postrealist period can be called instrumentalism. Rather than viewing the common law as seeking to develop over time an abstractly ideal set of legal doctrines – a natural law – instrumentalism sees the law as one of a collection of societal responses, or instruments, that can be deployed to try to solve current problems and to achieve desired goals. Thus, criminal law is seen less as the abstract working out of a catalog of undesirable behaviors that are philosophically deserving of formal societal sanction and more as a social system, necessarily working in tandem with other social systems, that seeks to reduce the occurrence of certain kinds of behavior and their resultant harm.

Far from being a slowly evolving and ever-improving body of bedrock legal principles and the more specific legal doctrines that logically flow from them, as one might view the ever more accurate and evolving body of scientific laws and principles in a natural science such as physics or chemistry, law would be expected, from an instrumentalist perspective, to readily change over time and across different jurisdictions, sometimes dramatically, in response to changes in the perception and prioritizing of current social needs and goals. In this context, the measure of the quality of a given legal doctrine is the degree to which it effectively responds to an existing social problem or helps to achieve a particular desirable goal. It is the practical consequence of the legal doctrine in the world, not its logical consistency with preexisting precedent and principle, that serves as the benchmark against which to measure its desirability and its quality.

Therefore, for example, in tort law, a court should determine whether a formal legal duty should exist for a therapist to warn another of the possible danger posed by a patient on the basis of its analysis of the practical costs and benefits that would

7 See Chapter 4 herein.
8 See Chapter 8 herein.

likely be generated by the adoption of such a duty, and alternatively by its absence. Similarly, a court should decide if the jurisdiction in question should embrace a formal duty to affirmatively aid as part of its tort law by comparing the societal costs and benefits of adopting such a rule with the likely practical consequences of not doing so.

Clearly, a legal scholar working in a postrealist era and within the instrumentalist paradigm who desires to do more than merely describe the analysis reported by a court in its opinion, and who also wants to evaluate that analysis and to perhaps offer suggestions for improvement, must now fully engage the world outside of the law library. In contrast to the far more philosophical and internal focus of traditional formalism, instrumentalism demands that normative legal scholarship take into consideration the practical costs and benefits of competing versions of legal doctrine. The question of how regulated individuals will respond to one legal rule as compared to another must now be asked and answered.

Was the court correct in the *Tarasoff* case that there would be fewer injuries experienced by potential victims if a formal tort duty exists for a therapist to warn the victim of a patient's possible violent behavior? Will the social cost of false warnings and greater involuntary commitments of the mentally ill be higher than the violent harm prevented? Is a formal duty to affirmatively aid likely to result in better or worse overall outcomes for those in peril? Would a tort duty alone generate a significantly different outcome than a criminal duty alone, or a tort law and a criminal law duty operating together?

This bedrock requirement inherent in instrumentalism – that normative legal analysis identify and analyze the practical consequences of legal rules – poses more of a threat to traditional legal scholarship than may at first appear. Legal scholars engaged in such work must literally and figuratively get out of the law library. They must move beyond the materials with which they are familiar and expert, and they must develop a sophisticated sense of the way in which different entities in society normally operate and how they perceive and respond to legal regulation. This is a fundamental change in the long-standing professional role of legal scholar, and there exists little tradition or precedent for it.

Given the enormity of this change, it is understandable that it may be initially denied, or ignored, or that alternatives to it would be sought. One possible response that may appear helpful is to take the position that legal scholars need not rush out into the world to discover how persons actually respond to legal rules and how they use them to resolve disputes because many of these persons, in fact, come to them. The thousands of volumes of appellate case reports that reside in the law library each contain hundreds of examples of actual disputes and their resolution in every imaginable area of the law. A scholar who has become familiar with even a modest percentage of these cases in a given area might be able to claim to have little left to learn about the interaction of the relevant legal rules with those who are regularly governed by them.

After all, would we not assume that a sitting judge who has for many years specialized in hearing criminal cases or domestic dispute cases would have developed over that time a deep instinct for the way in which criminals and couples misbehave? Is this not one of the reasons that experienced judges are generally preferred to novices? What better guide could there be than such a person for predicting the reaction of the relevant community to one possible legal rule or another? While scholars are not judges with such direct experience, they can claim the benefit of having access to the written accounts of judges performing their professional role in hundreds of thousands of cases in every jurisdiction in this country for more than 100 years.

At first blush, this position has significant appeal. Upon reflection, however, difficulties emerge. The focus of normative legal scholarship is not confined to the application of existing law to discrete disputes. It must also, of course, evaluate the way in which regulated communities respond to applicable law in the normal course and it must imagine how these communities might respond to alternative versions of that law or to entirely different regulatory approaches. Instrumentalism demands a keen sensitivity to the behavioral effect that legal doctrine exerts on the normal daily behavior of those who are regulated by it, and on the ways in which customary routines are established around existing legal requirements. The resolution of specific disputes covers only one limited aspect of the instrumentalist focus on the effect of law on ordinary life.

One can readily see the limitations of this position. As experienced as a judge may be, that experience is largely confined to the function of law as a means of resolving concrete disputes. Certainly, that is the dominant focus of the formal published reports of the courts' activities to which legal scholars have access. Thus, while a practicing jurist may well pick up enormous insight into the behavior of persons who are routinely subject to the area of law in which the judge presides, it is not likely that much of that instinctive insight will be included in the formal memoranda and decisions that fill the law reports that in turn fill the shelves of the law library.

Additionally, the court's focus is necessarily on the resolution of discrete disputes. This means that the experience from which the court extrapolates its notions of regulated community behavior is largely confined, at least professionally, to the behavior of parties engaged in ongoing litigation and parties who have been drawn into disputes that require formal litigation to resolve. It might be difficult, given this strongly weighted sample, to accurately imagine the dynamics of the regulated community as a whole. That would be like asking surgeons who specialize in cardiac bypass surgery how they believe people, in general, will respond to a new medication designed to decrease blood cholesterol or to a dietary regime that excludes all sugar.

Still another problematic matter is the fact that the overwhelming majority of the court materials that fill the shelves of the law library are appellate court reports. Appellate courts rarely have direct exposure to the parties in the case. They typically work only with the transcribed record from the proceedings below, the formal written briefs of attorneys, and, perhaps, a short period of oral argument. The experience of appellate courts with even the small segment of the regulated community that becomes involved in litigation is once removed and somewhat abstract.

There are also many reasons to believe that only a weak correspondence exists between the portrait of a regulated community presented in appellate court opinions and the actual reality of the situation. Factual investigation in litigation is conducted by the parties themselves and is infused with self-interest. The factual presentation made by each party to the trial court is profoundly influenced by the specific set of disputed facts and issues in the case, by the technical demands of proof required by the applicable legal doctrine, by the posturing of each party seeking an advantage in the settlement, and by the financial limitations of the parties. This is hardly reliable source material for a balanced view of a regulated community.

It is also true that the availability, and, in fact, the desirability, within an active litigation context of factual stipulations entered into by the parties, admissions, formal presumptions, and burdens of proof can all work to significantly skew the factual picture offered to the court. Moreover, the accuracy and the thoroughness of the factual presentations at trial are often burdened by the notorious unreliability of live witness testimony, and by long-standing rules of evidence that exclude from a trial the presentation of unquestionably true and relevant information if it is likely to be more prejudicial than probative, or if it falls under one of a number of recognized privileges.

Not only do all of these forces at work at the trial court level justify significant suspicion about the objective factual accuracy of the presentations of the parties, but the appellate judges do not even enjoy the benefit of direct observation and exposure to the parties' live presentations, as does the trial judge. Their experience is limited to the written record of the trial. Further, in cases of trials before juries who return with a general verdict, it is common for the appellate court to have before them only the written record of the conflicting testimony offered by the parties at trial and the jury's ultimate verdict, leaving them without a definitive legal version of what transpired between these particular parties in this specific case. Furthermore, even if the appellate court was presented with a version of the facts in the case that corresponded perfectly with what actually occurred, the court would have no way of knowing with confidence the extent to which the facts of this specific case could accurately be extrapolated to the larger regulated community.

For all of the foregoing reasons the published reports of courts, especially appellate courts, simply cannot serve as reliable guides to the likely behavior of the regulated community at large when performing serious instrumentalist analysis of legal doctrine. Legal scholars engaged in normative legal scholarship in the postrealist era have little choice but to look out and examine the world through sources not typically available in a law library. This is no small challenge to a profession that has little experience, little training, and virtually no tradition in this kind of academic work.

From this perspective, one can view two of the dominant trends that have emerged in legal scholarship in the latter half of the twentieth century as being, at least in part, responses to this critical challenge. One is the movement toward greater interdisciplinary legal scholarship. The other is the marked increase in interest and support for empirical legal scholarship. Both of these trends seek a path to an academic model of regulated community behavior that can be deployed in normative doctrinal analysis. Interdisciplinary work looks for these models in the existing work of other academic disciplines such as economics, sociology, history, psychology, and, interestingly, literature. Empirical legal scholarship seeks to develop the models directly.

While both movements offer reasonable responses to the challenges faced by normative instrumentalist legal analysis, and while both movements have thus far produced important and interesting work, significant issues are raised in the active pursuit of these strategies by legal scholars.

One significant difficulty, faced particularly by interdisciplinary legal scholarship, is that many of the academic disciplines in which help is sought do not offer a highly developed body of predictive work. The social sciences, in particular, have not been very successful in developing sophisticated models that can accurately predict the future actions and reactions of their subjects, except perhaps at the simplest level. Neither psychology nor sociology currently provide predictive theories of the sort that are likely to be valuable in instrumentalist legal analysis. The lone exception here is economics, and this surely helps to explain why law and economics has thus far been the breakout star of interdisciplinary legal scholarship. Moreover, if these traditional social sciences have yet to find success in this endeavor within their respective disciplines, why would one expect empirical work engaged in by legal scholars to be more successful?

Another serious difficulty with both interdisciplinary and empirical legal scholarship, at least when practiced by legal scholars, is that there is virtually nothing in the traditional training and experience of law professors, save for the acquisition of knowledge about law and legal processes, that would adequately prepare them to do such work in a serious way. The central tension here is between law schools as institutions engaged predominately in professional education and a widely accepted expectation that law professors should also be scholars who, as part of their normal professional portfolio, are regularly engaged in instrumentalist normative legal analysis. The consequence of this tension bears down on law professors from at least two directions.

The first is that it is still overwhelmingly the case that law professors receive their graduate training, most often their only graduate training, in law school, and are taught there by professors who also received the same graduate training in their youth. During their last two years of law school, they may have taken a few small seminars of as few as twenty students that provided them the opportunity for some sustained contact with a faculty member. They may have worked as a research assistant for a semester or a summer. They most likely completed a single writing project of no more than a compulsory thirty pages to satisfy the requirements for graduation. But on the whole, they enrolled in required first-year courses and core upper-level electives that were designed to introduce and survey the subject matter, that culminated in a final examination, and that were taught in a lecture hall to a large number of students who nearly all expected to engage in the practice of law after graduation.

Contrast this experience with the typical training expected of a professional scholar in the field of psychology, sociology, economics, finance, or literature. Academics in those fields typically complete both a master's program and then a highly specialized doctoral program that involves intensive apprenticeship with an established professor in the field and culminates in the production of a significant work of original scholarship in the form of a dissertation, traditionally subsequently published as the new academic's first book. This training, especially the doctoral program, is specifically designed to provide the graduate student with the skills and experience needed to successfully pursue a career as a professional scholar in that field.

Obviously, law schools could resolve this aspect of the tension by hiring only those individuals to serve on their faculty who have earned both a graduate law degree and an academic Ph.D. While there is some indication that the possession of a Ph.D. in addition to a J.D. is currently an advantage when seeking an appointment to a law faculty, and while the aforementioned analysis makes some sense of this postrealist trend, no law school, no matter how prestigious, has announced, or has even suggested, that it would henceforth hire only those with an academic Ph.D. as faculty members. Furthermore, to follow the inevitable flow of the argument, no one has seriously suggested that those law school faculty members who do possess a doctoral degree are engaged in meaningful scholarship, or are properly fulfilling their institutional role, only when they produce legal scholarship that reaches out in an interdisciplinary fashion to their doctoral field.

The reason for not requiring that law school faculty members possess a traditional academic doctoral degree, of course, despite the nearly ironclad logic in its favor, is that even those law schools that are most impressively represented by graduates currently employed as full-time law professors send only a tiny percentage of their graduates off to do such work. The overwhelming percentage of their graduates, like the overwhelming percentage of graduates at every American law school, pursue careers in the practice of the profession of law. American law schools are, at the beginning and the end of the day, institutions of professional education. Those who attend them, those who finance them, and those who hire their graduates all expect that they will provide at least a minimally adequate preparation for the practice of law. The possession of an academic Ph.D. in addition to a J.D. by members of the law school faculty is widely understood to be tangential to that fundamental mission.

Thus, law professors are generally, and quite understandably, insufficiently trained to engage in professional-level empirical or interdisciplinary scholarship. This might well be where the imperatives of modern instrumentalist legal analysis lead, but when they do they come into stark conflict with the teaching function of the law school and its faculty. Under the formalist paradigm, teachers, scholars, practitioners, and students alike were thought to be characterized by their focus on traditional legal analysis as the primary intellectual skill and this belief served to harmonize the teaching and the scholarship functions of law professors. In contrast, the skills required for serious instrumentalist analysis at a professional level are rather far removed from the skills needed to thrive in the practice of law or to effectively train future lawyers.

This then leads to a second source of the previously described tension that falls upon law faculty. The more they acquire training in empirical legal analysis, the more sophisticated they become in the tools of academic empirical research and the methods and understandings of other academic disciplines. As a result of this more sophisticated approach, the gap between their professional lives as scholars and their professional responsibilities as teachers of law students grows greater. It is almost certainly the case that some practicing attorneys in some practice niches encounter and must deal with empirical research and models of the sort used in academic scholarship. It is also equally certain that a seminar or an upper-level elective on empirical research and modeling would likely make a valuable addition to a law school's curriculum. But that is a far cry from implying that a facility with sophisticated empirical tools and models, and with the professional research techniques and current body of literature of other academic fields, is a necessary component of professional legal training. And yet, the nature of instrumentalist analysis in the postrealist era calls for exactly that of those who must engage in serious instrumentalist legal scholarship and must also simultaneously discharge the teaching function – the faculties of law schools.

Finally, and perhaps most importantly, the serious pursuit of instrumentalist research regarding law and legal regulation in our society will inexorably lead to a progressive, limitless broadening of the intellectual jurisdiction for law schools and for legal scholarship. There is essentially no human activity in our society that is not either touched by legal doctrine or legal regulation of some sort, or about which a conscious decision has been made to forgo legal regulation. If the postrealist understanding of the rationale for existing legal doctrine is an instrumentalist one, based ultimately not upon a deductive application of precedent and principle but on a balancing of practical costs and benefits, then one who would engage in sophisticated scholarship in a given area of law must also become fully conversant and expert in the nature and operation of the regulated community.

Perhaps for any one particular legal scholar, with the field of law sufficiently narrowly defined and with their training and skills uniquely suited to the special area of interest, this goal may be feasible. But for law schools and legal scholarship collectively, this newly understood scope of appropriate study and expertise is virtually unlimited. Once one fuses the nature of our modern administrative state with the prevailing postrealist instrumentalist paradigm, what kind of academic expertise about the nature of the world and its inhabitants could not arguably be made part of legal scholarship?

Practically everything that we can observe, and almost anything that we can imagine, is either the subject of legal regulation or is the subject of a conscious decision not to regulate. Should legal standards be established for automobile emissions or engine fuel efficiency in an effort to reduce global warming? Do laws prohibiting development on certain tracts of land in order to protect the continuing survival of an endangered species make sense and are there other possible versions of such regulation that would better achieve that goal? Is the development of a new drug sufficiently different from one or more existing drugs to deserve the issuance of a patent? Is this song, play, novel, or film sufficiently the same as one or more existing ones to constitute legal plagiarism? Would one or another possible version of a particular doctrine of matrimonial law most effectively minimize the rate of separations and divorces? Should a specific religious belief and practice that causes harm to another trigger civil liability? Should especially evil thoughts and intentions increase the possible penalty when those thoughts can be shown to motivate a criminal act?

Virtually every legitimate field of academic study could plausibly be shown to be relevant to instrumentalist legal analysis, and thus within the colorable province of normative legal scholarship. The fundamental issue, then, regarding interdisciplinary and empirical work should not be whether they can get a legitimate sustainable start in legal scholarship but just exactly where we might expect them to end.

Law schools would no longer reside in just a single building somewhere on campus, but would, at least intellectually, stand astride the entire university with normative instrumentalist legal scholarship serving as the gatekeeper whose academic expertise is to translate the knowledge of all of the other disciplines into regulatory prescriptions.

Such a vision, of course, is ridiculous. Yet that is where the logic of normative instrumentalist analysis inexorably leads. An expansion toward a boundless breadth of inquiry and ever greater required expertise for normative legal scholarship is more or less inevitable once an instrumentalist view of law is adopted. Nevertheless, no matter how latent it may remain, it is highly improbable that other academic disciplines, and actual legal decision-makers, will be willing to grant to legal scholars this virtually limitless academic jurisdiction and authority. Legal scholarship and legal scholars operating under such a conception are unlikely to be ushered to a place of preeminence in the modern university. It is more likely that normative legal scholarship will slide into increasing irrelevance and obscurity.

An additional problem this fundamental challenge presents is even more formidable. Given that the subject of academic legal scholarship is principally the law and legal processes, the search for an academic basis upon which to normatively analyze and evaluate the subject becomes essentially the search for an objective science of human governance. Just how, within an instrumentalist paradigm, could legal scholars plausibly hope to discover a sufficiently neutral and objective foundation that would provide to their normative work a genuinely academic status? Such a search, ironically, is an expression of one of the most powerful yearnings of traditional formalism. Among the most influential insights offered by legal realism is the implausibility, if not the impossibility, of such a quest.

Thus, legal scholarship in the postrealist era finds itself in a highly uncertain state. The recognized authority and expertise of the legal scholar to engage in a normative analysis of law has been sharply circumscribed by virtue of the shift from formalism to instrumentalism and as yet no plausible strategy exists to reclaim it.

While first-order descriptive legal scholarship is as available as before, the relative importance and prestige accorded it has dramatically declined. This leaves various kinds of second-order descriptive legal scholarship. Work of this sort, however, is descriptive in more of a heuristic sense than in the type of harder, falsifiable version of academic description that is normally associated with the natural sciences.

Postrealist legal scholarship can be, therefore, understood, on the basis of this analysis, to be a kind of soft social science or perhaps an academic discipline most closely aligned with the humanities. Sophisticated work in the area provides interesting and insightful perspectives on a recognized body of published materials. It identifies and develops possible themes and works out their implications. It is valued to the extent that it is perceived as novel, perhaps even counterintuitive, and elegantly presented. But it cannot really claim to be objectively true, and it suffers from declining relevance and influence outside the legal academy.

Those invested in legal scholarship need to begin a serious assessment of its possible roles and functions in this postrealist period. What unique expertise do law professors as legal scholars bring to the table and what kind of research and scholarship would be a productive application of that expertise? How might scholarship that better serves the needs of the bench and the practicing bar be identified and encouraged? What is the relationship between the pursuit of different kinds of legal scholarship and a law professor's concurrent professional obligations as an instructor of law students? These are important questions. As a practical matter, they may not need to be addressed for law schools and legal scholarship to continue much as they have, but they must eventually be addressed before legal scholarship can regain its respect and its influence in the larger world.

12

Conclusion

It is widely understood that in the process of deciding discreet and active disputes, appellate courts in this country can announce the adoption of general legal doctrine that then enjoys the status of authoritative and binding law, known as common law. That law exists on an equal status with the laws that are duly enacted by the legislature in that same jurisdiction. Unlike elected legislators, however, appellate judges, in their lawmaking capacity, are severely constrained. They only possess lawmaking authority when adjudicating active disputes that require the adoption of the general legal rule in question for their resolution. They cannot, as legislators can, make law speculatively by anticipating future problems and future possible disputes. They cannot go back and change or refine existing law without doing so in the context of dealing with an active dispute that requires resolution by the appellate court and also requires the adopted change or refinement to existing law to affect an appropriate resolution of that dispute. Unlike the legislature, an appellate court is at least expected, and is sometimes required, to produce and to make publicly available a formal written explanation of its resolution of the disputes that come before it and the common law that it creates.

This is a strange and fascinating time in the life of American common law. Since its inception, American common law has operated under a prevailing conventional conception, or paradigm, that could be called formalism. Under formalism, it was thought that appellate courts reviewed the legal decisions made by lower courts and created new common law by engaging in a distinctive form of abstract and technical legal analysis similar to formal logic. Much like a professional board of scientists reviewing specific empirical experiments, an appellate court was thought to be primarily checking the legal logic employed by the lower courts in making legal decisions in the case and ensuring that these judgments conformed to the existing common law in the jurisdiction; this in the same way that the review board might seek to ensure that the body of knowledge used by the scientists conducting the experiments conformed to the current science of the day. When the appellate court was required to make new common law, it was thought that it did so by deductively extending or elaborating upon existing common law. The hope was that by expanding and refining the existing law in this way, appellate courts would incrementally develop that law and move it ever closer to an ideal version of the law – sometimes called the natural law – much like a community of scientists hope to review experiments and to work over time to evolve their current version of, say, physics or chemistry, ever closer to the actual laws of nature. Critically, under formalism, appellate court judges are thought, similar to scientists, to be engaged in a dispassionate, technical, value-neutral, largely objective endeavor when they review the work of subordinate courts and create common law.

The structure of appellate courts and appellate procedure in America was designed and developed around and within this formalist paradigm. Thus, appellate court judges, while unquestionably functioning as lawmakers within a democratic republic, are generally not selected by popular election, nor do they stand for regular reelection. They are conventionally said to be appointed based on their experience and their perceived expertise in law and legal analysis. It is their asserted ability to engage in the distinctive analytical and technical method thought to be employed by appellate courts that justifies their status as makers of law. Their political authority to make binding law is grounded in their adherence to that objective, value-neutral method of appellate court review and analysis. It is the method, and its reliance upon an abstract, fully principled, scientific-like analysis, that substitutes for popular election as a source of legitimacy for the formal lawmaking power that is invested in appellate courts.

Similarly, the formalist analogy to the work of a scientific review board suggests that the materials with which appellate courts work to review the legal decisions of the lower courts and to create new common law be very limited in number and overwhelmingly abstract in nature, and, in fact, they are. Appellate courts do their work based only on a dry formal written transcript of the trial court activity in the case (known as the record), a small number of formal written arguments (known as legal briefs and usually submitted only by the parties to the case), and, often but not always, a brief period of live presentations by, and questioning of, the attorneys in the case (known as oral argument). Traditionally, these few formal inputs and the contents of a typical law library constitute the complete base of information upon which the appellate court does its work.

Both of these foundational attributes of appellate courts – lawmakers not selected and not regularly retained by popular electoral mandate and a markedly limited number of abstract formal inputs – are the consequence of, and rationalized by, the work of these courts being understood as technical, objective, highly constrained by formal logic, and essentially value-free in nature.

Starting in the first third of the twentieth century, the traditional and tidy world of legal formalism began to be questioned in a sustained and serious manner. A collection of challenges that are now commonly grouped under the name "legal realist movement" critiqued many of the tenets of formalism. Chief among the targets of the legal realists' criticism was the formalist claim that the work of appellate courts, including when they created new common law, was predominantly technical, objective, and free of outcome preferences. In contrast, the legal realists sought to demonstrate that a very large number of appellate court opinions, including nearly all of the most consequential and interesting ones, while presenting their ultimate judgments and results as logically inevitable deductions from widely accepted first principles, were, in fact, disguising the exercise and influence of social, moral, and practical policy preferences on the part of the deciding judges.

Most cases of any legal significance present to the courts issues that could plausibly be resolved in more than one way. Similarly, when needing to create new common law, or to possibly alter in some way existing common law, courts are faced with more than one reasonable alternative. Formalist appellate courts presented in their published opinions a logically deductive path from an asserted first principle or maxim of general acceptance to the court's conclusions and decisions in the case. The legal realists demonstrated, again and again, that a close and critical inspection of these cases revealed that there existed other, equally tenable, conclusions and results that could also be shown to be the product of a logically deductive path from a recognized larger principle or aphorism. Often this was because there exist a very large number of alleged first principles and dictums in the common law from which to choose, no small number of which are potentially in partial or nearly full conflict with others. This was also the case because a sizable number of these well-recognized common law precepts are vague enough in substance and nature to admit to a variety of more specific interpretations when used as the start of a deductive chain of inference.

Regardless of the specific rhetorical mechanism that was employed, formalist appellate court opinions were repeatedly shown by the legal realists to be offering an allegedly definitive analytical path to a uniquely correct conclusion when in fact equally logical and analytically sound paths of analysis could be constructed that would lead to quite different, and sometimes directly contradictory, conclusions. The decisional action in these formalist opinions did not lie in the deductive path of logic set forth by the court, but instead in the courts' unstated and unexamined choice of first principle by which to begin and to ground the deductive chain of reasoning. In choosing among the possible candidates to use as the first principle in a given instance, it is very likely that these formalist courts were influenced by the specific conclusions to which each first principle would necessarily lead. In making a choice for one conclusion or another among the possibilities, appellate judges were necessarily invoking and advancing personally held values, beliefs, and understandings that led them to a preference for one conclusion of the case, and one version of common law doctrine, over others. The realists pointed out that there was little or nothing objective or value-neutral about such appellate adjudication by the courts. In contrast, they argued, this was a value-laden expression and application of some particular values, beliefs, and social commitments over others, hidden under a veneer of supposedly technical, objective, logic-based formalist legal analysis.

There was a more theoretical branch of the legal realist movement that sought to establish that the kind of jurisprudence espoused by the formalists was not just inaccurate in describing what appellate courts were actually doing, but that it was not, as a philosophical matter, a possible means of developing concrete rules to govern and regulate human behavior. Regardless of the success of this larger project, the descriptive critique of formalism by the legal realists resonated with a large number of members of the legal community. It resonated with many attorneys who practiced before appellate courts and who found the realist account to be a more accurate description of what they experienced and observed than the traditional formalist account. It resonated also with law professors who invested large amounts of time reading and studying appellate court opinions and who often had great difficulty satisfactorily explaining them in formalist terms to their students and in their scholarship.

Over time, the legal realist critique of formalism came to enjoy acceptance by a consensus of the legal community. The former formalist paradigm had effectively been exposed and discredited by the legal realist movement. No longer did most members of the legal community believe that appellate courts were maintaining and creating the common law of this country in an objective, value-neutral manner.

If appellate courts were not, in fact, engaging in the kind of mechanistic and highly determined jurisprudence alleged by the formalist paradigm, then on what basis were they preferring one possible version of common law over others? The legal realist critique of formalism does not necessarily offer an answer to this question. The success of the legal realist movement effectively created a void, a vacuum, in which there resided no necessary answer to the question of what should be the proper basis upon which appellate courts choose one version of common law doctrine over others as the authoritative and binding law for the jurisdiction.

In the face of this vacuum, the legal community gravitated toward the other principled basis for creating law with which the governing system in this country was familiar. That was a version of a legislative balancing analysis that considers anticipated practical costs and benefits of various plausible versions of the law and then opts to elevate to the status of binding law the version that promises the most attractive mix of benefits and costs. By adhering to this approach, appellate courts would no longer focus on asserted abstract first principles and syllogistic logical deduction therefrom and would instead focus on the specific social purposes and policy sought to be achieved by a given area of common law and then analyze the degree to which each plausible version of the law under consideration might be expected to advance these purposes and policies.

This newer approach to appellate court lawmaking does not view the creation and evolution of common law, or any law, as being analogous to the scientific search for the true and eternal laws of nature. Instead, the law is viewed as a tool, one among many others, by which human societies strive to solve current problems and seek to achieve social goals. As external conditions change, and as social problems and aspirations change, the law might well appropriately and productively change as well. Thus, this understanding of jurisprudence is sometimes known as instrumentalism. So, one can recognize that American common law over and last half of the twentieth century has experienced a profound paradigm shift from formalism to instrumentalism.

One important and conventionally underappreciated aspect of the current period is that appellate courts continue to engage in routine common law lawmaking, but are doing so within an administrative structure and according to appellate procedures that were designed and developed during, and for, the prior formalist era. For example, once it is widely understood that appellate judges must regularly and repeatedly exercise preferences for some social values and outcomes over others when choosing which doctrinal alternatives to elevate to the status of authoritative and binding law, then the practice of having them selected on a supposedly merit-only basis by executive and legislative actors and not elected, and then reelected, by the citizens of a jurisdiction becomes problematic and difficult to justify. In addition, it is difficult to rationalize the continued practice of appellate judges creating binding law within an instrumentalist paradigm on the basis of a very small number of formal and abstract materials, most of which poorly serve the needs of instrumentalist analysis.

There are many possible reasons for this long and continuing delay in the American legal system coming to terms with these current contradictions. One such reason is that the kind of changes to both appellate judge selection and appellate court procedures required to make them more appropriate and productive for instrumentalist jurisprudence would be highly disruptive and exceptionally expensive, both in terms of the transition and then continuing going forward. Another such reason is that none of the actors who would need to be deeply involved in the initiation and implementation of these changes – including legislators, members of the practicing bar, and appellate judges themselves – have much professional incentive to do so.

In the case of current appellate judges, not only is there little incentive to seek changes to long-standing practices and procedures which resulted in their own selection as lawmakers and with which they are already familiar, but fear of a possible deterioration of public respect for their authority encourages them to continue to present their judgments in their published opinions in objective, value-neutral, logic-driven, formalist terms. This has resulted in a period of American appellate practice that is characterized by a discordant, cacophonous mix of disparate elements and approaches. Appellant briefs, oral arguments, and published opinions frequently contain an amalgam of formalist, instrumentalist, and still other kinds of considerations, both abstract and practical.

Much time and attention is often devoted to discussion of prior cases and precedents and the degree to which possible resolutions of the instant case either will or will not conform to them. This kind of analysis makes sense in terms of a concern for stare decisis and an exploration of whether the court's discretion in the instant case is appropriately constrained by that doctrine. But that is infrequently the way in which such discussion proceeds. More typically, the arguments of the parties and the opinions of the courts engage in this discussion in a vague formalist manner, treating the association of a given resolution of the instant case with some element, theme, argument, decision, or result in a previously published case as an importantly persuasive factor, without explaining why. Similarly, one can frequently observe arguments made by the attorneys, and rationales offered by the court, that focus on likely practical consequences of one possible version of common law doctrine or another without there being present any kind of serious, systematic, thorough instrumentalist analysis of the disputed issue.

Adjudication before appellate courts is a serious endeavor engaged in by highly educated and skilled attorneys and judges. There is no lack of intelligence at play either at the podium or on the bench. But a close examination of briefs often reveals a striking lack of clarity in terms of a consistent, coherent approach that the court is anticipated to take to its analysis and resolution of the issues raised by the case. Most briefs contain a hodgepodge of arguments and points that conform to no uniform and systematic notion of how the court is expected to analyze and decide these issues. What one often reads in appellate briefs is a mingling of various disjointed formalist and instrumentalist arguments that are, individually, thought to be advantageous to the party represented by the authoring attorneys. Rarely is there an organized overall analytical framework that is pursued consistently and conscientiously throughout the brief.

One repeatedly sees the same phenomenon when reading published appellate opinions. The authoring court often supports its judgments and conclusions by citing a loose and unfocused collection of arguments, some of which have meaning within a formalist paradigm and others that address the anticipated practical consequences of the version of common law that the court has adopted. Unsurprisingly, because savvy attorneys look to published opinions for guidance on how best to persuade the judges, the rationales offered by the courts in their published opinions and the unfocused mélange of arguments that one sees presented in the attorneys' briefs share essentially the same character.

What harm is there in the current lack of coherence in appellate common law jurisprudence? Why does it matter if appellate attorneys present, and appellate judges rely upon, a jumble of considerations and arguments that speak to profoundly different criteria for legal judgment and that fail to follow a structured and ordered analysis? The primary answer to this question is that the current practice of appellate common law lawmaking has ended up nodding to the success of the legal realist movement by including instrumentalist style arguments in the mix while still retaining many of the problematic qualities of formalism. There are two primary kinds of social costs associated with this situation.

The first is that the current circumstance shares with traditional formalism a lack of transparency. Attorneys offer to the court a conflicting assortment of formalist, instrumentalist, and miscellaneous arguments. The court makes its decisions and then justifies those decisions in a published opinion by offering some subset of the overall assortment as its rationale, perhaps adding a few of its own. Had the court chosen to embrace a different set of decisions, it could have presumably supported those different outcomes in the case by offering a different subset of the same overall assortment as its rationale. Why did the court opt to decide in one way rather than the other? Because under such an approach, a facial rationale is available to the court to justify multiple possible outcomes, the court's own public written explanation for its decisions and judgments does not necessarily reveal the actual basis for those decisions, much as with traditional formalism. As explained in Chapter 7 herein, this means that the multiple policies and purposes supporting the custom of requiring appellate courts to justify the exercise of their unelected power in published written opinions are badly compromised or thwarted.

The second problem with the current state of appellate jurisprudence is both a profound cost on its own and is also the root cause of the lack of transparency. This is the lack of a constraining discipline that is such a prominent feature of the current analytical approach. Much like traditional formalism, the current court practice of constructing a public rationale by assembling and presenting a selection of isolated, conceptually unconnected arguments can almost always be used to rationalize a variety of different outcomes in the case and virtually never requires the court to choose a particular one among them. It does not meaningfully constrain judges' application of personal preference in exercising formal political power.

One implicit and basic trade-off contained within the formalist paradigm was that unelected appellate judges were invested with the formal power to make general binding law in exchange for the expectation that they would exercise such power while adhering to a jurisprudential method that was thought to rely upon formal logic and deductive reasoning to lead them to a unique and inescapable legal conclusion. When the legal realists demonstrated that the method that resided at the heart of the paradigm did not operate as was thought, the legal community stopped trusting that the formalist paradigm possessed the ability to impose a constraining discipline on the exercise of appellate court lawmaking power and to support court transparency – and the paradigm crumbled. The current practice shares these same methodological flaws with traditional formalism and does not improve upon that discarded paradigm in either respect.

Instrumentalism does not provide a constraining discipline in that sense either. It does not offer an approach to appellate jurisprudence that prevents the exercise of personal preferences and personal values by appellate judges. It does, however, prescribe a specific and particular method of analysis. Adherence to this particular method of legal analysis recognizes that appellate judges will rely upon their personal judgment, perceptions, and values in creating common law, but it mandates that they do so within the constraining discipline of fidelity to the social purposes and policy sought to be advanced by the particular law under consideration, combined with a practical cost-benefit approach to that inquiry. In so doing, instrumentalism promotes consistency of jurisprudential approach by appellate courts in the exercise of their power, which promotes reliability, and reliance, and the ability of advocates to predict those arguments most relevant and persuasive to these courts. That consequence improves the utility and potency of appellate adjudication. Furthermore, instrumentalism, by prescribing a specific, even if substantively indeterminate, method of analysis, establishes the expectation that courts will adhere to that analytical method when explaining their decisions in their published opinions. This serves to meaningfully increase transparency.

The currently amorphous, vague, undisciplined, and unconstrained consideration of a motley assortment of arguments fails to provide to the system of common law lawmaking either the surface consistency of formalism or the constraining methodological discipline and transparency of instrumentalism. It is, in some ways, the worst of both worlds.

What, then, might one expect moving forward? Are there reasons to expect that the current and prolonged denial of the underlying paradigm shift from common law formalism to instrumentalism might weaken or give way?

As noted earlier, the kinds of systemic changes required to make appellate practice more compatible with the instrumentalist paradigm are extensive, disruptive, and expensive. The rules of evidence and trial practice seek to advance their own legitimate objectives. They are understandably focused on providing the disputing parties with a fair forum and an equitable set of procedures for the adjudication of their claims, not on developing a written record upon which appellate courts can better engage in instrumentalist common law lawmaking. Would it make sense to admit at trial factually accurate evidence that is likely to unfairly prejudice the judgment of jurors because it might better inform the appellate courts in their lawmaking function? Should the important values and social policies that justify various formal privileges, such as the physician–patient and the spousal privileges, be compromised in favor of possibly improving an instrumentalist appellate court methodology of common law lawmaking? Probably not.

It would be possible to enhance instrumentalist lawmaking by appellate courts without altering the rules of evidence and trial practice by providing appellate courts with their own means of empirical factfinding and investigation. Staffs could be built to engage in such work. Expert witnesses could be called to provide empirical information, and to respond to cross-examination-style questioning. In addition to the enormous expense of such an endeavor, multiplied by the hundreds and hundreds of appellate courts that exist in this country, making such changes would have the consequence of more or less duplicating the standard model of legislative lawmaking in the judicial branch at the appellate court level – including regular fact-finding hearings, witnesses, subpoenas, and substantial research and investigative staffs. Such a project would result in expensively highlighting the degree to which instrumentalist appellate court lawmaking duplicates legislative lawmaking, except with politically unaccountable lawmakers making the critical decisions. Again, probably not.

It therefore seems unlikely that significant changes to the procedures or inputs by which appellate courts operate and create common law will be implemented in at least the medium term. If greater numbers of appellate courts become more consistently and transparently instrumentalist in their approach, then it is possible that legal briefs will come to look more like the model of the Brandeis brief, but this would not be a major change, more like a modest shift in the customary practice of brief writing. The current practice of appellate oral argument is certainly questionable as it is especially unsuited to careful instrumentalist analysis, and it is arguably ripe for change, but it is unlikely that it will move anytime soon to more closely resemble a serious empirical inquiry.

So, the instrumentalist elements of appellate practice will most likely remain as they have been for at least the last fifty to seventy-five years – formally presented arguments and analysis regarding the likely practical consequences of various plausible versions of the common law (and statutory interpretations) based on the intuitions and common sense of the arguing attorneys and the deciding judges, exercised without the aid of reliable or sophisticated empirical data or research support. That was the methodology employed by the California Supreme Court in the *Tarasoff* case some fifty years ago, and it remains the prevailing methodology employed by appellate courts to this day.

Given this, one modest and plausibly achievable reform that might be pursued is consciously increasing the diversity of class, gender, education, ethnicity, race, and other attributes of those who are nominated to serve as appellate judges. To the extent that instrumentalist analysis will continue to be the product of the normative social values and intuitive understanding of how the world works possessed by appellate judges, it will be more poorly performed, and the resulting common law will suffer, when appellate judges represent only a narrow slice of societal experience and opinion. A more broadly diverse appellate judiciary is likely to bring a fuller spectrum of intuition and experience to appellate instrumentalist analysis and thereby to improve a court's ability to identify and evaluate a broader spectrum of practical consequences of those legal doctrines under consideration. This should improve the quality of the common law (and statutory interpretations) produced by more diverse appellate courts working within an instrumentalist paradigm.

With regard to changing the facially merit-based selection of appellate court judges, and the possible reduction in the respect accorded to the lawmaking product of the appellate courts, the current experience of the United States Supreme Court can be instructive. Here, in the latter half of 2024, there is no question that the Supreme Court enjoys far less general presumptive regard and respect than it did fifty and seventy-five years ago. The overwhelming perception that Supreme Court justices decide relevant cases based on their personal political and social-value commitments and beliefs has filtered down from academia, and other regular observers of the Court, to even the casually engaged general public. While the future remains unpredictable, it seems right now very unlikely that the Court as a political institution enjoys a plausible path to regaining its former cultural legitimacy, and thus its former societal status, in the foreseeable future.

In this respect, however, the United States Supreme Court may be unique. It is probably fair to presume that only a small percentage of the not-legally-trained public are even aware that appellate courts in this country routinely create binding law equal in status to the law enacted by state and federal legislatures. Fewer still are probably aware of the paradigm shift from formalism to instrumentalism in the making of that common law. Therefore, the likelihood of state appellate courts, and federal appellate courts other than the United States Supreme Court, suffering from a loss of prestige or respect based on that paradigm shift is low.

Even with the vertiginous decline in automatic respect for the objectivity and non-partisan nature of the United States Supreme Court, and even with the recent striking increase in the number and seriousness of proposals for change in the size, composition, tenure, jurisdiction, and means of appointment to that Court, strikingly little momentum has developed for direct popular election of Supreme Court justices. Given this, it appears all but certain that any meaningful pressure for increased direct election of any other appellate judges is a very long way off, if it is even on the horizon at all.

How might one reasonably try to reconcile this state of affairs? Belief in the objective and value-neutral nature of formalist common law analysis and lawmaking is long gone, and there are no indications that it is likely to return anytime soon. Dramatic change to appellate court composition, selection of judges, basic inputs, or operating procedures appears to be unlikely. So, too, does the emergence of any meaningful constituency, including the general public, that will be motivated to advocate for paying the high financial price and absorbing the profound disruption of traditional appellate practice that would be required to more rationally and appropriately accommodate the currently prevailing instrumentalist paradigm.

The best cold-eyed view looking forward is that things will remain much as they have been since the success of the legal realist revolution. Appellate judges will be selected by executive and legislative branch actors with only very limited opportunity for election, or reelection, by the general public. These judges will engage in legal analysis that will include elements of instrumentalism, and will also often include vague and loosely defined elements of formalism as well. Instrumentalist analysis will identify the likely practical consequences of one version of common law or another based on appellate judges' casual and untested intuitions about how the world works and what anticipated practical consequences are more and less attractive.

What useful functions might appellate court lawmaking of this nature perform in our democratic republic? It can offer a source of binding law that is an alternative to the legislature. It is a source, unlike the legislature, that has no choice but to confront and to resolve actual problems requiring the creation and application of binding law to be settled, whether or not the resolution of such problems or the creation of such law offer an opportunity for political gain. It can be a source that is expected to create binding general law without regard to party politics, constituency service, lobbying pressure, or legislative logrolling. It can remain a source of law-making that is expected, and often required, to explain itself in published writing when it exercises its authority.

The societal value of these functions can be enhanced by dropping the pretense of technical-merit-only selection, and perhaps also increasing modestly the role of public confirmation, or reconfirmation, of appellate judges by general election. They can be enhanced by striving to make both states and the federal appellate judiciary more diverse in class, background, education, sex, ethnicity, and race. They can be enhanced by pressuring appellate courts to be more specific and more transparent about the method of legal analysis that they employ, being more disciplined in that analysis, and being more candid and thorough in the presentation of that analysis and the basis for their decisions in their published opinions. Finally, they can be enhanced by resisting efforts to allow unelected appellate judges to exercise their political power while either not producing written explanations for that exercise in the form of published opinions or having the ability to say that any such explanation that is produced does not count in the usual way as regular precedent in the jurisdiction. This would mean a curtailment in the permitted use of unpublished appellate opinions.

Index

www.ingramcontent.com/pod-product-compliance
Lightning Source LLC
LaVergne TN
LVHW011814200926
848484LV00005B/1195

* 9 7 8 1 0 0 9 5 8 9 2 6 0 *